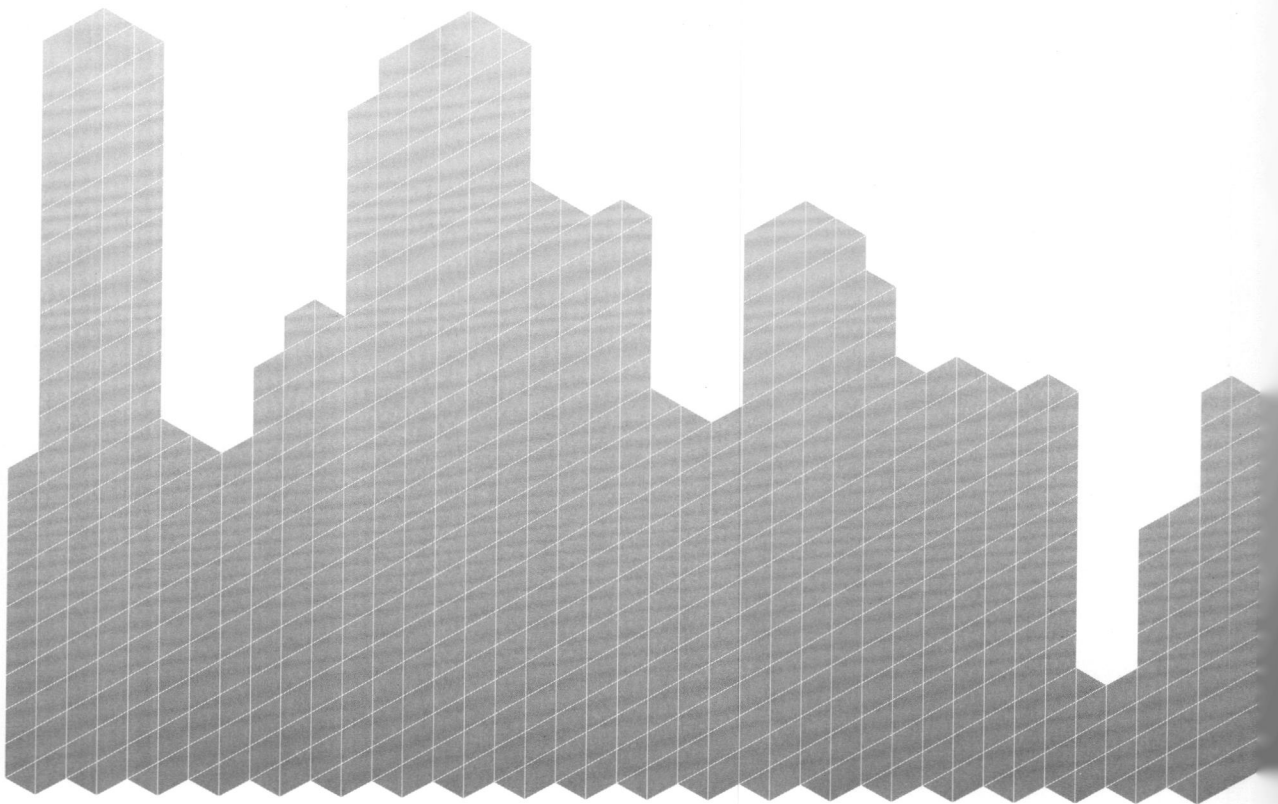

高职高专经济管理类规划教材

浙江省高等教育重点建设教材

外贸单证实训

Documents Practice for Foreign Trade

朱春兰 主 编

ZHEJIANG UNIVERSITY PRESS

浙江大学出版社

前　　言

外贸单证员是外贸企业开展业务的基础人才。因此外贸单证员的培养至关重要。为了更好地适应职业教育的发展和要求，遵循高职教育"以岗位为基础，以能力为本位"的原则，加强学生职业能力培养，特编写《外贸单证实训》教材。

本书在编写过程中注重知识的时效性，采用最新版本的规章、制度、规定等，如《代理报检委托书》采用 2010 年 6 月 1 日起正式使用的格式。本书的图片、合同、单据、信用证等都来自外贸企业，但涉及的原交易当事人、交易内容等关键信息均已虚化。所述内容如不慎与真实生活中的人物、组织或事件雷同，纯属巧合。

本书由浙江经贸职业技术学院朱春兰担任主编并统稿，浙江凯喜雅股份有限公司单证科的李韶辉科长参加了审稿。参加编写的人员有：朱春兰（模块一、模块二之实训六、七），翁旭青（模块二之实训一、二、三、四），李韶辉（模块二之实训五）。

本书可作为高职高专国际贸易、国际商务、商务英语、英用英语等相关专业的教学用书，也可作为外贸行业单证岗位培训用书，还可供经贸类管理人员和从业人员的参考用书。

本书在编写和出版过程中得到了有关外贸公司领导和专家的大力支持和帮助，他们提供了大量外贸单证材料，在此表示衷心的感谢。本书也得到了浙江经贸职业技术学院丁珏、罗俊勤、方巧云等教师的帮助，谢谢他们的不吝赐教。同时，为丰富本书内容，在编写过程中，还参阅和引用了国内外有关论著、网站的资料和观点，书中未一一列出，在此一并向有关作者致谢。

由于编者学识水平和能力所限，书中的谬误及疏忽之处在所难免，敬请广大读者批评指正，以便再版时予以修正、完善。

编者
2010 年 11 月

目 录
Contents

模块一

单项能力训练

＞＞＞　＞

项目一　信用证条款分析

实训目标

能够分析信用证条款。

实训任务

§ **实训一**

1.浙江凯喜雅股份有限公司收到了由中国银行浙江省分行发出的信用证通知书和随附的信用证。要求:仔细阅读信用证通知书及随附的信用证,并找出下列内容。

(1)信用证的种类

(2)信用证号码

(3)开证日期

(4)信用证的有效期、到期地点

(5)开证申请人

(6)受益人

(7)付款行

(8)开证行

(9)通知行

(10)信用证金额及货币单位

(11)分批装运、转运

(12)装运港(地)、目的港(地)

(13)最迟装运期

(14)货名及规格

(15)货物数量

(16)价格术语

(17)海运提单种类

(18)交单期限

(19)信用证要求的单据

(20)信用证特别条款

（一）信用证通知书

中国银行
BANK OF CHINA

ZHEJIANG BRANCH   EB02

ADDRESS：321 FENGQI ROAD, HANGZHOU

CABLE：6892

TELEX：35019 BOCHZ CN   信用证通知书

SWIFT：BKCH CNBJ 910   NOTIFICATION OF DOCUMENTARY CREDIT

FAX：85010842   2009/05/04

TO 致：2099530 ZHEJIANG CATHAYA INT'L CO.,LTD. 117 TIYU CHANG ROAD,HANGZHOU,CHINA TEL：0571－85199162 FAX：85199159	WHEN CORRESPONDING PLEASE QUOTE OUR REF. NO AD91009103334
ISSUING BANK 开证行 8000974 BANK OF TOKYO-MITSUBISHI UFJ,LTD. OSAKA	TRANSMITTED TO US THROUGH 转递行 REF. NO. REIM BANK

中国银行浙江省分行
出口业务专用章
9100101

L/C NO. 信用证号 S-441-2000029	DATED 开证日期 2009/04/30	AMOUNT 金额 USD30,000.00	EXPIRY PLACE 有效地 LOCAL
EXPIRY DATE 有效期 2009/07/30	TENOR 期限 0 DAYS	CHARGE 未付费用 RMB200.00	CHARGE BY 费用承担人 BENE
RECEIVED VIA 来证方式 SWIFT	信用证是否生效 VALID	印押是否相符 YES	我行是否保兑 NO

DEAR SIRS,迳启者：

WE HAVE PLEASURE IN ADVISING YOU THAT WE HAVE RECEIVED FROM THE A/M BANK A(N) LETTER OF CREDIT,CONTENTS OF WHICH ARE AS PER ATTACHED SHEET(S).

THIS ADVICE AND THE ATTACHED SHEET(S) MUST ACCOMPANY THE RELATIVE DOCUMENTS WHEN PRESENTED FOR NEGOTIATION.

兹通知贵司,我行收自上述银行信用证一份,现随附通知。贵司交单时,请将本通知书及信用证一并提示。

REMARKS 备注：

PLEASE NOTE THAT THIS ADVICE DOES NOT CONSTITUTE OUR CONFIRMATION OF THE ABOVE L/C NOR DOES IT CONVEY ANY ENGAGEMENT OR OBLIGATION ON OUR PART.

THIS L/C CONSISTS OF ____ SHEET(S), INCLUDING THE COVERING LETTER AND AT-TACHMENT(S).

本信用证连同面函及附件共____纸。

IF YOU FIND ANY TERMS AND CONDITIONS IN THE L/C WHICH YOU ARE UNABLE TO COMPLY WITH AND OR ANY ERROR(S), IT IS SUGGESTED THAT YOU CONTACT APPLICANT DIRECTLY FOR NECESSARY AMENDMENT(S) SO AS TO AVOID ANY DIFFICULTIES WHICH MAY ARISE WHEN DOCUMENTS ARE PRESENED.

如本信用证中有无法办到的条款及/或错误,请迳与开证申请人联系,进行必要的修改,以排除交单时可能发生的问题。

THIS L/C IS ADVISED SUBJECT TO ICC UCP PUBLICATION NO. 600.

本信用证之通知系遵循国际商会跟单信用证统一惯例第 600 号出版物办理。

> YOURS FAITHFULLY,
>
> FOR BANK OF CHINA, ZHEJIANG

(二)信用证

2009APR30 13:47:51　　　　　　　　　　　　LOGICAL TERMINAL H020

MT S700　　　　ISSUE OF A DOCUMENTARY CREDIT　　PAGE 00001

　　　　　　　　　　　　　　　　　　　　　　　　FUNC MSG700

　　　　　　　　　　　　　　　　　　　　　　　　UMR 40501961

MSGACK　DWS765I AUTH OK, KEY DIGEST, BKCHCNBJ BOTKJPJT RECORD

BASIC HEADER　　　　F 01 BKCHCNBJA910 1751 951800

APPLICATION HEADER　0 700 1447 090430 BOTKJPJTAOSA 1569 057082 090430 1347 N

　　　　　　　　　　* BANK OF TOKYO-MITSUBISHI UFJ, LTD.

　　　　　　　　　　* THE OSAKA

USER HEADER　　　　SERVICE CODE　　103:

　　　　　　　　　　BANK. PRIORITY　　113:

　　　　　　　　　　MSG USER REF.　　108:

　　　　　　　　　　INFO. FROM CI　　115:

SEQUENCE OF TOTAL　　*27　: 1/1

FORM OF DOC. CREDIT　*40A : IRREVOCABLE

DOC. CREDIT NUMBER　*20　: S-441-2000029

DATE OF ISSUE　　　　31C　: 090430

APPLICABLE RULES　　*40E : UCP LATEST VERSION

EXPIRY　　　　　　　*31D : DATE 090730　PLACE IN BENEFICIARIES' COUNTRY

APPLICANT　　　　　*50　: HOEI SEN-I CO., LTD

　　　　　　　　　　　172 MOTOKITAKOJI-CHO, IMADEGAWA

　　　　　　　　　　　OMIYA NISHIIRU, KAMIGYO-KU, KYOTO

BENEFICIARY　　　　*59　: ZHEJIANG CATHAYA INTERNATIONAL CO., LTD.

　　　　　　　　　　　117 TIYU CHANG ROAD, HANGZHOU, CHINA

AMOUNT　　　　　　*32B : CURRENCY USD AMOUNT 30.000,

POS./NEG. TOL. (%)　39A : 10/10

AVAILABLE WITH/ BY　*41D : ANY BANK

　　　　　　　　　　　BY NEGOTIATION

```
DRAFTS AT ···          42C : AT SIGHT
                             IN DUPLICATE
                             INDICATING THIS L/C NUMBER
DRAWEE                 42D : ISSUING BANK
PARTIAL SHIPMENTS      43P : ALLOWED
TRANSHIPMENT           43T : PROHIBITED
PORT OF LOADING        44E : SHANGHAI,CHINA
PORT OF DISCHARGE      44F : OSAKA
LATEST DATE OF SHIP.   44C : 090709
DESCRIPT. OF GOODS     45A :
SILK KNITTED GARMENTS
FOB SHANGHAI
```

DOCUMENTS REQUIRED   46A :
+SIGNED COMMERCIAL INVOICES IN 3 ORIGINALS
+FULL SET NOT LESS ONE ORIGINAL OF CLEAN ON BOARD OCEAN BILLS OF LADING MADE OUT TO ORDER OF SHIPPER AND BLANK ENDORSED MARKED FREIGHT COLLECT NOTIFY APPLICANT.
+BENEFICIARY'S CERTIFICATE STATING THAT ONE SET OF ORIGINAL DOCUMENTS INCLUDING 1/3 ORIGINAL B/L HAVE BEEN SENT DIRECTLY TO THE APPLICANT.

ADDITIONAL COND.   47A :
+INSURANCE IS TO BE EFFECTED BY BUYER.

DETAILS OF CHARGES   71B :
+ ALL BANKING CHARGES OUTSIDE JAPAN ARE FOR ACCOUNT OF BENEFICIARY.

PRESENTATION PERIOD   48 :
+DOCUMENTS MUST BE PRESENTED WITHIN 21 DAYS AFTER THE DATE OF SHIPMENT, BUT WITHIN THE VALIDITY OF THE CREDIT.

CONFIRMATION   * 49 : WITHOUT
INSTRUCTIONS   78 :
+REIMBURSEMENT BY TELECOMMUNICATION IS PROHIBITED.
+ THIS CREDIT IS AVAILABLE ON SIGHT BASIS. ALL DOCUMENTS MUST BE SENT TO US, I. E. THE BANK OF TOKYO-MITSUBISHI UFJ, LTD. GLOBAL SERVICE CENTRE 1-1 KAWARAMACHI 2-CHOME,CHUO-KU,OSAKA 541-0048 JAPAN IN ONE LOT BY COURIER SERVICE. IN REIMBURSEMENT WE SHALL REMIT PROCEEDS ACCORDING TO YOUR INSTRUCTIONS.
+ A DISCREPANCY FEE OF USD45.00 WILL BE DEDUCTED FROM THE PROCEEDS IF DOCUMENTS CONTAINING DISCREPANCIES ARE PRESENTED TO US UNDER THIS CREDIT.

TRAILER   ORDER IS <MAC:> <PAC:> <ENC:> <CHK:> <TNG:> <PDE:>
               MAC: 8EC9ADEA
               CHK: E57C9DA0353D

2.浙江凯喜雅股份有限公司对信用证进行了认真审核,发现一些不能接受而需要修改的条款,于是向买方提出改证的要求。过后,浙江凯喜雅股份有限公司收到由中国银行浙江省分行发出的信用证修改通知书及随附的修改。要求:仔细阅读信用证修改通知书及随附的修改,比较与原证的区别,并填写信用证分析单。

(一)信用证修改通知书

中国银行 BANK OF CHINA

ZHEJIANG BRANCH   NEA3

ADDRESS:321 FENGQI ROAD, HANGZHOU

CABLE:6892

TELEX:35019 BOCHZ CN   修改通知书

SWIFT:BKCH CNBJ 910   NOTIFICATION OF AMENDMENT

FAX:85010842   2009/07/20

| TO 致:2099530
ZHEJIANG CATHAYA INT'L CO. ,LTD.
117 TIYU CHANG ROAD,HANGZHOU,CHINA
TEL:0571-85199162   FAX:85199159 | WHEN CORRESPONDING
PLEASE QUOTE OUR REF. NO | AD91009103334 |
| ISSUING BANK 开证行 8000974
BANK OF TOKYO-MITSUBISHI UFJ,LTD. OSAKA | TRANSMITTED TO US THROUGH 转递行
REF. NO.
REIM BANK | |

中国银行浙江省分行
出口业务专用章
9100101

L/C NO. 信用证号 S-441-2000029	DATED 开证日期 2009/04/30	AMOUNT 金额 USD30,000.00	EXPIRY PLACE 有效地 LOCAL
EXPIRY DATE 有效期 2009/10/15	TENOR 期限 0 DAYS	CHARGE 未付费用 RMB100.00	CHARGE BY 费用承担人 BENE
RECEIVED VIA 来证方式 SWIFT	信用证是否生效 VALID	印押是否相符 YES	我行是否保兑 NO
AMEND NO 修改次数 1	AMEND DATE 修改日期 2009/07/17	INCREASE 增额 USD23,000.00	DECREASE 减额 USD0.00

DEAR SIRS,迳启者:

WE HAVE PLEASURE IN ADVISING YOU THAT WE HAVE RECEIVED FROM THE A/M BANK A(N) AMENDMENT TO THE CAPTIONED L/C,CONTENTS OF WHICH ARE AS PER AT-TACHED SHEET(S).

兹通知贵司,我行自上述银行收到修改一份,内容见附件。

THIS AMENDMENT SHOULD BE ATTACHED TO THE CAPTIONED L/C ADVISED BY US,

OTHERWISE, THE BENEFICIARY WILL BE RESPONSIBLE FOR ANY CONSEQUENCES ARISING THEREFROM.

本修改须附于有关信用证,否则,贵公司须对因此而产生的后果承担责任。

REMARKS 备注:

THIS AMENDMENT CONSISTS OF ＿＿ SHEET(S), INCLUDING THE COVERING LETTER AND ATTACHMENT(S).

本修改连同面函及附件共＿＿纸。

KINDLY TAKE NOTE THAT THE PARTIAL ACCEPTANCE OF THE AMENDMENT IS NOT ALLOWED.

本修改不能部分接受。

THIS AMENDMENT IS ADVISED SUBJECT TO ICC UCP PUBLICATION WHICH APPLY TO THE ORIGINAL L/C.

本修改之通知系遵循原信用证适用的国际商会跟单信用证统一惯例。

> YOURS FAITHFULLY,
> FOR BANK OF CHINA, ZHEJIANG

（二）随附的修改

```
2009JUL17 12：47：51                          LOGICAL TERMINAL H020
MT S707     AMENDMENT TO A DOCUMENTARY CREDIT  PAGE 00001
                                              FUNC MSG700
                                              UMR 41710126

MSGACK  DWS765I AUTH   OK, KEY DIGEST, BKCHCNBJ BOTKJPJT RECORD
BASIC HEADER          F 01 BKCHCNBJA910 1778 261570
APPLICATION HEADER   0 707 1328 090717 BOTKJPJTAOSA 1584 815346 090717 1228 N
                      * BANK OF TOKYO-MITSUBISHI UFJ, LTD.
                      * THE OSAKA
USER HEADER          SERVICE CODE      103：
                     BANK. PRIORITY    113：
                     MSG USER REF.     108：
                     INFO. FROM CI     115：
SENDER'S REF.        * 20 ：S-441-2000029
RECEIVER'S REF.      * 21 ：NONREF
DATE OF ISSUE         31C ：090430
DATE OF AMENDMENT     30 ：090717
NUMBER OF AMENDMENT 26E ：01
APPLICABLE RULES     * 40E：UCP LATEST VERSION
BENEFICIARY          * 59 ：ZHEJIANG CATHAYA INTERNATIONAL CO., LTD.
                            117 TIYU CHANG ROAD, HANGZHOU, CHINA
NEW DATE OF EXPIRY    31E ：091015
INCREASE DOC CREDIT   32B ：CURRENCY USD AMOUNT 23.000,
NEW AMOUNT            34B ：CURRENCY USD AMOUNT 53.000,
POS./NEG. TOL. (%)    39A ：10/10
```

LATEST DATE OF SHIP.　44C　：090924

　　＊＊REPEATABLE SEQUENCE 001＊＊＊＊＊＊＊＊＊＊＊OCCURRENCE 00001

TRAILER　　　　　ORDER IS ＜MAC：＞ ＜PAC：＞ ＜ENC：＞ ＜CHK：＞ ＜TNG：＞ ＜PDE：＞

　　　　　　　　　MAC：F02FD807

　　　　　　　　　CHK：B81919F459DB

信用证分析单

信用证分析单　　　　　　　(1)编号： (2)本证　　　年　　月　　　日收到							
开证行(3)			开证日(4)				
申请人(5)			受益人(6)				
信用证金额(7)			信用证号码(8)				
汇票付款人(9)			汇票期限(10)				
可否转运(11)			可否分批(12)				
装运期限(13)		信用证有效期(14)			到期地点(15)		
运输标志(16)			交单期(17)				
单据名称	提单 (18)	发票 (19)	装箱单 (20)	保险单 (21)	检验证 (22)		
银行							
客户							
提单或 承运单据	抬头(23)						
	通知(24)						
	注意事项						
保险	险别(25)						
	加成(26)						
其他注意事项：							

§ 实训二

仔细阅读信用证通知书及随附的信用证,并找出下列内容。

（1）信用证的种类

（2）信用证号码

（3）开证日期

（4）信用证的有效期、到期地点

（5）开证申请人

（6）受益人

（7）付款行

（8）开证行

（9）通知行

（10）信用证金额及货币单位

（11）分批装运、转运

（12）装运港（地）、目的港（地）

（13）最迟装运期

（14）货名及规格

（15）货物数量

（16）价格术语

（17）海运提单种类

（18）交单期限

（19）信用证要求的单据

（20）信用证特别条款

- -

（一）信用证通知书

NatWest

TELEPHONE	:020 7672 7230	LONDON TRADE SERVICES CENTRE
FACSIMILE	:020 7672 6221	DOCUMENTARY CREDITS
S. W. I. F. T	:NWBKGB2L	PO BOX 39971,GROUND FLOOR
		DEVONSHIRE SQUARE
		LONDON EC2M 4XB

NOBLECONTROL LTD

T/A FIGURE CLOTHING

25－31 CHEETHAM HILL ROAD

MANCHESTER M4 4FY

18 DECEMBER 2009
DEARS SIRS,
OUR REFERENCE：DOCUMENTARY CERDIT NO. TFPCYF922786
VALUE：USD80,350.00
IN FAVOUR OF：HANGZHOU DALI GARMENT COMPANY
YOUR REFERENCE：

IN ACCORDANCE WITH YOUR INSTRUCTIONS WE HAVE ISSUED THE ABOVE DOCUMENTARY CREDIT WITH CHANGES AS AGREED AND ARE PLEASED TO ENCLOSE A COPY FOR YOUR RECORDS.

WE NOTE THAT ALL CHARGES UNDER THIS DOCUMENTARY CREDIT ARE FOR ACCOUNT OF THE BENEFICIARY. HOWEVER, IN ACCORDANCE WITH ARTICLE 18C OF THE UCP WE RESERVE THE RIGHT TO DEBIT YOUR ACCOUNT WITH ALL CHARGES, INCLUDING OURS AS MENTIONED IN THE ENCLOSED DOCUMENTARY CREDIT, IN THE EVENT OF NON PAYMENT BY THE BENEFICIARY.

WE ARE PLEASED TO ADVISE THAT THIS LETTER OF CREDIT IS SUBJECT TO OUR SPECIAL PROCESSING ARRANGEMENT WITH STANDARD CHARTERED BANK, HONGKONG, THE DETAILS OF WHICH HAVE PREVIOUSLY BEEN ADVISED TO YOU.

YOU MAY BE AWARE THAT THE ICC HAS UPDATED THE CURRENT UNIFORM CUSTOMS AND PRACTICE FOR DOCUMENTARY CREDITS, THEREFORE PLEASE NOTE THAT ALL CREDITS ARE AUTOMATICALLY ISSUED SUBJECT TO UCP600 WITH EFFECT FROM 1ST JULY 2007. THIS OVERRIDES ANY REFERENCE TO UCP500 THAT MAY BE MENTIONED IN YOUR APPLICATION.

KINDLY QUOTE OUR ABOVE REFERENCE NUMBER IN ANY CORRESPONDENCE. SHOULD YOU HAVE ANY QUERIES PLEASE CONTACT LONDON TRADE SERVICE CENTRE CUSTOMER SERVICE TEAM ON 020 7672 7230.

YOURS FAITHFULLY,

JULIE HARRIS

AUTHORISED SIGNATORY

(二)信用证

DATE：18 DEC 2009   SWIFT MESSAGE-MT700
STANDERD CHARTERED BANK (HONG KONG) LTD.
15TH FLOOR, STANDARD CHARTERED TOWER,
388 KWUN TONG ROAD, KWUN TONG, HONGKONG
{1：F01NWBKGB2LXXXX0000000000}{2：1700SCBLHKHHXXXXN1005}{4：

:27 : SEQUENCE OF TOTAL

1/1

:40A: FORM OF DOCUMENTARY CREDIT

IRREVOCABLE

:20 : DOCUMENTARY CREDIT NUMBER

TFPCYF922786

:31C: DATE OF ISSUE

091218

:40E: APPLICABLE RULES

UCP LATEST VERSION

:31D: DATE AND PLACE OF EXPIRY

100320 CHINA

:50 : APPLICANT

NOBLECONTROL LTD

T/A FIGURE CLOTHING

25—31 CHEETHAM HILL ROAD

MANCHESTER M4 4FY

:59 : BENEFICIARY

HANGZHOU DALI GARMENT COMPANY

37 HUANGTANG ROAD

HANGZHOU,CHINA 311100

:32B: CURRENCY CODE, AMOUNT

USD80350,

:41D: AVAILABLE WITH … BY …

ANY BANK IN CHINA BY NEGOTIATION

:42C: DRAFTS AT …

SIGHT

:42D: DRAWEE

THE ROYAL BANK OF SCOTLAND PLC HONGKONG

:43P: PARTIAL SHIPMENTS

PARTIAL SHIPMENTS ARE ALLOWED

:43T: TRANSHIPMENT

TRANSHIPMENT ARE ALLOWED

:44E: PORT OF LOADING/AIRPORT OF DEPARTURE

SHANGHAI PORT

:44F: PORT OF DISCHARGE/AIRPORT OF DESTINATION

ANY U. K. PORT

: 44C: LATEST DATE OF SHIPMENT

100228

:45A: DESCRIPTION OF GOODS AND/OR SERVICES

COVERING: LADIES GARMENTS

STYLES LL4936/FIG21

TOTAL VALUE OF GOODS USD 80,350.00

SHIPPING TERMS: FOB SHANGHAI

:46A: DOCUMENTS REQUIRED

+1) INVOICE IN 3 COPIES EACH INDIVIDUALLY SIGNED.

+2) FULL SET OF CLEAN ON 'BOARD OCEAN'MARINE BILLS OF LADING ISSUED TO ORDER AND BLANK ENDORSED AND EVIDENCING FREIGHT COLLECT AND NOTIFY PARTY—NOBLECONTROL LTD T/A FIGURE CLOTHING,25—31 CHEETHAM HILL ROAD MANCHESTER M4 4FY.

+3) COPY PACKING LIST

+4) COPY CERTIFICATE OF ORIGIN

+5) COPY CERTIFICATE OF ORIGIN GSP FORM 'A'

+6) BENS CERTIFICATE CONFIRMING THAT THE FOLLOWING DOCUMENTS HAVE BEEN SENT BY REGISTERED COURIER (COPY OF COURIER RECEIPT TO BE ATTACHED) AT SENDERS RISK TO THE L/C APPLICANT (ALL DOCUMENTS TO BE ORIGINAL).

A. INVOICE IN TRIPLICATE EACH INDIVIDUALLY SIGNED

B. PACKING LIST

C. CERTIFICATE OF ORIGIN GSP FORM 'A'

D. CERTIFICATE OF ORIGIN

+7) BENS CERT CONFIRMING PRODUCTION SAMPLES COVERING ALL STYLES, COLOURS AND SIZES ON ORDER HAVE BEEN SENT TO L/C APPLICANT FOR THE APPROVAL BY ANUJ VIJ.

+8) INSPECTION REPORT PURPORTED TO BE ISSUED AND SIGNED BY ANUJ VIJ APPROVING THE PRODUCTION SAMPLES AND CONFIRMING THAT THE GOODS CAN BE DESPATCHED.

:47A: ADDITIONAL CONDITIONS

+WE UNDERSTAND THAT THE INSURANCE IS BEING CARED FOR BY THE APPLICANT.

+A DOCUMENT HANDLING FEE OF USD40 OR EQUIVALENT AND A REIMBURSEMENT FEE OF USD60 OR EQUIVALENT ARE TO BE PAID ON ALL DRAWINGS.

+A DISCREPANCY FEE OF USD65 OR EQUIVALENT AND ANY RELATED CABLE CHARGES FOR DISCREPANT DOCS ARE FOR BENEFICIARYS ACCOUNT.

+ALL DOCUMENTS CALLED FOR UNDER THIS L/C OTHER THAN

THOSE WHICH BY ITS TERMS ARE PERMITTED TO BE COPIES MUST BE ISSUED CLEARLY MARKED ORIGINAL ON THEIR FACE.

＋ALL DOCUMENTS AND DRAFTS MUST BE SENT IN ONE LOT BY COURIER THROUGH YOUR BANKERS TO 7TH FLOOR, STANDARD CHARTERED TOWER, 388 KWUN TONG ROAD, KWUN TONG, HONG KONG ATTN THE ROYAL BANK OF SCOTLAND PLC HONG KONG, L/C PROCESSING CENTRE.

＋ANY COMMUNICATION CAN BE SENT BY FAX 852 23771823, TELEX 77923 SCHNKHX OR SWIFT SCBLHKHH WITH REQUEST TO RELAY MESSAGE TO THE ROYAL BANK OF SCOTLAND PLC HONG KONG, L/C PROCESSING CENTRE.

＋THE NUMBER AND DATE OF THE CREDIT AND NAME OF OUR BANK MUST BE QUOTED ON ALL DRAFTS REQUIRED.

＋ALL BANKING CHARGES INCLUDING OPENING COMMISSION OF USD340.42 AND EXAMINATION COMMISSION CALCULATED AT 0.125 PER CENT PER PRESENTATION（MINIMUN USD75）ARE FOR THE BENEFICIARYS ACCOUNT.

:71B：CHARGE

ALL BANKING CHARGES ARE FOR ACCOUNT OF BENEFICIARY.

:48　：PERIOD FOR PRESENTATION

21 DAYS AFTER SHIPMENT DATE

:49　：CONFIRMATION INSTRUCTIONS：

WITHOUT

:78　：INSTRUCTIONS TO PAYING/ACCEPTING/NEGOTIATING BANK

THIS L/C IS ISSUED BY THE ROYAL BANK OF SCOTLAND PLC HONG KONG WHO UNDERTAKE TO HONOUR DRAFTS ACCOMPANIED BY DOCUMENTS IF PRESENTED IN CONFORMITY WITH CREDIT TERMS.

:57D："ADVISE THROUGH"BANK：

SHANGHAI PUDONG DEVELOPMENT BANK

HANGZHOU

CHINA

:72　：SENDER TO RECEIVER INFORMATION

PRIV/RBOS

ORIGINATING IBC CITY

—}

§ 实训三

1. 杭州万盛国际贸易有限公司收到了由上海浦东发展银行杭州分行余杭支行发出的信用证通知书和随附的信用证。要求：仔细阅读信用证通知书及随附的信用证，并找出下列内容。

(1) 信用证的种类
(2) 信用证号码
(3) 开证日期
(4) 信用证的有效期、到期地点
(5) 开证申请人
(6) 受益人
(7) 付款行
(8) 开证行
(9) 通知行
(10) 信用证金额及货币单位
(11) 分批装运、转运
(12) 装运港（地）、目的港（地）
(13) 最迟装运期
(14) 货名及规格
(15) 货物数量
(16) 价格术语
(17) 海运提单种类
(18) 交单期限
(19) 信用证要求的单据
(20) 信用证特别条款

（一）信用证通知书

LETTER OF CREDIT ADVICE

OUR REF.：EX951107001107
DATED：2009-12-14

TO：HANGZHOU WANSHENG INTERNATIONAL TRADING INC.
致：杭州万盛国际贸易有限公司
ISSUING BANK ：SOCIETE GENERALE
开证行　　　　　75009 PARIS
RECEIVED VIA：
转递行/转让行
L/C NO.　　　：22001-0061642LLM
信用证编号

L/C AMT 　　　 : USD32240.00
信用证金额

WE HAVE PLEASURE IN ADVISING YOU THAT WE HAVE RECEIVED FROM THE ABOVE BANK THE CAPTIONED CREDIT, IN FULL DETAILS, CONTENTS OF WHICH ARE AS PER THE ATTACHED.

PLEASE NOTE THAT UNLESS OTHERWISE STAMPED ON THE ATTACHED CREDIT, THIS CREDIT DOES NOT BEAR OUR CONFIRMATION NOR INVOLVE ANY UNDERTAKING(S) ON OUR PART.

THIS ADVICE AND THE ATTACHED (AND ANY SUBSEQUENT AMENDMENT) MUST ACCOMPANY ALL PRESENTATIONS. IN THE CASE OF MESSAGES RECEIVED BY CABLE OR TELEX, WE ACCEPT NO RESPONSIBILITY OR LIABILITY FOR ANY ERRORS, OMISSION OR DELAYS IN THE TRANSMISSION OF THE CABLE OR TELEX.

IF YOU FIND ANY TERMS IN THIS CREDIT YOU ARE UNABLE TO COMPLY WITH OR ANY ERRORS IN YOUR NAME AND/OR ADDRESS, PLEASE COMMUNICATE(DIRECT WITH YOUR) BUYERS IMMEDIATELY WITH A VIEW TO ARRANGING ANY DEFINED AMENDMENTS AND THUS AVOID DIFFICULTIES WHICH WOULD OTHERWISE ARISE WHEN DOCUMENTS ARE PRESENTED.

　　我行荣幸地通知贵公司，兹收到来自上述银行的全电信用证，信用证内容附后。

　　提请贵公司注意，除非我行在随附的信用证上盖章注明，否则我行对该证不加具保兑，也不承担任何责任。

　　此信用证通知及随附的信用证，包括今后可能有的信用证修改，在所有交单中都应一并提交。若收到的信息以电报或电传方式发送，则我行对电讯（报）和电传传递过程中发生的任何错误、遗漏和延迟都不负有责任。

　　请仔细阅读随附的信用证，若您发现有无法执行的条款或您的名称、地址有错误，请迅速与买方取得直接联系，安排其进行修改，以避免将来交单时可能遇到的困难。

　　　　　　　　　　　FOR SHANGHAI PUDONG DEVELOPMENT BANK
　　　　　　　　　　　上海浦东发展银行

THIS LETTER OF CREDIT IS SUBJUCT TO UCP LATEST VERSION.

上海浦东发展银行杭州分行
余杭支行
信用证通知章

（二）信用证

Eximbills Enterprise Incoming Swift

==

Message Type：700
Send Bank ： SOGEFRPPXXX
SOCIETE GENERALE
75009 PARIS
Recv Bank ： SPDBCNSH336
SHANGHAI PUDONG DEVELOPMENT BANK
310006 HANGZHOU
User Name ： 11001183 PRINT TIMES：1
Print Date ： 2009-12-14 15：01：01 MIR：091214SOGEFRPPLXXX1509651532

==

:27 ： SEQUENCE OF TOTAL
1/1
:40A： FORM OF DOCUMENTARY CREDIT
IRREVOCABLE
:20 ： DOCUMENTARY CREDIT NUMBER
22001-0061642LLM
:31C： DATE OF ISSUE
091214
:40E： APPLICABLE RULES
UCP LATEST VERSION
:31D： DATE AND PLACE OF EXPIRY
100219 CHINA
:51A： APPLICANT BANK
SOGEFRPPLLM
:50 ： APPLICANT
CAMAIEU INTERNATIONAL
211 AVENUE JULES BRAME
BP 229
59054 ROUBAIX CEDEX 1
:59 ： BENEFICIARY
HANGZHOU WANSHENG INTERNATIONAL TRADING INC
37 LONGHUANGTANG ROAD
LINPING，HANGZHOU
CHINA 311100
:32B： CURRENCY CODE，AMOUNT
USD32240，

:39A: PERCENTAGE CREDIT AMOUNT TOLERANCE
05/05
:41D: AVAILABLE WITH ⋯ BY ⋯
ANY BANK BY NEGOTIATION
:42C: DRAFTS AT ⋯
60 DAYS AFTER SHIPMENT DATE
:42A: DRAWEE
SOGEFRPP
:43P: PARTIAL SHIPMENTS
ALLOWED PER COMPLETE ORDER
:43T: TRANSHIPMENT
ALLOWED
:44E: PORT OF LOADING/AIRPORT OF DEPARTURE
SHANGHAI PORT
:44F: PORT OF DISCHARGE/AIRPORT OF DESTINATION
ROTTERDAM OR ANTWERP PORT
:44C: LATEST DATE OF SHIPMENT
100129
:45A: DESCRIPTION OF GOODS AND/OR SERVICES
FOB SHANGHAI PORT
+5200 PIECES LADIES 70 PCT VISCOSE 30 PCT POLYAMIDE KNITTED
PULLOVER（CAT 5）STYLE-ARIZONA － AT THE UNIT PRICE OF
USD6. 20 AS PER CAMAIEU ORDER 500431, LATEST SHIPMENT
DATE BY SEA 29/01/2010
:46A: DOCUMENTS REQUIRED
+ORIGINAL OF DULY DATED AND SIGNED DETAILED COMMER-
CIAL INVOICE IN 3 FOLDS MENTIONING FOR EACH CAMAIEU OR-
DER NUMBER THE PRECISE DESCRIPTION OF THE GOODS (COMPO-
SITION, MENTION PRECISING IF THE GARMENTS ARE WOVEN OR
KNITTED), THE QUANTITY OF ITEMS, THE UNIT PRICE AND THE
TOTAL AMOUNT WITH THE TOTALS OF ALL THE ORDERS.
+ORIGINAL OF DETAILED PACKING LIST (ONE SHEET PER OR-
DER) IN 2 FOLDS INDICATING THE FOLLOWING INFORMATION:
ORDER NO. , QUANTITY AND REFERENCE OF CARTONS, STYLE,
COLOR, QUANTITY OF ITEMS BY SIZE WITH THE TOTALS.
+PHOTOCOPY OF TEXTILE PRODUCTS CERTIFICATE OF ORIGIN
ISSUED BY CHINESE OFFICIAL AUTHORITY MENTIONING THE CA-
MAIEU ORDERS NUMBERS.
+PHOTOCOPY OF EXPORT LICENCE ISSUED BY CHINESE OFFICIAL

AUTHORITY BEARING THE CATEGORY IF IT INDICATED IN THE DESCRIPTION OF THE GOODS AND MENTIONING THE CAMAIEU ORDERS NUMBERS.

+ORIGINAL OR COPY OF DULY DATED STAMPED AND SIGNED IN-SPECTION CERTIFICATE ISSUED BY CAMAIUE CHINA.

+ ORIGINAL DATED AND SIGNED BENEFICIARIES ATTESTATION CERTIFYING THAT ALL ORIGINAL DOCUMENTS (INCLUDING 2/3 O-RIGINAL OF BILL OF LADING BUT EXCEPTED INSPECTION CERTIFI-CATE) HAVE BEEN SENT BY EXPRESS MAIL TO CAMAIEU FEMME 211 AVENUE BRAME B. P. 229 59054 ROUBAIX CEDEX FRANCE ATTN MRS SERVANE DUTHOIT WITHIN 7 DAYS AFTER SHIPMENT DATE (EXPRESS MAIL RECEIPT REQUIRED) AND THAT COPIES OR PHOTOCOPIES OF COMMERCIAL INVOICE, DETAILED PACKING LIST, TEXTILES PROD-UCTS CERTIFICATE OF ORIGIN, EXPORT LICENCE HAVE BEEN SENT TO CAMAIEU FEMME ATTN MRS SERVANE DUTHOIT WITHIN 3 DAYS AF-TER SHIPMENT DATE BY EMAIL TO SDUTHOITATCAMAIEU. FR(COPY OF EMAIL IS REQUIRED).

+1/3 ORIGINAL OF CLEAN ON BOARD BILLS OF LADING ISSUED BY SEDIS LOGISTICS CHINA LTD. , DULY DATED AND SIGNED MADE OUT TO ORDER OF CAMAIEU INTERNATIONAL 211 AVENUE BRAME 59054 ROUBAIX FRANCE SHOWING FREIGHT COLLECT NO-TIFY:

1) SEDIS LOGISTICS SA BLANDAIN TEL32. (0). 69. 33. 27. 27

2) CAMAIEU FEMME MRS SERVANE DUTHOIT TEL 33. 3. 20. 99. 53. 14

AND ONE NOT NEGOTIABLE COPY

:47A: ADDITIONAL CONDITIONS

+MORE OR LESS 5 PCT IN QUANTITY ACCEPTABLE

+A COPY OF CERTIFICATE NAMED-NEW TRANSPORT CONDITIONS-IS-SUED,DULY DATED, SIGNED AND STAMPED BY CAMAIEU FEMME IS REQUIRED IN CASE OF:

A/ LATE SHIPMENT

AND/OR

B/ CHANGE OF FORWARDERS AGENT PREVIOUSLY STATED ON L/C

THIS DOCUMENT MUST INDICATE THE FOLLOWING MENTION:

• L/C NUMBER

• ORDER NUMBER

• BENEFICIARY'S NAME

• NEW DATE OF SHIPMENT

• THE NEW FORWARDERS

      • THE ISSUER OF DOCUMENT CHECK LIST AND RECIEPT CERTIFI-
CATE (IN CASE OF AIR SHIPMENT)

IN CASE OF ERASURE THIS DOCUMENT WILL BE CONSIDERED AS
DISABLED.

THIS DOCUMENT WILL CANCEL ANY DISCREPANCIES ABOUT
LATE SHIPMENT DATE OF FORWARDER NAME DIFFERENT THAN
L/C REQUIREMENTS EXCEPT IN CASE OR CREDIT EXPIRED.

+THIS DOCUMENTARY CREDIT IS SUBJECT TO UCP 600(2007 REVI-
SION).

+THIS CREDIT IS TRANSFERABLE BY SHANGHAI PUDONG DEVEL-
OPMENT BANK

:71B: CHARGE

ALL BANKING CHARGES OUTSIDE FRANCE ARE FOR ACCOUNT OF
BENEFICIARY.

A FEE OF USD30.00 WILL BE DEDUCTED FOR EACH DISCREPANCY.

:48 : PERIOD FOR PRESENTATION

21 DAYS AFTER SHIPMENT DATE

:49 : CONFIRMATION INSTRUCTIONS:

WITHOUT

:78 : INSTRUCTIONS TO PAYING BANK

+WE HEREBY ENGAGE WITH DRAWERS, ENDORSERS OR BONA FIDE
HOLDERS THAT DRAFT(S) DRAWN AND NEGOTIATED ON PRESENTA-
TION AND THAT DRAFT(S) ACCEPTED WITHIN THE TERMS OF THIS
CREDIT WILL BE DULY HONOURED AT MATURITY.

:57D: "ADVISE THROUGH"BANK:

SHANGHAI PUDONG DEVELOPMENT BANK
YUHANG, HANGZHOU
CHINA

:72 : SENDER TO RECEIVER INFORMATION

/REC/FAXBEN:+86.571.85803670

:999 : {NULL}

IM9901080007958/0/9511

—}{5:00000000}{CHK:D86FAB7A4C35}{DLM:}{S:{SAC:}{COP:P}}

:

    2.杭州万盛国际贸易有限公司对信用证进行了认真审核,发现一些不能接受而需要修改的条款,于是向买方提出改证的要求。过后,杭州万盛国际贸易有限公司收到由上海浦东发展银行杭州分行余杭支行发出的信用证修改通知书及随附的修改。要求:仔细阅读信用证修改通知书及随附的修改,比较与原证的区别,并填写信用证分析单。

（一）信用证修改通知书

上海浦東發展銀行
SHANGHAI PUDONG DEVELOPMENT BANK

ADVICE OF LETTER OF CREDIT AMENDMENT

OUR REF.：EX951107001107-1

DATED：2010-1-3

TO：HANGZHOU WANSHENG INTERNATIONAL TRADING INC.

致：杭州万盛国际贸易有限公司

ISSUING BANK：SOCIETE GENERALE

开证行　　　　　75009 PARIS

RECEIVED VIA：

转递行/转让行

L/C NO.　　　　：22001-0061642LLM

信用证编号

L/C AMT　　　　：USD32240.00

信用证金额

WE HAVE PLEASURE IN ADVISING YOU THAT WE HAVE RECEIVED FROM THE ABOVE BANK THE REFERENCED AMENDMENT CONTENTS OF WHICH ARE AS PER THE ATTACHED.

PLEASE NOTE THAT UNLESS OTHERWISE STAMPED ON THE ATTACHED CREDIT, THIS CREDIT DOES NOT BEAR OUR CONFIRMATION NOR INVOLVE ANY UNDERTAKING(S) ON OUR PART.

THIS ADVICE AND THE ATTACHED（AND ANY SUBSEQUENT AMENDMENT）MUST ACCOMPANY ALL PRESENTATIONS. IN THE CASE OF MESSAGES RECEIVED BY CABLE OR TELEX, WE ACCEPT NO RESPONSIBILITY OR LIABILITY FOR ANY ERRORS, OMISSION OR DELAYS IN THE TRANSMISSION OF THE CABLE OR TELEX.

　　我行荣幸地通知贵公司，兹收到来自上述银行的上述编号的信用证修改，内容附后。

　　提请贵公司注意，除非我行在随附的信用证上盖章注明，否则我行对该证不加具保兑，也不承担任何责任。

　　此信用证修改通知及随附的修改，包括今后可能有的其他信用证修改，在所有交单中都应一并提交。若收到的信息以电报或电传方式发送，则我行对电讯（报）和电传传递过程中发生的任何错误、遗漏和延迟都不负有责任。

FOR SHANGHAI PUDONG DEVELOPMENT BANK
上海浦东发展银行

THIS LETTER OF CREDIT IS SUBJUCT TO UCP LATEST VERSION.

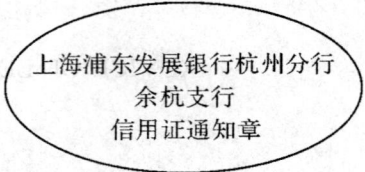

上海浦东发展银行杭州分行
余杭支行
信用证通知章

（二）随附的修改

Eximbills Enterprise Incoming Swift

===

Message Type：707

Send Bank　　：SOGEFRPPXX

　　　　　　　SOCIETE GENERALE

　　　　　　　75009 PARIS

Recv Bank　　：SPDBCNSH336

　　　　　　　SHANGHAI PUDONG DEVELOPMENT BANK

　　　　　　　310006 HANGZHOU

User Name　　：11001183　　PRINT　TIMES：1

Print Date　　：2010-01-03　14：58：10　MIR：100102SOGEFRPPCXXX4056550275

===

:20　: SENDER'S REFERENCE NUMBER

　　　22001-0061642LLM

:21　: RECEIVER'S REFERENCE

　　　UNKNOWN

:31C: DATE OF ISSUE

　　　091214

:26E: NUMBER OF AMENDMENT

　　　01

:59　: BENEFICIARY(BEFORE THIS AMENDMENT)

　　　HANGZHOU WANSHENG INTERNATIONAL TRADING INC

　　　37 LONGHUANGTANG ROAD

　　　LINPING，HANGZHOU

　　　CHINA 311100

:31D：NEW EXPIRY DATE

　　　100308

:44E: PORT OF LOADING/AIRPORT OF DEPARTURE

　　　SHANGHAI PORT

:44F: PORT OF DISCHARGE/AIRPORT OF DESTINATION

BRUSSELS BELGIUM OR LILLE LESQUIN FRANCE AIRPORT

:44C: LATEST DATE OF SHIPMENT

100227

:79 : NARRATIVE

+LATEST SHIPMENT DATE BY AIR FROM SHANGHAI AIRPORT TO LILLE LESQUIN AIRPORT 27/02/2010.

+FCA SHANGHAI AIRPORT

+PERIOD FOR PRESENTATION 10 DAYS AFTER SHIPMENT DATE AND NEW DOCUMENTS REQUIRED:

+ORIGINAL OF HOUSE AIRWAYBILL ISSUED BY KAOSCO EXPRESS CO. LTD. ,DULY DATED AND SIGNED CONSIGNED TO CAMAIEU INTERNATIONAL 211 AVENUE BRAME 59054 ROUBAIX FRANCE SHOWING ALL COLLECT,NOTIFY:

1) NIPPON EXPRESS BELGIUM ATTN MR HANS COOLS TEL32. 2. 753. 02. 41

2) CAMAIEU FEMME MRS SERVANE DUTHOIT TEL33. 3. 20. 99. 53. 14

+PHOTOCOPY OR FAX OF-DOCUMENTS CHECK-LIST AND RECEIPT CERTIFICATE-DOCUMENT DULY FILLED IN, DATED, SIGNED AND STAMPED BY THE FORWARDER KAOSCO EXPRESS CO. ,LTD. CERTIFYING THE RECEIPT BY THEM OF ALL THE ORIGINAL DOCUMENTS EXCEPT TEXTILE PRODUCTS CERTIFICATE OF ORIGIN, EXPORT LICENCE, HOUSE AIRWAYBILL AND INSPECTION CERTIFICATE NOT LATER THAN THE SHIPMENT DATE.

+ORIGINAL DATED, STAMPED AND SIGNED BENEFICIARIES ATTESTATION CERTIFYING THAT ORIGINAL OF TEXTILE PRODUCTS CERTIFICATE OF ORIGIN AND EXPORT LICENCE HAVE BEEN SENT BY EXPRESS MAIL BEFORE SHIPMENT DATE TO CAMAIEU FEMME 211 AVENUE BRAME B. P. 229 59054 ROUBAIX CEDEX FRANCE ATTN MRS SERVANE DUTHOIT (EXPRESS MAIL RECEIPT REQUIRED) AND THAT COPIES OR PHOTOCOPIES OF COMMERCIAL INVOICE, DETAILED PACKING LIST, TEXTILES PRODUCTS CERTIFICATE OF ORIGIN, EXPORT LICENCE HAVE BEEN SENT TO CAMAIEU FEMME ATTN MRS SERVANE DUTHOIT BY EMAIL TO SDUTHOITATCAMAIEU. FR THE SAME DAY THAN SHIPMENT DATE AT THE LATEST(COPY OF EMAIL IS REQUIRED).

:72 : SENDER TO RECEIVER INFORMATION

ALL OTHER TERMS UNCHANGED

:999 : {NULL}

IM9901080004329/0/9501

一}{5:{MAC:00000000}{CHK:3CD7D3E8D6F4}{DLM:}{S:{SAC:}{COP:P}}

:

信用证分析单

信用证分析单			(1)编号：			
(2)本证　　　年　　月　　日收到						
开证行(3)				开证日(4)		
申请人(5)				受益人(6)		
信用证金额(7)				信用证号码(8)		
汇票付款人(9)				汇票期限(10)		
可否转运(11)				可否分批(12)		
装运期限(13)		信用证有效期(14)			到期地点(15)	
运输标志(16)				交单期(17)		

单据名称	提单(18)	发票(19)	装箱单(20)	保险单(21)	检验证(22)		
银行							
客户							

提单或承运单据	抬头(23)	
	通知(24)	
	注意事项	
保险	险别(25)	
	加成(26)	

其他注意事项：

实训指导

一、信用证的基本内容

（一）关于信用证本身的说明

主要有信用证号码（L/C NO.）、开证日期和地点（Date of Issue and Place）、有效期和有效地点（Expiry Date and Place）、交单期（Presentation Period）、信用证种类（Form of Documentary Credit）、信用证当事人、信用证金额和币种（L/C Amount and Currency）、费用条款（Details of Charges）等。

有效期指交单付款、承兑或议付的最后期限。未规定到期日/有效期的信用证是无效的。凡过有效期提交的单据，开证行有权拒收。

有效地点是指有效期应以受益人向何地银行的交单日期为准。在我国的出口业务中，原则上应争取在我国到期，以便我方在交付货物后能及时办理议付、要求付款或承兑。

交单期是指向银行提交单据要求付款、承兑或议付的特定期限。如信用证无规定交单期，按惯例，单据在运输单据签发日后 21 天内提交，但不得迟于信用证的有效期。

信用证当事人主要有开证行（Opening Bank/Issuing Bank）、开证申请人/开证人（Applicant/Opener）、受益人（Beneficiary）、通知行（Advising Bank/Notifying Bank）、议付行（Negotiating Bank）等内容。

（二）对汇票说明

主要用来说明 L/C 对汇票的要求，如出票人（Drawer）、付款人/受票人（Payer/Drawee）、汇票金额（Draft Amount）、汇票期限（Tenor）、出票条款（Drawn Clause）等。不需汇票的信用证没有此项内容。

（三）对装运说明

主要包括装运港（Port of Loading/Loading in Charge）、目的港（Port of Discharge/for Transport to）、装运期（Latest Date of Shipment）、分批装运（Partial Shipments）和转运（Transhipment）规定。

（四）对货物说明

一般包括货物名称和规格（Description and Specification）、数量（Quantity）、单价（Unit Price）、总值（Total Amount）、包装（Packing）等。

（五）对单据要求

主要规定应提交单据名称、份数和具体要求。常见单据有:商业发票（Commercial Invoice）、提单（Bill of Lading）、保险单（Insurance Policy）、原产地证书（Certificate of Origin）、检验证书（Inspection Certificate）、受益人证明书（Beneficiary's Certificate）、装船通知（Shipping Advice）、装箱单（Packing List）等。

单据份数英文表述为:IN DUPLICATE(TRIPLICATE, QUADRUPLICATE, QUINTUPLICATE, SEXTUTPLICATE, SEPTUPLICATE, OCTUPLICATE, NONUPLICATE, DECUPLICATE)一式两份（三、四、五、六、七、八、九、十份）。

（六）特殊条款

特殊条款主要是根据进口国政治经济贸易情况的变化或每一笔具体交易的需要而作

出的特别规定。

(七)其他内容

1.给议付行/付款行/承兑行的指示

给议付行/付款行/承兑行的指示(Instructions to Negotiating Bank/Paying Bank/Accepting Bank)一般包括偿付方式、寄单方式和议付金额、背书条款等。如:

YOU ARE AUTHORIZED TO REIMBURSE YOURSELF FOR THE AMOUNT OF YOUR NEGOTIATION BY DRAWING AS PER ARRANGEMENT ON OUR ACCOUNT WITH UNITED BANK LIMITED, LONDON. 兹授权你行索偿你行议付金额,按约定办法请向伦敦联合银行我账户内支取。

2.开证行保证付款

常见的条款有:

WE HEREBY UNDERTAKE TO HONOUR ALL DRAFTS DRAWN AND PRESENTED IN ACCORDANCE WITH TERMS OF THIS CREDIT. 凡按本信用证所列条款开具并提示的汇票,我行保证承兑。

WE HEREBY ENGAGE WITH DRAWERS AND /OR BONA FIDE HOLDERS THAT DRAFT(S) DRAWN AND NEGOTIATED ON PRESENTATION AND THAT DRAFT(S) ACCEPTED WITHIN THE TERMS OF THIS CREDIT WILL BE DULY HONOURED AT MATURITY.

我行向对出票人及/或善意持有人保证:凡按本证条款开具及议付的汇票一经提交即予承兑;凡依本证条款承兑的汇票,到期即予照付。

WE HEREBY ENGAGE WITH DRAWERS, ENDORSERS AND BONA FIDE HOLDERS OF DRAFTS DRAWN UNDER AND IN COMPLIANCE WITH THE TERMDS OF THIS CREDIT THAT SUCH DRAFTS SHALL BE DULY HONOURED ON THE PRESENTATION AND DELIVERY OF DOCUMENTS AS SPECIFIED.

我行向根据本信用证并符合本信用证所开立的汇票的出票人、背书人及善意持票人保证,一旦提交规定的有关单据,汇票将被支付。

3.适用惯例

在信用证中,一般要明确该信用证所适用的国际惯例,作为买卖双方遵守的原则和依据。完整的适用惯例条款规定为:

THIS CREDIT IS SUBJECT TO THE UNIFORM CUSTOMS AND PRACTICE FOR DOCUMENTARY CREDITS(2007 REVISION) INTERNATIONAL CHAMBER OF COMMERCE PUBLICATION NO. 600.

本证根据国际商会 2007 年修订本第 600 号出版物《跟单信用证统一惯例》办理。

二、信用证种类辨别

(1)根据开证行对所开出的信用证所负的责任,信用证分为不可撤销信用证(Irrevocable L/C)和可撤销信用证(Revocable L/C)。

《UCP500》规定,信用证应明确注明是可撤销的或是不可撤销的。如无此注明,应视为不可撤销的。《UCP600》规定:信用证都是不可撤销的。

（2）根据受益人对信用证权利可否转让，信用证分为可转让信用证（Transferable Credit）和不可转让信用证（Non-transferable Credit）。

凡可转让信用证，必须注明"可转让"（Transferable）字样。如未注明，则被视为不可转让信用证。

（3）根据是否有另一家银行加以保兑，信用证分为保兑信用证（Confirmed L/C）和不保兑信用证（Unconfirmed L/C）。

凡使用保兑信用证，应在该证上注明"不可撤销"的字样和保兑行加保的文句。

（4）根据信用证使用方法（付款方法/兑付方式），信用证分为付款信用证（Payment Credit）、承兑信用证（Acceptance Credit）和议付信用证（Negotiation Credit）。

信用证中应标明是即期付款、延期付款、承兑或议付，即 CREDIT AVAILABLE WITH ×××

□BY PAYMENT AT SIGHT 即期付款；

□BY DEFERRED PAYMENT AT 延期付款；

□BY ACCEPTANCE OF DRAFTS AT 承兑；

□BY NEGOTIATION 议付。

（5）根据付款时间不同，信用证分为即期信用证和远期信用证。

付款时间规定方法大致有：

AT SIGHT 见票即付；

AT……DAYS AFTER SIGHT 见票后若干天付款；

AT……DAYS AFTER DATE OF B/L 提单日后若干天付款；

AT……DAYS AFTER DATE OF DRAFT 汇票日后若干天付款。

如采用第一种规定方法，即为即期信用证；如采用后三种方法，即为远期信用证。

（6）根据结算过程中有无货运单据，信用证分为跟单信用证和光票信用证。

项目二　信用证审核与修改

实训目标

能够根据合同和国际贸易惯例审核与修改信用证。

实训任务

§ 实训一

根据出口合同对信用证进行审核,指出信用证存在的问题并提出具体的改证要求。

(一)售货确认书

售货确认书

SALES CONFIRMATION

NO. LT09060

DATE：AUG. 10，2009

The sellers：AAA IMPORT AND EXPORT CO.　The buyers：BBB TRADING CO.

222 JIANGUO ROAD　　　　　　　　　　P. O. BOX 203

DALIAN, CHINA　　　　　　　　　　　　GDANSK，POLAND

下列签字双方同意按以下条款达成交易:

The undersigned Sellers and Buyers have agreed to close the following transactions according to the terms and conditions stipulated below：

品名与规格 COMMODITY AND SPECIFICATION	数量 QUANTITY	单价 UNIT PRICE	金额 AMOUNT
LADIES SKIRTS 65% POLYESTER 35% COTTON		CIF GDANSK	
STYLE NO. A101	200DOZ	USD60/DOZ	USD12000.00
STYLE NO. A102	400DOZ	USD84/DOZ	USD33600.00
	TTL：600DOZ		USD45600.00
ORDER NO.　HMW0901			

总值 TOTAL VALUE：U. S. DOLLARS FORTY FIVE THOUSAND AND SIX HUNDRED ONLY

装运口岸PORT OF LOADING：DALIAN

目的地 DESTINATION：GDANSK

转运TRANSSHIPMENT：ALLOWED

分批装运PARTIAL SHIPMENTS：ALLOWED

装运期限SHIPMENT：DECEMBER，2009

保险 INSURANCE：BE EFFECTED BY THE SELLERS FOR 110％ INVOICE VALUE COVERING F. P. A. RISKS OF PICC CLAUSE

付款方式PAYMENT：BY TRANSFERABLE CONFIRMED L/C PAYABLE 60 DAYS AFTER B/L DATE，REACHING THE SELLERS 45 DAYS BEFORE THE SHIPMENT

一般条款GENERAL TERMS：

1.合理差异：质地、重量、尺寸、花形、颜色均允许合理差异，对合理范围内差异提出的索赔，概不受理。

Reasonable tolerance in quality，weight，measurements，designs and colors is allowed，for which no claims will be entertained.

2.卖方免责：买方对下列各点所造成的后果承担全部责任：

（甲）使用买方指定包装、花形图案等；

（乙）不及时提供生产所需的商品规格或其他细则；

（丙）不按时开信用证；

（丁）信用证条款与售货确认书不符而不及时修改。

The buyers are to assume full responsibilities for any consequences arising from：

（a) the use of packing，designs or pattern made of order；

（b) late submission of specifications or any other details necessary for the execution of this sales confirmation；

（c) late establishment of L/C；

（d) late amendment to L/C inconsistent with the previsions of this sales confirmation.

买方（the buyers）　　　　　　　　　　卖方（the sellers）

BBB TRADING CO.　　　　　　　　AAA IMPORT AND EXPORT CO.

　David King　　　　　　　　　　　　　王大齐

请在本合同签字后寄回一份

Please sign，and return one copy

（二）信用证

LETTER OF CREDIT

FORM OF DOC. CREDIT ＊40A：IRREVOCABLE

DOC. CREDIT NUMBER ＊20：70/1/5822

DATE OF ISSUE ＊31：091007

EXPIRY ＊31D：DATE 100115 PLACE POLAND

ISSUING BANK ＊51D：SUN BANK，

P. O. BOX 201 GDANSK，POLAND

APPLICANT ＊50：BBB TRADING CO.

	P. O. BOX 303, GDANSK, POLAND
BENEFICIARY	*59: AAA EXPORT AND IMPORT CO.
	222 JIANGUO ROAD, DALIAN, CHINA
AMOUNT	*32B: CURRENCY HKD AMOUNT 45,600.00
AVAILABLE WITH/BY	*41A: BANK OF CHINA,DALIAN BRANCH
	BY DEFERRD PAYMENT
DEFERRED PAYM. DET.	*42P: 60 DAYS AFTER SIGHT
PARTIAL SHIPMENTS	*43P: NOT ALLOWED
TRANSSHIPMENT	*43T: ALLOWED
LOADING IN CHARGE	*44A: SHANGHAI
FOR TRANSPORT TO	*44B: GDANSK
LATEST DATE OF SHIPMENT	*44: 091131
DESCRIPT OF GOODS	*45A: LADIES SHIRTS
	65% POLYESTER 35% COTTON
	STYLE NO. 101　200DOZ@USD60/PC
	STYLE NO. 102　400DOZ@USD84/PC
	ALL OTHER DETAILS OF GOODS ARE
	AS PERCONTRACT NO. LT 09060 DAT-
	ED AUG 10, 2009
	DELIVERY TERMS: CIF GDANSK(IN-
	CONERMS 2000)

DOCUMENTS REQUIRED　　*46A:

1. COMMERCIAL INVOICE MANUALLY SIGNED IN 2 ORIGINALS PLUS 1 COPY MADE OUT TO DDD TRADING CO., P. O. BOX 211, GDANSK, POLAND.

2. FULL SET(2/3) OF ORIGINAL CLEAN ON BOARD BILL OF LADING PLUS 3/3 NON-NEGOTIABLE COPIES, MADE OUT TO ORDER OF ISSUING BANK AND BLANK ENDORSED, NOTIFY THE APPLICANT, MARKED FREIGHT COLLECT, MENTIONING GROSS WEIGHT AND NET WEIGHT.

3. ASSORTMENT LIST IN 2 ORIGINALS PLUS 1 COPY.

4. CERTIFICATE OF ORIGIN IN 1 ORIGINAL PLUS 2 COPIES SIGNED BY CCPIT.

5. MARINE INSURANCE POLICY IN THE CURRENCY OF THE CREDIT ENDORSED IN BLANK FOR CIF VALUE PLUS 30 PCT MARGIN COVERING ALL RISKS OF PICC CLAUSES INDICATING CLAIMS PAYABLE IN POLAND.

6. BENEFICIARY'S CERTIFICATE STATED THAT 1/3 SET OF ORIGINAL BILL OF LADING HAS BEEN AIRMAILED DIRECTLY TO APPLICANT WITHIN 48 HOURS AFTER SHIPMENT.

ADDITIONAL COND.　　　＊47A：

　　＋ALL DOCS MUST BE ISSUED IN ENGLISH.

　　＋SHIPMENTS MUST BE EFFECTED BY FCL.

　　＋B/L MUST SHOWING SHIPPING MARKS：BBB，S/C LT09060，GDAND，C/NO.

　　＋ALL DOCS MUST NOT SHOW THIS L/C NO. 70/1/5822

　　＋FOR DOCS WHICH DO NOT COMPLY WITH L/C TERMS AND CONDITIONS，WE SHALL DEDUCT FROM THE PROCEEDS A CHARGE OF EUR 50,00 PAYABLE IN USD EQUIVALENT PLUS ANY INCURED SWIFT CHARGES IN CONNECTION WITH.

　　＋THIS CREDIT IS NON-OPERATIVE UNLESS THE NAME OF CARRYING VESSEL HAS BEEN APPROVED BY APPLICANT AND TO BE ADVISED BY L/C ISSUING BANK IN FORM OF A L/C AMENDMENT TO BENIFICIARY.

DETAILS OF CHARGES　　　＊71B：ALL BANKING COMM/CHRGS OUTSIDE POLAND ARE ON BENEFICIARY'S ACCOUNT.

PERIOD FOR PRESENTATION　＊48：15 DAYS AFTER B/L DATE，BUT WITHIN THE VALIDITY OF THE CREDIT.

CONFIRMATION　　　＊49：WITHOUT

INSTRUCTIONS　　　＊78：WE SHALL REIMBURSE AS PER YOUR INSTRUCTIONS

SENT TO REC. INFO　　　＊72：CREDIT SUBJECT TO ICC PUBL. 600/2007 REV

§　实训二

根据出口合同对信用证进行审核，指出信用证存在的问题并提出具体的改证要求。

- -

（一）售货合同

SALES CONTRACT

BUYER：JAE&SONS PAPERS COMPANY　　　　NO. ST05-016

　　　　203 LODIA HOTEL OFFICE 1546，DONG-GU，DATE：AUGUST 08,2009

　　　　BUSAN, KOREA　　　　　　　　　PLACE：NANJING,CHINA

SELLER：BLUESKY INTERNATIONAL TRADE COMPANY LIMITED

　　　　NO. 529, QIJIANG ROAD HE DONG DISTRICT,

　　　　NANJING, CHINA

　　　THIS CONTRACT IS MADE BY THE SELLER；WHEREBY THE BUYER AGREE TO BUY AND THE SELLER AGREE TO SELL THE UNDER-MEN-

TIONED COMMODITY ACCORDING TO THE TERMS AND CONDITIONS STIPULATED BELOW:

1. COMMODITY: UNBLEACHED KRAFT LINERBOARD

   UNIT PRICE: USD390.00/PER METRIC TON, CFR BUSAN KOREA

   TOTAL QUANTITY: 100 METRIC TONS, ±10% ARE ALLOWED

   PAYMENT TERM: BY IRREVOCABLE L/C 90 DAYS AFTER B/L DATE

2. TOTAL VALUE: USD39,000.00 (SAY U.S. DOLLARS THIRTY NINE THOUSAND ONLY. ***10% MORE OR LESS ALLOWED)

3. PACKING: TO BE PACKED IN STRONG WOODEN CASE(S), SUITABLE FOR LONG DISTANCE OCEAN TRANSPORTATION.

4. SHIPPING MARK: THE SELLER SHALL MARK EACH PACKAGE WITH FADELESS PAINT THE PACKAGE NUMBER, GROSS WEIGHT, MEASUREMENT AND THE WORDING: "KEEP AWAY FROM MOISTURE", "HANDLE WITH CARE", ETC. AND THE SHIPPING MARK: ST05-016

   BUSAN

   KOREA

5. TIME OF SHIPMENT: ON OR BEFORE OCTOBER 31,2009

6. PORT OF SHIPMENT: MAIN PORTS OF CHINA

7. PORT OF DESTINATION: BUSAN, KOREA

8. INSURANCE: TO BE COVERED BY THE BUYER AFTER SHIPMENT. (F.O.B TERM)

9. DOCUMENT:

   +SIGNED INVOICE INDICATING L/C NO. AND CONTRACT NO.

   +FULL SET (3/3) OF CLEAN ON BOARD OCEAN BILL OF LADING MARKED "FREIGHT TO COLLECT"/"FREIGHT PREPAID" MADE OUT TO ORDER BLANK ENDORSED NOTIFYING THE APPLICANT.

   +PACKING LIST/WEIGHT LIST INDICATING QUANTITY/GROSS AND NET WEIGHT.

   +CERTIFICATE OF ORIGIN.

   +NO SOLID WOOD PACKING CERTIFICATE ISSUED BY MANUFACTURER.

10. OTHER CONDITIONS REQD IN L/C:

    +ALL BANKING CHARGES OUTSIDE THE OPENING BANK ARE FOR BENEFICIARY'S A/C.

    +DO NOT MENTION ANY SHIPPING MARKS IN YOUR L/C.

    +PARTIAL AND TRANSSHIPMENT ALLOWED.

11. REMARKS: THE LAST DATE OF L/C OPENING: 20 AUGUST, 2009

（二）信用证

BANK OF KOREA LIMITED，BUSAN

SEQUENCE OF TOTAL　　　　＊27：1/1

FORM OF DOC. CREDIT　　　＊40 A：IRREVOCABLE

DOC. CREDIT NUMBER　　　 ＊20：S100-108085

DATE OF ISSUE　　　　　　＊31C：20090825

EXPIRY　　＊31D：DATE 20091001 PLACE APPLICANTS COUNTRY

APPLICANT　＊50：JAD&SONS PAPERS COMPANY

　　　　　　　203 LODIA HOTEL OFFICE 1564，DONG-GU，

　　　　　　　BUSAN，KOREA

BENEFICIARY＊59：BLUESKY COMPANY LIMITED

　　　　　　　NO. 529，QIJIANG ROAD HE DONG DISTRICT，

　　　　　　　NANNING，CHINA

AMOUNT　　　　＊32B：CURRENCY HKD AMOUNT 39,000.00

AVAILABLE WITH/ BY ＊41D：ANY BANK IN CHINA BY NEGOTIATION

DRAFTS AT…　　　＊42C：DRAFTS AT 90 DAYS AT SIGHT FOR FULL

　　　　　　　　　　　　INVOICE COST

DRAWEE　　　　＊42A：BANK OF KOREA LIMITED, BUSAN

PARTIAL SHIPMENTS　　　＊43P：ALLOWED

TRANSSHIPMENT　　　　　＊43T：NOT ALLOWED

LOADING ON BOARD　　　 ＊44A：MAIN PORTS OF CHINA

FOR TRANSPORTATION TO　＊44B：MAIN PORTS OF KOREA

LATEST DATE OF SHIPMENT ＊44C：20091031

DESCRIPT OF GOODS　　　＊45A：

　　　　　　+COMMODITY：UNBLEACHED KRAFT LINERBOARD

　　　　　　U/P：USD 390.00/MT　TOTAL：100MT±10％ ARE ALLOWED

　　　　　　PRICE TERM：CIF BUSAN KOREA

　　　　　　COUNTRY OF ORIGIN：P. R. CHINA

　　　　　　PACKING：STANDARD EXPORT PACKING

　　　　　　SHIPING MARK：ST05-016

　　　　　　　　　BUSAN KOREA

DOCUMENTS REQUIRED　　　＊46 A：

　　1. COMMERCIAL INVOICE IN 3 COPIES INDICATING LC NO. CONTRACT NO. ST05-018

　　2. FULL SET （3/3）OF CLEAN ON BOARD OCEAN BILL OF LADING MADE OUT TO ORDER AND BLANK ENDORSED, MARKED FREIGHT TO COL-LECT, NOTIFYING THE APPLICANT

　　3. PACKING LIST/ WEIGHT LIST IN 3 COPIES INDICATING QUANTITY/ GROSS AND NET WEIGHT

　　4. CERTIFICATE OF ORIGIN IN 3 COPIES

ADDITIONAL COND.	* 47 B: ALL DOCUMENTS ARE TO BE PRESENT-ED TO US IN ONE LOT BY COURIER/SPEED POST.
DETAILS OF CHARGES	* 71 B: ALL BANKING CHARGES OUTSIDE OPEN-ING BANK ARE FOR ACCOUNT OF BEN-EFICIARY.
PERIOD FOR PRESENTATION	* 48: DOCUMENTS TO BE PRESENTED WITH-IN 2 DAYS AFTER THE DATE OF SHIP-MENT BUT WITHIN THE VALIDITY OF THE CREDIT.
CONFIRMATION	* 49: WITHOUT
INSTRUCTIONS	* 78: WE HEREBY UNDERTAKE THAT DRAFTS DRAWN UNDER AND IN COMPLY WITH THE TERMS AND CONDITIONS OF THIS CREDIT WILL BE PAID MATURITY.
SEND. TO REC. INFO.	* 72:/SUBJECT U. C. P. 2007 ICC PUBLICATION 600.

§ 实训三

将信用证内前后矛盾、我方不宜接受的条款指出来,并提出具体的改证要求。

DOCUMENTARY CREDIT NO. 8169/26598
　ISSUING: KOREA EXCHANGE BANK, SEOUL
　APPLICANT: G AND Y TRADING CO. , LTD.
　　　　　RM 908 PHOENIX BLDG. 702-23
　　　　　YUKSAM-DONG KANGNAM-KU SEOUL KOREA
　ADVISING: BANK OF CHINA TIANJIN
　BENEFICIARY: TIANJIN SUNSHINE INTERNATIONAL TRADING CO. , LTD.
　　　　　　HUASHENG BLDG. NO. 85 LIUWEI RD. HEDONG DISTRICT
　　　　　　TIANJIN CHINA 300112
　AMOUNT: USD33,264.00
　SAY US DOLLARS THIRTY THREE THOUSAND TWO HUNDRED SIXTY ONLY
　DATE OF ISSUE: APR. 2, 2009
　EXPIRY: MAY 15, 2009 IN KOREA
　　WE HEREBY ISSUE IN YOUR FAVOR THIS IRREVOCABLE DOCUMEN-TARY CREDIT WHICH IS AVAILABLE BY NEGOTIATION OF YOUR DRAFT AT SIGHT DRAWN ON BENEFICIARY BEARING THE CLAUSE: "DRAWN UNDER DOCUMENTARY CREDIT NO. 8169/26589 DATED APR. 5, 2009 OF KOREA EXCHANGE BANK SEOUL" ACCOMPANIED BY THE FOLLOWING DOCUMENTS:

+SIGNED COMMERCIAL INVOICE IN TRIPLICATE SHOWING FOB,
FREIGHT AND INSURANCE COSTS SEPARATELY

+PACKING LIST IN TRIPLICATE

+FULL SET OF CLEAN ON BOARD AIRWAY BILLS OF LADING MADE
OUT TO ORDER MARKED FREIGHT PREPAID AND NOTIFY APPLICANT

+FORM A CERTIFICATE OF ORIGIN

+INSURANCE POLICY/CERTIFICATE IN DUPLICATE ENDORSED IN BLANK
FOR 150 PCT OF THE INVOICE VALUE WITH CLAIMS PAYABLE IN KO-
REA IN THE CURRENCY OF DRAFT, COVERING THE INSTITUTE CAR-
GO CLAUSE ALL RISKS

+CERTIFICATE OF SHIPPING CO. INDICATING THAT THE CARRYING
STEAMER IS A NEW VESSEL NOT EXCESS OF TEN YEARS OLD

DESCRIPTION OF GOODS:

+ORIGIN CHINA

+65PCT POLYESTER 35PCT COMBED COTTON BLENDED WOVEN FABRIC
45 * 45　110 * 7 647 ″ IN GREY

P/LENGTH: 90PCT 117-121 YDS 10PCT 40 YDS UP

WEIGHT: ABOUT 110GR/YD

100,000YDS IN TWO SHIPMENTS AT CFR BUSAN USD0.5/YD

SHIPMENT: FROM TIANJIN TO TOKYO BY STEAMER NOT LATER THAN
MAY 20, 2009 AND MUST REACH THE PORT OF DESTINA-
TION ON OR BEFORE THE END OF MAY 2009

PARTIAL SHIPMENTS & TRANSSHIPMENT: PROHIBITTED

SPECIAL CONDITIONS:

+ALL BANKING CHARGES INCLUDING REIMBURSING CHARGE ARE
FOR ACCOUNT OF BENEFICIARY

+SHIPPER MUST FAX ADVISE BUYER SHIPMENT PARTICULARS IM-
MEDIATELY AFTER SHIPMENT

+ONE COPY OF SIGNED COMMERCIAL INVOICE AND NON-NEGOTIA-
BLE B/L TO BE AIRMAILED IN ADVANCE TO BUYER

+NO HOOKS USED

INSTRUCTIONS TO THE NEGOTIATING BANK:

+T/T REIMBURSEMENT NOT ALLOWED

+THE DISCREPANCY FEE OF USD 60.00 (OR EQUIVALENT) SHOULD
BE DEDUCTED FROM YOUR REIMBURSEMENT CLAIM TO THE REIM-
BURSING BANK OR WILL BE DEDUCTED FROM PROCEEDS BY US IF
DOCUMENTS ARE PRESENTED WITH DISCREPANCY

+ALL DOCS MUST BE DESPATCHED TO US IN ONE LOT

+DOCUMENTS MUST BE PRESENTED WITHIN 2 DAYS AFTER SHIP-

PING DATE SHOWN ON B/L, BUT WITHIN THE VALIDITY OF THE L/C

+ THE DOCUMENTS BENEFICIARY PRESENT SHOULD INCLUDE AN INSPECTION CERTIFICATE SIGNED BY APPLICANT OR ITS AGENT

§ 实训四

根据销售合同对信用证进行审核,指出信用证存在的问题并提出具体的改证要求。

(一)销售合同

销售合同

SALES CONTRACT

Contract No. : RT05342

Date: Mar. 20, 2010

Signed at: SHANGHAI

Sellers: SHANGHAI TOOL IMPORT& EXPORT CO., LTD Tel: 021—65756156

Address: 31, GANXIANG ROAD SHANGHAI, CHINA Fax: 021—65756155

Buyers: MAMUT ENTERPRISESAV Tel: 024—4536—2453

Address: TARRAGONA75-3ER, BARCELONA, SPAIN Fax: 024—4536—2452

THIS CONTACT IS MADE BY AND BETWEEN THE SELLERS AND BUYERS, WHEREBY THE SELLERS AGREE TO SELL AND THE BUYERS AGREE TO BUY THE UNDER-MENTIONED GOODS ACCORDING TO THE CONDITIONS STIPULATED BELOW:

(1)货号、品名及规格 NAME OF COMMODITY AND SPECIFICATIONS	(2)数量 QUANTITY	(3)单价 UNIT PRICE	(4)金额 AMOUNT
HAND TOOLS		FOB	SHANGHAI
1) 9PC EXTRA LONG HEX KEY SET	1200 SETS	USD1. 76	USD2112. 00
2) 8PC DOUBLE OFFSET RING SPANNER	1200 SETS	USD3. 10	USD3720. 00
3) 12PC DOUBLE OFFSET RING SPANNER	800 SETS	USD7. 50	USD6000. 00
4) 12PC COMBINATION SPANNER	1200 SETS	USD3. 55	USD4260. 00
5) 10PC COMBINATION SPANNER	1000 SETS	USD5. 80	USD5800. 00
AS PER PROFORM INVOICE NO 20100329 DATED MARCH 10, 2010			
TOTAL AMOUNT	5400 SETS		USD21892. 00

(5)PACKING: 8PC DOUBLE OFFSET RING SPANNER

PACKED IN 1 PLASTIC CARTON OF 16 SET EACH;

9PC EXTRA LONG HEX KEY SET，12PC COMBINATION SPANNER，10PC COMBINATION SPANNER

PACKED IN 1 PLASTIC CARTON OF 10 SETS EACH；

12PC DOUBLE OFFSET RING SPANNER

PACKED IN 1 PLASTIC CARTON OF 8 SETS EACH.

PACKED IN THREE 40' CONTAINER

(6)DELIVERY FROM SHANGHAI, CHINA TO BARCELONA, SPAIN

(7)SHIPPING MARKS M. E

BARCELONA

C/NO. 1-UP

(8)TIME OF SHIPMENT：LATEST DATE OF SHIPMENT MAY. 10，2010

(9)PARTIAL SHIPMENTS：NOT ALLOWED

(10)TRANSSHIPMENT：ALLOWED

(11)TERMS OF PAYMENT：BY 100% CONFIRMED IRREVOCABLE LETTER OF CREDIT TO BE AVAILABLE AT 30 DAYS AFTER SIGHT.

DRAFT TO BE OPENED BY THE SELLERS.

L/C MUST MENTION THIS CONTRACT NUMBER.

L/C ADVISED BY BANK OF CHINA SHANGHAI BRANCH.

ALL BANKING CHARGES OUTSIDE CHINA (THE MAINLAND OF CHINA) ARE FOR ACCOUNT OF DRAWEE.

(12)ARBITRATION：ANY DISPUTE ARISING FROM THE EXECUTION OF OR IN CONNECTION WITH THIS CONTRACT SHALL BE SETTLED AMICABLY THROUGH NEGOTIATION. IN CASE NO SETTLEMENT CAN BE REACHED THROUGH NEGOTIATION, THE CASE SHALL THEN BE SUBMITTED TO CHINA INTERNATIONAL ECONOMIC & TRADE ARBITRATION COMMISSION IN SHANGHAI (OR IN BEIJING) FOR ARBITRATION IN ACCORDANCE WITH ITS ARBITRATION RULES. THE ARBITRATION AWARD IS FINAL AND BINDING UPON BOTH PARTIES. THE FEE FOR ARBITRATION SHALL BE BORNE BY LOSING PARTY UNLESS OTHERWISE AWARDED.

The Seller：SHANGHAI TOOL IMPORT& EXPORT CO. , LTD

LILI

The Buyer：MAMUT ENTERPRISESAV

JHON

（二）信用证

DOCUMENTARY CREDIT

SEQUENCE OF TOTAL   * 27: 1/1

FORM OF DOC. CREDIT   * 40A: REVOCABLE

DOC. CREDIT NUMBER   * 20: 31173

DATE OF ISSUE   31C: 100401

DATE AND PLACE OF EXPIRY   * 31D: DATE 100531 PLACE SPAIN

APPLICANT   * 50: MAMUT ENTERPRISESAV
                           TARRAGONA 75-3ER

ISSUING BANK   52A: CREDIT ANDORRA
                           ANDORRA LA VELLA, ANDORRA

BENEFICIARY   * 59: SHANGHAI TOOL EXPORT & IMPORT CO., LTD.
                           31, GANXIANG ROAD
                           SHANGHAI, CHINA

AMOUNT   * 32 B: CURRENCY EUR AMOUNT 21892.00

AVAILABLE WITH/ BY   * 41 D: ANY BANK IN CHINA
                           BY NEGOTIATION

DRAFTS AT…   42 C: AT SIGHT

DRAWEE   42 A: CREDIT ANDORRA
                           ANDORRA LA VELLA, ANDORRA

PARTIAL SHIPMENTS   43 P: ALLOWED

TRANSSHIPMENT   43T: NOT ALLOWED

LOADING ON BOARD   44 A: SHANGHAI

FOR TRANSPORTATION TO   44 B: BARCELONA (SPAIN)

LATEST DATE OF SHIPMENT   44 C: 100510

DESCRIPT OF GOODS   45 A: HAND TOOLS
                           AS PER PROFORMA INVOICE NO. 20100339
                           DATED MARCH 10, 2010
                           FOB BARCELONA

DOCUMENTS REQUIRED   46 A:

+SIGNED COMMERCIAL INVOICE, 1 ORGINAL AND 4 COPIES.

+PACKING LIST, 1 ORGINAL AND 4 COPIES.

+CERTIFICATE OF ORIGINA GSP CHINA FORM A, ISSUED BY THE CHAMBER OF COMMERCE OR OTHER AUTHORITY DULY ENTITLED FOR THIS PURPOSE.

+FULL SET OF B/L, (2 ORIGINAL AND 5 COPIES) CLEAN ON BOARD, MARKED "FREIGHT COLLECT", CONSIGNED TO: MAMUT ENTERPRISES-AV, TARRAGONA 75-3ER BARCELONA, SPAIN, TEL+376 823 323 FAX+376 860 914-860807, NOTIFY: BLUE WATER SHIPING ESPANA, ER 2NA,

A，08003 BARCELONA (SPAIN) TEL 34 93 295 4848，FAX 34 93 268 16 81.
CHARGES   71 B：ALL BANKING CHARGES OUTSIDE SPAIN ARE FOR
ACCOUNT OF BENEFICIARY.
PERIOD FOR PRESENTATION   48：
DOCUMENTS MUST BE PRESENTED WITHIN 15 DAYS
AFTER THE DATE OF SHIPMENT BUT WITHIN THE VA-
LIDITY OF THE CREDIT.

实训指导

一、审证负责者

信用证审核由通知行和受益人分别进行。通知行在收到信用证后主要负责审核开证行的背景、资信、L/C真假等内容。出口公司在收到信用证后，对照合同并依据《跟单信用证统一惯例》，审核信用证是否符合合同规定和业务做法。

二、出口公司审证注意事项

(一)审核信用证是否符合合同规定

1.货物条款的审核

信用证中关于货物的名称、质量、数量、包装等规定必须与合同一致。如有错误,都应提出修改。

2.价格条件、币种、金额的审核

首先,要审核信用证中的价格条件、币种与合同规定是否一致。其次,要核对信用证金额与合同是否相符。信用证金额可以超过合同金额,但信用证金额不能低于合同金额。如数量有溢短装,信用证金额应相应增减;如有佣金或折扣的,应核对是按减除佣金或折扣后的净值开证,还是按不减佣金或折扣的毛值开证。另外,有的信用证订明部分金额以信用证付款、余额以托收付款,那么信用证金额仅是部分的金额。此外,信用证金额一般包括大写和小写,应核对大小写是否一致,避免发生纠纷。

3.装运时间、地点、转运、分批装运的审核

装运时间、地点、转运、分批装运的审核要结合实际情况审核清楚。根据《UCP600》规定,信用证如果没有规定是否可以分批装运和转运,应理解为允许分批装运和转运。

4.保险险别、投保金额的审核

信用证中保险条款的规定应与合同相符,保险险别、投保金额不得超出合同规定。

5.L/C种类的审核

信用证中种类的规定应与合同相符。

6.汇票的付款期限审核

汇票的付款期限原则上应与合同规定一致,但也可接受更有利于我方融资的付款期限。如成交时为即期支付,而来证时却要求远期付款并加付远期利息,这实际上成了出口方自垫资金,而不是开证行或偿付行的资金融通,应予以注意并改为利息与承兑费用由买

方负担。

7.受益人、开证人的名称地址的审核

受益人应特别注意信用证上的受益人名称和地址应与其印就好的文件上的名称和地址内容相一致,买方的公司名称和地址写法是不是也完全正确。在填写发票时,照抄信用证上写错了的买方公司名号和地址是有可能的,如果受益人的名称不正确,将会给今后的收汇带来不便。

(二)审核信用证是否符合业务做法

1.L/C 是否有限制生效的条款

按惯例,信用证在送到受益人时即生效,但有些信用证中有不合理的限制性或保留条款。如信用证规定"This credit is non-operative unless the opening bank give further advice";又如 L/C 规定信用证要"获得有关当局的进口许可证后方生效(This credit is operative only after the buyer obtains the import license)"或"等收到货物的样品并以函电确认后方能生效"等类似条款,这些在审证时都要注意。另外,简电本不是有效的信用证,在简电本后一般都注有"随寄证实书"字样,证实书则是随后寄来的信开信用证。

2.L/C 是否有到期日(有效期)、到期地点

信用证中必须有到期日,没有规定到期日的信用证为无效信用证。为掌握交单时间以保证安全收汇,我国出口业务中应争取到期地点在中国境内。

3.到期日和装运期关系是否合理

信用证的有效期一般应与装运期有一定的合理间隔(通常是 15 天),以便在装运后有足够的时间办理制单结汇。如果最后装运期和到期日为同一天,则称为"双到期"。在这种情况下,应在信用证到期日前提早几天将货物装上运输工具或交给承运人,以便留出足够时间制备单据向银行交单办理议付、承兑或付款。

4.汇票付款人是否合理

汇票付款人应是开证行或其指定的付款行,因信用证是银行信用,开证行或付款行承担第一性付款责任。

5.银行费用规定是否合理

银行费用一般包括通知费、保兑费、承兑费、议付费、修改费等。我国的习惯做法是出口地的银行费用由出口方负担,进口地的银行费用由进口方负担。

6.单据种类是否与交易条件相符

如空运方式下要求提供海运提单、FOB 下要求提供保险单、CIF 下漏列保险单。

7.B/L 运费规定是否与成交条件矛盾

CFR 、CIF 术语下,B/L 运费规定为"freight prepaid/paid";FOB 术语下,B/L 运费规定为"freight to collect"。

8.运输工具限制是否过严

如果信用证对船龄、船籍、船公司或港口等有限制条款,则要考虑能否办到。

9.信用证中的单据条款是否合理

特别要注意一些软条款,如商业发票经买方复签生效、正本 B/L 全部或部分直接寄交客户、要求由开证行或开证行指定的人在检验证书上签字、要求提供一些需要特别机构认证的单据等。

项目三 商业发票缮制

实训目标

能够根据有关资料缮制商业发票。

实训任务

§ 实训一

根据下列资料缮制商业发票。

(一)信用证资料

ISSUING BANK：NATIONAL COMMERCIAL BANK,JEDDAH

ADVISING BANK：BANK OF CHINA, ZHEJIANG BRANCH

DATE OF ISSUE：JAN. 3,2010

L/C NO.：DC668839

L/C AMOUNT：USD29,040.00

APPLICANT：JEDDAH XYZ FOOD COMPANY, JEDDAH

BENEFICIARY：HANGZHOU ABC FOOD COMPANY,HANGZHOU

PARTIAL SHIPMENTS：NOT ALLOWED

MERCHANDISE：ABOUT 48000CANS OF MEILING BRAND CANNED OR-ANGE JAM,250 GRAM/CAN,12CANS IN A CARTON

UNIT PRICE：USD0. 55/CAN CIFC5 JEDDAH

COUNTRY OF ORIGIN：P. R. CHINA

DOCUMENTS REQUIRED：

+MANULLY SIGNED COMMERCIAL INVOICES IN 3 COPIES DATED THE SAME DATE AS THAT OF L/C ISSUANCE DATE INDICATING COUNTRY OF ORIGIN OF THE GOODS AND CERTIFIED TO BE TRUE AND CORRECT,INDI-CATING CONTRACT NO. SUM356/2010 AND L/C NO.

......

ADDITIONAL CONDITIONS：

+ALL DOCUMENTS MUST INDICATE SHIPPING MARKS AS JAM IN DI-AMOND JEDDAH

+ALL DOCUMENTS INCLUDING INVOICE MUST BE IN NAME OF JED-DAH EFG FOOD COMPANY, JEDDAH

+5% COMMISSION TO BE DEDUCTED FROM INVOICE VALUE

+INVOICE SHOULD SHOW FOB VALUE,FREIGHT CHARGES AND IN-SURANCE PREMIUM SEPARATELY

（二）其他资料

INVOICE NO.：ABC123/2010

受益人有权签字人为吴一帆

出仓单显示：50000 CANS OF MEILING BRAND CANNED ORANGE JAM

提单显示货物从宁波运往吉达

船名：LINDA V.123

海运运费：USD54.00

保险费：USD28.00

COMMERCIAL INVOICE		
SELLER1)	INVOICE NO. 3)	INVOICE DATE4)
BUYER2)	L/C NO. 5)	S/C NO. 6)
TRANSPORT DETAILS 7) FROM TO PARTIAL SHIPMENTS: TRANSSHIPMENT： BY:	TERMS OF PAYMENT 8)	

9)MARKS	10)DESCRIPTION OF GOODS	11)QTY.	12) UNIT PRICE	13)AMOUNT

TOTAL AMOUNT IN WORDS：14)

ISSUED BY   15)

SIGNATURE

§ 实训二

根据下列资料缮制商业发票。

(一)信用证资料

FROM：NATIONAL BANK LIMITED, DHAKA (MOHAKHALI BRANCH)

TO：WACHOVIA BANK，NA，SHANGHAI

DATE OF ISSUE：090719

L/C NO. ：094709060309

EXPIRY DATE AND PLACE：090826 CHINA

APPLICANT：AFG APPARELS LTD.

JOYNABARI,HEMAYETPUR,SAVAR,DHAKA,BANGLADESH

BENEFICIARY：ZHEJIANG FANTA TRADING CO. ，LTD.

NO.158 ZHONGSHAN ZHONG ROAD, HANGZHOU, CHINA

L/C AMOUNT：USD48513,00

POS. /NEG. TOL(%)：03/03

PARTIAL SHIPMENT：ALLOWED

TRANSHIPMENTS：ALLOWED

TAKING CHARGE PLACE：ANY PORT OF CHINA

FINAL DESTINATION：CHITTAGONG SEAPORT

LATEST DATE OF SHIP. ：090805

DESCRIP. OF GOODS：FABRIC FOR 100PCT EXPORT ORIENTED READY-
MADE GARMENTS INDUSTRY AS PER BENEFICIARY'S PROFOR-
MA INVOICE NO. OCL-09043-CK02-V4 DTD. 15JUL09 AS UNDER：

DESCRIPTION	COLOR	QTY YDS	U/PRICE USD/YD	TOTAL AMT. IN USD
100PCT COTTON TWILL	STONE	8950	1,57	
S/D，16X12/108X56	OLIVE	8450	1,57	
WD：57/58″	BLACK	13500	1,57	
STYLE NO. S/33335				
TOTAL： CFR CHITTAGONG		30900YDS		48513,00

DOCUMENTS REQUIRED：

+ SIGNED COMMERCIAL INVOICES IN OCTUPLICATE CERTIFYING MER-
CHANDISE ARE STRICTLY IN ACCORDANCE WITH THE PROFORMA IN-
VOICE AS STATED ABOVE

……

ADDITIONAL CONDITIONS：

01—L/C AUTHORIZATION FORM NO. N8LAB-46109

IRC NO. BA-124933

H. S. CODE NO. 5407. 52. 00

IMPORT UNDER EXPORT L/C NO. 1572603 DTD 13JUL09

OUR L/C NO. 094709060309 DTD 19JUL09 MUST APPEAR IN ALL DOCS.

02—SHIPMENT /TRANSHIPMENT ON FLAG VESSEL OF IRAQ/LIBYA/IS-RAEL/CUBA PROHIBITED.

03—DISCREPANT DOCS MUST NOT BE NEGOTIATED.

04—NEGOTIATING BANK MUST FORWARD DOCS TO NATIONAL BANK LIMITED, MOHAKHALI BRANCH 9-MOHAKHALI C/A, DHAKA, BANGLADESH IN TWO SEPARATE LOTS BY COURIER SERVICES.

05—ONE SET OF NON-NEGOTIABLE COPY OF DOCS TO BE SENT THE APPLICANT WITHIN 7 DAYS AFTER SHIPMENT BY COURIER, COURIER RECEIPT MUST ACCOMPANY WITH SHIPPING DOCS.

06—SHORT FORM/STALE/CHARTERED PARTY/BLANK BACKED/THIRD PARTY BL/FCR/FBL NOT ACCEPTABLE.

07—IN CASE OF DISCREPANT/COLLETION DOCS AN AMOUNT OF USD50, 00 AND SWIFT CHARGES USD50, 00 WILL BE DEDUCTED FROM BILL VALUE AT THE TIME OF SETTLEMENT OF THE BILL.

08—BENEFICIARY MUST CERTIFY THAT INVOICE PRICE IS NET AND DOES NOT INCLUDE ANY COMMISSION FOR THEIR AGENT IN BANGLADESH.

09—PRE-SHIPMENT INSPECTION CERTIFICATE ISSUED BY SGS/LLOYDS/ OR ANY INTERNATIONAL REPUTED ORGANISATION/BENEFICIARY/ MANUFACTURER ACCEPTABLE.

10—INTEREST FOR THE ACTUAL USANCE PERIOD TO BE PAID AT LIBOR BY THE APPLICANT.

11—MATURITY DATE TO BE COUNTED FROM THE DATE OF NEGOTIATION.

12—CONTINUOUS LENGTH OF FABRICS MUST NOT BE LESS THAN 20 YDS. A CERTIFICATE TO THIS EFFECT SHOULD ACCOMPANY SHIPPING DOCS.

(二)其他资料

INVOICE NO. : 9109H69R038

INVOICE DATE: 2009/07/21

SC NO. : 09EJFR039

出口公司有权签字人为百灵

出仓单显示：

STONE	8950YDS	114BALES
OLIVE	8450YDS	107BALES
BLACK	13500YDS	171BALES

装运港：青岛

船名：YM UTILITY   V.0004M

PACKING IN 392 BALES

NET W. : 11432.1KGS

GROSS W. : 11628.2KGS

MEASUMENT：23.520M³
SHIPPING MARKS：
　　AFG APPARELS LTD.
　　CHITTAGONG，BANGLADESH
　　COLOR：KHAKI
　　QTY：YDS
　　C/T NO.：
　　MADE IN CHINA

浙江纺大贸易有限公司

ZHEJIANG FANTA TRADING CO.，LTD.

NO.158 ZHONGSHAN ZHONG ROAD，HANGZHOU，CHINA

COMMERCIAL　INVOICE

TO：			NO.：	
			DATE：	
			L/C NO.：	
			S/C NO.：	
FROM		TO		
MARKS&NOS	DESCRIPTIONS OF GOODS KIND & NUMBER OF PACKAGE	QUANTITY	UNIT PRICE	AMOUNT

§ 实训三

根据下列资料缮制商业发票。

（一）信用证资料

FROM：UBI BANCA (UNIONE DI BANCHE ITALIANE) S. C. P. A. BERGAMO

TO：BANK OF CHINA LIMITED, ZHEJIANG BRANCH

DATE OF ISSUE：091113

L/C NO. ：0946CIM2002454R0

EXPIRY DATE AND PLACE：100309 CHINA

APPLICANT：CALZEDONIA S. P. A.

VIA MONTE BALDO 20 37062 DOSSOBUONO DI VILLAFRANCA VR

BENEFICIARY：ZHEJIANG CHUBO TRADING CO. , LTD.

NO. 35 HUSHU ROAD, HANGZHOU, CHINA

L/C AMOUNT：USD733,920. 00

POS. /NEG. TOL(%)：05/05

AVAILABLE WITH/BY：BANCA REGIONALE EUROPEA SPA (UBI BANC GROUP), PAVIA

(MAIN BRANCH)

BY DEF. PAYMENT

DEFERRED PAYM. DET. ：PAYMENT AT 60 DAYS FROM TRANSPORT DOCUMENTS DATE

PARTIAL SHIPMENTS：ALLOWED

TRANSHIPMENT：ALLOWED

PORT OF LOADING：SHANGHAI, CHINA

PORT OF DISCHARGE：VENEZIA, ITALY

LATEST DATE OF SHIP. ：100222

DESCRIP. OF GOODS：CLOTHING

PO NO.	ART. CODE	QUANTITY	TOT. VALUE	DATE OF SHIPMENT
2000004151	CL020A	8940PCS	USD108. 174,00	30/11/09
2000004661	CL020A	8940PCS	USD108. 174,00	30/11/09
2000004552	AI018S	10000PCS	USD192. 072,00	22/02/10
2000004577	CM020A	30000PCS	USD325. 500,00	25/12/09

TATAL AMOUNT：USD 733. 920,00

INCOTERMS 2000：FOBSHANGHAI

DOCUMENTS REQUIRED：

+ COMMERCIAL INVOICE DULY SIGNED AND DATED EVIDENCING THAT INVOICE AND SHIPPED GOODS ARE IN CONFORMITY WITH ORDERS NO. 2000004151/4661/4552/4577：ORIGINAL AND 2 COPIES.

……

ADDITIONAL COND. ：

　　＋ALL DOCUMENTS MUST BE WORDED IN ENGLISH

　　＋ALL DOCUMENTS MUST REPORT OUR L/C NUMBER AND ISSUING BANK NAME：BANCA REGIONALE EUROPEA SPA

　　＋NO DRAFT IS REQUIRED, IF ANY IT WILL RETURNED TO YOU AND EUR50. 00 OUR CHARGES DEDUCTD FROM PAYMENT

　　＋ONE EXTRACOPY OF ALL DOCUMENTS IS REQUIRED FOR ISSUING BANK'S FILE. IF NOT PRESENTED EUR10. 00 WILL BE DEDUCTED FROM PROCEEDS

　　＋PENALTY FOR POSSIBLE DELAYS：

10 PERCENT DISCOUNT FOR DELIVERIES FROM 7 DAYS AFTER LAST DELIVERY DATE, TILL 14 DAYS AFTER LAST DELIVERY DATE. 20 PERCENT DISCOUNT FOR DELIVERIES FROM 15 DAYS AFTER LAST DELIVERY DATE, TILL 40 DAYS AFTER LAST DELIVERY DATE.

（二）其他资料

INVOICE NO. ：BP919A520301

INVOICE DATE：2009/12/22

出仓单显示：

PO NO. 2000004577　　ART. CODE CM020A　　5500PCS　　80CTNS

SHIPPING MARKS：CALZEDONIA/VERONA/NO. 1-80

S/C NO. ZSD095010339

提示：本批出运货物为 PO NO. 2000004577 的货物，请注意发票的批注内容为：INVOICE AND SHIPPED GOODS ARE IN CONFORMITY WITH ORDERS NO. 2000004577。

浙江楚帛贸易有限公司
ZHEJIANG CHUBO TRADING CO., LTD.
NO. 35 HUSHU ROAD, HANGZHOU, CHINA

COMMERCIAL INVOICE

TO:			NO. :	
			DATE:	
			L/C NO. :	
			S/C NO. :	
FROM		TO		
MARKS&NOS	DESCRIPTIONS OF GOODS KIND & NUMBER OF PACKAGE		QUANTITY	UNIT PRICE	AMOUNT

§ 实训四

根据以下资料，审核并修改已填制的商业发票，在已填制的 17 个栏目（标号 1—17）中找出若干处填制错误，并说明原因。

（一）来自信用证的资料

THE ROYAL BANK OF CANADA

CABLE ADDRESS：ROYAL BANK

PLACE & DATE OF ISSUE：CANADA　APR. 20，2010

OPEN TYPE：CABLE

ADVISING BANK：BANK OF CHINA SHANGHAI BRANCH

CREDIT NUMBER：LC0501-FTC

EXPIRY：DATE JUN. 22，2010　FOR NEGOTIATION IN CHINA

APPLICANT：MAURICIO DEPORTS INTERNATIONAL S. A.

　　　　890 FINCH，STREE，TORONTO，CANADA

BENEFICIARY：ZHEJIANG SUMING IMPORT AND EXPORT CO. ，LTD

　　　　RM1900 JUXING BLDG，NO. 807 JIAOGONG ROAD，

　　　　HANGZHOU，310012，CHINA

AMOUNT：CURENCY USD AMOUNT17250. 00

DRAFTS AT：15 DAYS SIGHT FOR FULL INVOICE VALUE

PARTIAL SHIPMENTS：ALLOWED

TRANSHIPMENT：ALLOWED

PORT OF LOADING：SHANGHAI，CHINA

FOR TRANSPORT TO：TORONTO，CANADA

LATEST DATE OF SHIPMENT：JUN. 15，2010

DESCRIPTION OF GOODS：VALVE SEAT INSERT

　　　　W77T6　1050PCS@USD5. 00/PC

　　　　W88T9　2000PCS@USD6. 00/PC

　　AS PER SALES CONTRACT NO. ZJ2010-HZ08 DATED MAR. 31，2010

　　CIFTORONTO

DOCUMENTS REQUIRED：

＋ORIGINAL SIGNED COMMERCIAL INVOICE IN TRIPLICATE AND SHOULD BEAR THE FOLLOWING CLAUSE："WE HEREBY CERTIFY THAT THE CONTENTS OF INVOICE HEREIN ARE TRUE AND CORRECT. "

……

（二）装箱资料

NOS AND KINDS OF PACKAGES：61 WOODEN CASES

GROSS WEIGHT/VOLUME：8000KGS/12CBM

（三）已缮制的商业发票

浙江山名进出口公司（1）

ZHEJIANG SUMING IMPORT AND EXPORT CO. ,LTD

RM1900 JUXING BLDG，NO. 807 JIAOGONG ROAD，

HANGZHOU，310012，CHINA

COMMERCIAL INVOICE（2）

TO：(3) MAURICIO DEPORTS INTERNATIONAL S. A. 890 FINCH，STREE，TORONTO，CANADA	NO. ：(4) ZS35789
	DATE：(5) JUN. 23,2010
	S/C NO. ：(6) ZJ2001-HZ08
	L/C NO. ：(7)

FROM： SHANGHAI,CHINA TO：TORONTO,CANADA (8)				
MARKS&NOS (9)	DESCRIPTIONS OF GOODS (10)	QUANTITY (11)	UNIT PRICE (12)	AMOUNT (13)
M. D. TORONTO NO. 1-61	VALVE SEAT INSERT	3050PCS	CIF TORONTO USD5. 00/PC USD6. 00/PC	USD17250. 00
		3050PCS		USD17250. 00

TOTAL AMOUNT：SAY U. S. DOLLARS SEVENTEEN THOUSAND TWO HUNDRED AND FIFTY ONLY (14)

PACKING IN 61 WOODEN CASES (15)

(16)

E. & O. E.

浙江山名进出口公司(17)

ZHEJIANG SUMING IMPORT AND EXPORT CO. ,LTD

✿ 实训指导

一、商业发票缮制说明

商业发票无统一的格式,其各栏目的内容缮制如下。

1. 出票人名称与地址

一般情况下,出票人即为出口公司,制单时应标出出票人的中英文名称和地址。当企业采用印刷空白发票或电脑制单时,都已预先印上或在程序中编入出票人的中文名称和地址。

2. 发票名称

发票名称必须用粗体标出"COMMERCIAL INVOICE"或"INVOICE"。

3. 发票抬头人名称与地址(Messrs To)

当采用信用证支付货款时,如果信用证上有指定抬头人,则按来证规定制单。否则,根据《UCP600》第 18 条 a 款的规定,必须出具成以申请人为抬头;当采用托收方式支付货款时,填写合同买方的名称和地址。填写时,名称和地址不应同行放置。

4. 出票人名称与地址(Exporter)

填写出票人的英文名称和地址。

5. 运输资料(Transport Details)

填写货物实际的起运港(地)、目的港(地)以及运输方式。如果货物需经转运,应把转运港的名称表示出来。如:FROM GUANGZHOU TO HELSINKI W/T HONGKONG BY VESSEL

6. 发票号码(Invoice No.)

发票号码由出口公司根据本公司的实际情况自行编制。

7. 发票日期(Invoice Date)

在所有结汇单据中,发票是签发日期最早的单据,该日期可以早于开证日期,但不得迟于信用证的议付有效期(Expiry Date)。

8. 信用证号码(L/C No.)

当采用信用证支付货款时,填写信用证号码。

9. 开证日期(L/C Date)

填写信用证的开证日期。

10. 合同号码(S/C No.)

合同号码应与信用证上列明的一致。一笔交易牵涉几个合同的,应在发票上表示出来。

11. 支付方式(Terms of Payment)

填写该笔业务的付款方式。如 L/C、T/T 等。

12. 唛头及件号(Marks and Number)

发票的唛头应按信用证或合同的规定填写,并与托运单、提单等单据唛头保持严格一致。若为裸装货或散装货,可填写"N/M"(No Mark 的缩写)。如信用证或合同没有指定唛头,出口商可自行设计唛头,也可打上"N/M"。

13. 货物内容（Description of Goods）

货物内容一般包括货物的名称、规格、数量、单价、贸易术语、包装等项目。制单时应与信用证的内容严格一致，省略或增加货名的字或句，都会造成单证不符，开证银行有权拖延或拒付货款。

14. 商品的包装、件数（Quantity）

填写实际装运的数量及包装单位，并与其他单据相一致。

15. 单价（Unit Price）

完整的单价由计价货币、计量单位、单位金额、价格术语四个部分组成。根据《UCP600》第 18 条 a 款的规定，发票中显示的单价和币种必须与信用证的要求一致。

16. 总金额（Amount）

总金额应为数量和单价的乘积。总金额一般要有大、小写，大、小写金额应相等。发票总金额一般不应超过信用证金额。

17. 价格术语（Trade Terms）

价格术语涉及买卖双方的责任、费用和风险的划分问题，同时，也是进口地海关核定关税的依据，因此，商业发票必须标出价格术语。信用证中的价格术语一般在货物内容的单价中表示出来。

18. 声明文句

信用证要求在发票内特别加列船名、原产地、进口许可证号码等声明文句的，制单时必须一一详列。常用的声明字句有：

①证明所到货物与合同或订单所列货物相符；

②证明原产地；

③证明不装载于或停靠限制的船只或港口；

④证明货真价实；

⑤证明已经航邮有关单据。

19. 出单人签名或盖章（Name of beneficiary and signature）

商业发票由出口商或信用证中规定的受益人出具。如果信用证没有规定，用于对外收汇的商业发票不需要签署（但用于报关、退税等国内管理环节的发票必须签署）。当信用证要求"SIGNED COMMERCIAL INVOICE …"，发票需要签署。若来证要求"MANULLY SIGNED"，则必须手签。如果以影印、自动或电脑处理或复写方法制作的发票作为正本者，应在发票上注明"正本"（ORIGINAL）字样，并由出单人签字。

项目四 装箱单缮制

实训目标

能够根据有关资料缮制装箱单。

实训任务

§ **实训一**

根据以下资料缮制装箱单。

1.客户名称地址：AL. BALOUSHI TRADING EST JEDDAH.

              PO BOX 31248, JEDDAH 21497

              KINGDOM OF SAUDI ARABIA

2.付款方式：20% T/T BEFORE SHIPMENT AND 80% D/P AT SIGHT

3.装运信息：指定 APL 承运,装运期：不迟于 2010.04.29；起运港：NINGBO,目的港：JEDDAH

4.价格条款：CFR JEDDAH

5.唛头：ROYAL

       10AR225031

       JEDDAH

       C/N：1-460

6.货物描述：

P. P INJECTION CASES 14″/22″/27″/31″ 230SET@USD42.00/SET USD9660.00

P. P INJECTION CASES 14″/19″/27″/31″ 230SET@USD41.00/SET USD9430.00

（中文品名：注塑箱四件套）

7.装箱资料：

箱号	货号	包装	件数	毛重(KGS)	净重(KGS)	体积
1-230	ZL0322+BC05	CTNS	230	18.5/4255	16.5/3795	$34M^3$
231-460	ZL0319+BC01	CTNS	230	18.5/4255	16.5/3795	$34M^3$

8.合同号：10AR225031 签订日期：2010 年 3 月 30 日

9.商业发票号：AC08AR031

10.商业发票日期：2010 年 4 月 23 日

11.出口商名称地址：JIANGNAN LIGHT INDUSTRIAL PRODUCTS CORPORATION

                NO.188 EAST ZHONGSHAN ROAD, NINGBO, CHINA

江南轻工业品公司
JIANGNAN LIGHT INDUSTRIAL PRODUCTS CORPORATION
NO. 188 EAST ZHONGSHAN ROAD, NINGBO, CHINA
PACKING   LIST

1) SELLER:	3) INVOICE NO. :	4) INVOICE DATE:
	5) FROM:	6) TO:
	7) TOTAL PACKAGES (IN WORDS)	
2) BUYER:	8) MARKS & NOS.	

9)C/NOS.	10) NOS. & KINDS OF PKGS.	11) ITEM	12) QTY.	13) G. W.	14) N. W.	15) MEAS

16)

17) ISSUED BY:

18) SIGNATURE:

§实训二

根据以下资料缮制装箱单。

1.出口商公司名称：SHANGHAI JINHAI IMP& EXP CORP. LTD.

          720 DONGFENG ROAD,SHANGHAI,CHINA

2.进口商公司名称：ANTAK DEVELOPMENT LTD.

          STUTTGART STIR. 5,D-84618，SCHORNDORF，GERMANY

3.支付方式：20% T/T BEFORE SHIPMENT AND 80% L/C AT 30 DAYS AFTER SIGHT

4.装运条款：FROM SHANGHAI TO HAMBURG NOT LATER THAN SEP. 30, 2009

5.价格条款：CFR HAMBURG

6.货物描述：MEN'S COTTON WOVEN SHIRTS

货号/规格	装运数量及单位	单　价	毛重/净重（件）	尺　码
1094L	700DOZ	USD27.4/DOZ	33KGS/31KGS	68×46×45CM
286G	800DOZ	USD39.6/DOZ	45KGS/43KGS	72×47×49CM
666	160DOZ	USD34.0/DOZ	33KGS/31KGS	68×46×45CM

包装情况：一件一塑料袋装，6件一牛皮纸包，8打或10打一外箱。

尺码搭配：1094L：　M　　　L　　　XL

              3　　　3　　　4＝10打/箱

       286G：　M　　　L　　　XL

              1.5　　3　　　3.5＝8打/箱

       666：　M　　　L　　　XL

              1.5　　3.5　　3＝8打/箱

7.唛头由卖方决定（要求使用标准化唛头）。

8.L/C NO.123456 DATED AUG.18，2009 ISSUED BY BANK OF CHINA, HAM-BURG BRANCH

9.ADVISING BANK：BANK OF CHINA, SHANGHAI

10.船名：HONGHE　V. 188

11.B/L DATED SEP. 20,2009

12.S/C NO.00SHGM3178B DATED AUG. 2，2009

13.INVOICE NO：SHGM70561

14.FREIGHT FEE：USD160.00

15.DOCUMENT：

     +PACKING LIST IN ONE ORIGINAL PLUS 5 COPIES INDICATING THIS L/C NUMBER, ALL OF WHICH MUST BE MANUALLY SIGNED.

     ……

SHANGHAI JINHAI IMP & EXP CORP. LTD.
720 DONGFENG ROAD, SHANGHAI, CHINA
PACKING   LIST

Marks & Nos	Quantity and Descriptions of Goods	Net Weight	Gross Weight	Meas.
TO：		NO.：		
		Date：		

§ **实训三**

根据以下资料缮制装箱单。

信用证资料：

DOCUMENTS REQUIRED：

+PACKING LIST REQUIRED IN FIVE COPIES

……

其他内容：参考项目三（商业发票缮制）实训二资料

浙江纺大贸易有限公司
ZHEJIANG FANTA TRADING CO., LTD.
NO. 158 ZHONGSHAN ZHONG ROAD, HANGZHOU, CHINA
PACKING　LIST

TO:	NO. :
	DATE:
SHIPPING MARKS:	S/C NO. :
	L/C NO. :

C/NOS.	NOS. & KINDS OF PKGS.	ITEM	QTY.	G. W.	N. W.	MEAS. (M³)

✿ 实训指导

<h1 style="text-align:center">一、装箱单缮制说明</h1>

装箱单(重量单/尺码单)无统一的格式,其各栏目的内容填制如下。

第1栏:单据名称

单据名称应符合信用证规定。如信用证要求提供重量单,则名称应写为"WEIGHT LIST";如信用证要求提供尺码单,则名称应写为"MEASUREMENT LIST"。

第2栏:抬头

除非信用证特别要求,否则银行可接受装箱单表面无抬头(即无开证申请人名称和地址)的表示。

第3栏:号码

一般填发票号码。

第4栏:日期

即装箱单填制日期,一般与发票相同。如信用证未作规定,也可不注明出单日。

第5栏:唛头

填写唛头,且须与发票、信用证及实物印刷完全一致;如无唛头,填"N/M"。

第6栏:货物描述

装箱单中所标明的货物应与发票中所描述的货物一致,但可用与其他单据无矛盾的统称表示。

第7栏:数量及包装数

数量按商品的正常计量单位填写,包装填写最大包装种类和件数。

第8栏:净重、毛重、体积

填写商品的净重、毛重、体积。注意净重和毛重是以千克为单位。商品的体积,单位是立方米,且保留三位小数。

第9栏:其他

根据信用证中关于装箱单的特殊要求条款,制作时应在装箱单上注明。

第10栏:签署

当信用证没有规定装箱单签名时,可以不盖章签名,当然也可以盖章签名。盖章签名时,填出口公司名称及法定代表签名。

项目五 运输单据缮制

实训目标

能够根据有关资料缮制海运提单和航空运单。

实训任务

§ 实训一

根据下列资料缮制海运提单。

信用证资料:

DOCUMENTS REQUIRED:

+ FULL SET OF CLEAN SHIPPED ON BOARD OCEAN BILL OF LADING DRAWN OR ENDORSED TO THE ORDER OF NATIONAL BANK LIMITED, MOHAKHALI BRANCH 9-MOHAKHALI C/A, DHAKA, BANGLADESH SHOWING FREIGHT PREPAID AND NOTIFY L/C APPLICANT AND US GIVING FULL NAME AND ADDRESS.

……

其他内容:参考项目三(商业发票缮制)实训二资料。

其他资料:

货物装 1×20′集装箱 FCL

装运日:2009/07/23

CONTAINER NO.:HJCU8430166

SEAL NO.:S/6046374

SHIPPER'S LOAD AND COUNT

B/L NO.:HJSCTAOI14391305

Shipper			B/L NO.	
Consignee			**HANJIN SHIPPING** Beyond the Ocean **BILL OF LADING**	
Notify party				
Place of receipt		Pre-carriage by	CONTAINERIZED(vessel only) ☐ Yes　　☐ No	
Vessel voy.		Port of loading		
Port of discharge		Place of delivery	Final destination	

PARTICULARS FURNISHED BY SHIPPER				
Container NO. Seal NO. Marks & NOS.	NO. & kind of packages or containers	Description of goods	G. W. (KGS)	Meas. (CBM)

Total No. of packages or containers(in words)

Freight & charges	Rate as	Rate		Per	Prepaid	Collect

RECEIVED by the Carrier from the Shipper in apparent good order and condition unless otherwise indicated herein, the Goods, or the container(s) or package(s) said to contain the cargo herein mentioned, to be carried subject to all the terms and conditions provided for on the face and back of this Bill of Lading by the Vessel named herein or any substitute at the Carrier's option and/or other means of transport, from the place of receipt or the port of loading to the port of discharge or the place of delivery shown herein and there to be delivered to Consignee or on-carrier on payment of all charges due thereon.

If REQUIRED by the Carrier, this Bill of Lading duly endorsed must be surrendered in exchange for the Goods or delivery order None of the terms of this Bill of Lading can be waived by or for the Carrier except by written waiver signed by a duly authorized agent of the Carrier.

IN ACCEPTING THIS BILL OF LADING the Merchant agrees to be bound by all the stipulations, exceptions, terms and conditions on the face and back hereof, whether written, typed, stamped or printed, as fully as if signed by the Merchant any local custom or privilege to the contrary notwithstanding.

IN WITNESS WHEREOF, the undersigned, on behalf of Hanjin Shipping Co,,Ltd. the master and the owner of the Vessel has signed the number of Bill(s) of Lading stated above all of the same tenor and date, one of which being accomplished, the others to stand void. (Terms of Bill of Lading Continued on Back Hereof)

Total	
At	

Loading on board the vessel
Date
By

Place of B(s)/L issue

NO. of original B(S)/L signed

Date of B(S)/L issue

HANJIN SHIPPING CO., LTD.
As carrier
By

§ 实训二

根据下列资料缮制海运提单。

信用证资料：

+2/3 ORIGINAL BILL OF LADING ISSUED TO THE ORDER OF CALZEDONIA S. P. A. MARKED FREIGHT COLLECT NOTIFY APPLICANT

......

其他内容：参考项目三（商业发票缮制）实训三资料。

其他资料：

B/L NO. :SIN7890

VESSEL VOY. ：VICTORY V. 090

ON BOARD DATE：2009/12/24

ETA DATE:2010/01/16

G. W. :416KGS

N. W. :352.30KGS

MEASUREMENT：3.936CBM

Shipper	SINOTRANS	B/L No.
Consignee or order	中国对外贸易运输总公司 CHINA NATIONAL FOREIGN TRADE TRANSPORTATION CORP. 直运或转船提单 **BILL OF LADING** **DIRECT OR WITH TRANSSHIPMENT**	
Notify address	SHIPPED on board in apparent good order and condition (unless otherwise indicated) the goods or packages specified herein and to be discharged at the mentioned port of discharge or as near thereto as the vessel may safely get and be always afloat.	
	The weight, measure, marks and numbers, quality, contents and value, being particulars furnished by the Shipper, are not checked by the carrier on loading.	

Pre-carriage by	Place of loading
Vessel	Port of transshipment
Port of discharge	Final destination

The Shipper, Consignee and the Holder of this Bill of Lading hereby expressly accept and agree to all printed, written or stamped provisions, exceptions and conditions of this Bill of Lading including those on the back hereof.

IN WITNESS Where of the number of original Bills of Lading stated below have been signed, one of which being accomplished, the other(s) to be void.

Container, seal No. or marks & Nos.	Number & kind of packages	Description of goods	Gross weight (kgs)	Measurement (m³)
ABOVE PARTICULARS FURNISHED BY SHIPPER				

Freight & charges		Regarding transshipment information please contact	
Ex. rate	Prepaid at	Freight payable at	Place and date of issue
	Total Prepaid	Number of original B(s)/L	Signed for or on behalf of the master 　　　　　　　　as Agents

§ 实训三

根据下列资料缮制航空运单。

FROM：UFJ BANK，TOKYO

TO：BANK OF CHINA，ZHEJIANG BRANCH

DATE OF ISSUE：DEC. 28,2009

L/C NO.：UF7896

EXPIRY DATE AND PLACE：FEB. 15，2010

APPLICANT：SAKURA COMPANY,6-2 OHTEMACHI, 1-CHOME, CHIYADA-KU,TOKYO

BENEFICIARY：ZHEJIANG RONGXIN MEDICINES AND HEALTH PRODUCTS COMPANY,NO. 89, SHAOXING ROAD, SHAOXING, CHINA

L/C AMOUNT：USD22912. 50

TAKING CHARGE PLACE：SHANGHAI,SHANGHAI

FOR TRANSPORTATION TO：TOKYO,JAPAN

LATEST DATE OF SHIPMENT：JAN. 31,2010

DOCUMENTS REQUIED：

+AWB CONSIGNED TO APPLICANT MARKED FREIGHT PEPAID INDICATING ACTUAL FLIGHT DATE.

其他资料：

航空公司 2010 年 1 月 17 日对托运人的航空托运单予以确认：

SHIPPER：ZHEJIANG RONGXIN MEDICINES AND HEALTH PRODUCTS COMPANY

GOODS：5250PCS HOSPITAL UNIFORM

FLIGHT：CA1908

ACTUAL FLIGHT DATE：JAN. 18,2010

FROM SHANGHAI AIRPORT TO TOKYO AIRPORT

G. W.：1232KGS

MEAS.：4. 20CBM

PACKED IN 88 CARTONS

SHIPPING MARKS：S. C. /TOKYO/1-88

空运单据由上海佳达航空国际货运代理有限公司（BEST INTERNATIOAL AIR FREIGHT CO. ,LTD)签发。

签发日期：2010 年 1 月 18 日

Shipper's name and address	Shipper's Account Number	Not negotiable
		Air Waybill 中国东方航空公司
		ISSUED BY　CHINA EASTERN AIRLINES
		Copies 1，2 and 3 of　this Air Waybill are originals and have the same validity

Consignee's name and address	Consignee's Account Number	It is agreed that the goods described herein are accepted in apparent good order and condition (except as noted) for carriage SUBJECT TO THE CONDITIONS OF CONTRACT ON THE REVERSE HEREOF, ALL GOODS MAY BE CARRIED BY ANY OTHER MEANS, INCLUDING ROAD OR ANY OTHER CARRIER UNLESS SPECIFIC CONTRARY INSTRUCTIONS ARE GIVEN HEREON BY THE SHIPPER. THE SHIPPER'S ATTENTION IS DRAWN TO THE NOTICE CONCERNING CARRIER'S LIMITATION OF LIABILITY. Shipper may increase such limitation of liability by declaring a higher value for carriage and paying a supplemental charge if required.

Issuing Carrier's Agent Name and City	Accounting Information

Agents IATA Code	Account No.	

Airport of Departure(Addr. of First Carrier) and Requested Routing

Reference number	Optional shipping information

To	By First Carrier	Routing and Destination	To	by	To	by	Currency	CHGS Code	WT/VAL		Other		Declared Value for Carriage	Declared Value for Customs
									PPD	COLL	PPD	COLL		

Airport of Destination	Flight/Date	For Carrier Use only	Flight/Date	Amount of Insurance	INSURANCE-If carrier offers insurance and such insurance is requested in accordance with the conditions thereof indicate amount to be insured in figures in box marked "Amount of Insurance".

Handling Information

SCI

No.of Pieces RCP	Gross Weight	Kg lb	Rate Class / Commodity Item No.	Chargeable Weight	Rate / Charge	Total	Nature and Quantity of Goods (incl. Dimensions or Volume)

Prepaid	Weight charge	Collect	Other Charges
	Valuation Charge		
	Tax		
Total Other Charges Due Agent			Shipper certifies that the particulars on the face hereof are correct and that insofar as any part of the consignment contains dangerous goods, such part is properly described by name and is in proper condition for carriage by air according to the applicable Dangerous Goods Regulations Charges at Destination
Total Other Charges Due Carrier			
			Signature of　Shipper or his agent
Total Prepaid	Total Collect		
Currency　Conversion	CC Charges in dest Currency		Executed on(date)　At(place)　Signature of issuing Carrier or as Agent
For Carrier's Use Only at Destination	Charges at Destination	Total Collect Charges	AWB No.

§ 实训四

2010 年 4 月 7 日，南京食品贸易公司（NANJING FOOD TRADING CO. ，LTD. ）的货物从南京起运，航班为 FX0910，请根据下列资料作空运提单。

信用证资料：

2010MAR22 09：18；11   LOGICAL TERMINALE102

MT S700   ISSUE OF A DOCUMENTARY CREDIT

PAGE   00001
FUNC   MSG700
UMR   06881051

MSGACK DWS765I AUTH OK，KEY B198081689580FC5，BKCHCNBJ RJHISARI RECORO

BASIC HEADER F 01 BKCHCNBJA940 0588 550628

APPLICATION HEADER 0 700 1057 010320 RJHISARIAXXX 7277 977367 020213 1557 N

    * ALRAJHI BANKING AND INVESTMENT
    * CORPORATION
    * RIYADH
    * (HEAD OFFICE)

USER HEADER   SERVICE CODE   103：   （银行盖信用证通知专用章）
      BANK. PRIORITY   113：
      MSG USER REF.   108：
      INFO. FROM CI   115：

SEQUENCE OF TOTAL   *27：1 / 1

FORM OF DOC. CREDIT   *40A：IRREVOCABLE

DOC. CREDIT NUMBER   *20：0011LC123756

DATE OF ISSUE   31C：100322

DATE/PLACE EXP.   *31 D：DATE 100515 PLACE CHINA

APPLICANT   *50：NEO GENERAL TRADING CO.
      P. O. BOX 99552，RIYADH 22766，KSA
      TEL：00966-1-4659220 FAX：00966-1-4659213

BENEFICIARY   *59：NANJING FOOD TRADING CO. ，LTD.
      HUARONG MANSION RM2901 NO. 85 GUANJIAQIAO，
      NANJING 210005，CHINA
      TEL：0086-25-4715004 FAX：0086-25-4711363

AMOUNT   *32 B：CURRENCY USD AMOUNT 13260，

AVAILABLE WITH/BY *41 D：ANY BANK IN CHINA，
      BY NEGOTIATION

DRAFTS AT… 42 C：SIGHT

DRAWEE   42 A：RJHISARI
    * ALRAJHI BANKING AND INVESTMENT
    * CORPORATION
    * RIYADH
    * (HEAD OFFICE)

PARTIAL SHIPMTS	43 P：	NOT ALLOWED
TRANSSHIPMENT	43 T：	NOT ALLOWED
LOADING ON BRD	44 A：	NANJING，CHINA
FOR TRANSPORT TO	44 B：	DAMMAM PORT，SAUDI ARABIA
LATEST SHIPMENT	44 C：	100430
GOODS DESCRIPT.	45 A：	

ABOUT 1700 CARTONS CANNED MUSRHOOM PIECES & STEMS
24 TINS X 425 GRAMS
NET WEIGHT (D. W. 227 GRAMS) AT USD7. 80 PER CARTON
ROSE BRAND

DOCS REQUIRED 46 A：

+SIGNED COMMERCIAL INVOICE IN TRIPLICATE ORIGINAL AND MUST SHOW BREAK DOWN OF THE AMOUNT AS FOLLOWS：FOB VALUE, FREIGHT CHARGES AND TOTAL AMOUNT C AND F.

+FULL SET AIR WAYBILL EVIDENCING NEO GENERAL TRADING CO. , MARKED FREIGHT PREPAID.

+PACKING LIST IN ONE ORIGINAL PLUS 5 COPIES, ALL OF WHICH MUST BE MANUALLY SIGNED.

+INSPECTION (HEALTH) CERTIFICATE FROM C. I. Q. (ENTRY-EXIT INSPECTION AND QUARANTINE OF THE PEOPLES REP. OF CHINA) STATING GOODS ARE FIT FOR HUMAN BEING.

+CERTIFICATE OF ORIGIN DULY CERTIFIED BY C. C. P. I. T. STATING THE NAME OF THE MANUFACTURERS OF PRODUCERS AND THAT GOODS EXPORTED AR WHOLLY OF CHINESE ORIGIN.

+THE PRODUCTION DATE OF THE GOODS NOT TO BE EARLIER THAN HALF MONTH AT TIME OF SHIPMENT. BENEFICIARY MUST CERTIFY THE SAME.

+SHIPMENT TO BE EFFECTED BY CONTAINER AND BY REGULAR LINE. SHIPMENT COMPANY'S CERTIFICATE TO THIS EFFECT SHOULD ACCOMPANY THE DOCUMENTS.

DD. CONDITIONS 47 A：

A DISCREPANCY FEE OF USD50. 00 WILL BE IMPOSED ON EACH SET OF DOCUMENTS PRESENTED FOR NEGOTIATION UNDER THIS L/C WITH DISCREPANCY. THE FEE WILL BE DEDUCTED FROM THE BILL AMOUNT.

CHARGES 71 B：

ALL CHARGES AND COMMISSIONS OUTSIDE KSA ON BENEFICIARIES' ACCOUNT INCLUDING REIMBURSING BANK COMMISSION, DISCREPANCY FEE (IF ANY) AND COURIER CHARGES.

CONFIRMAT INSTR　＊49：WITHOUT

REIMBURS. BANK　53 D：ALRAJHI BANKING AND INVESTMENT CORP RIYADH (HEAD OFFICE)

INS PAYING BANK 78：

DOCUMENTS TO BE DESPATCHED IN ONE LOT BY COURIER.

ALL CORRESPONDENCE TO BE SENT TO ALRAJHI BANKING AND IN-
VESTMENT COPRORATION RIYADH（HEAD OFFICE）
TRAILER　ORDER IS ＜MAC：＞ ＜PAC：＞ ＜ENC：＞ ＜CHK：＞ ＜TNG：＞ ＜PDE：＞
　　　　MAC：E55927A4
　　　　CHK：7B505952829A
　　　　HOB：
补充资料：
商品毛重：19074.44KGS
体积：36.85CBM
Rate Class 运价分类代号：M
Rate/Charge 费率：20.61
Other Charge 其他费用：AWC（运单费）USD50.00

Shipper's name and address	Shipper's Account Number	Not Negotiable **Air Waybill** Issued by	中国国际航空公司 **AIR CHINA** BEIJING CHINA
		Copies 1, 2 and 3 of this Air Waybill are originals and have the same validity	

Consignee's name and address	Consignee's Account Number	It is agreed that the goods described herein are accepted in apparent good order and condition (except as noted) for carriage SUBJECT TO THE CONDITIONS OF CONTRACT ON THE REVERSE HEREOF, ALL GOODS MAY BE CARRIED BY ANY OTHER MEANS, INCLUDING ROAD OR ANY OTHER CARRIER UNLESS SPECIFIC CONTRARY INSTRUCTIONS ARE GIVEN HEREON BY THE SHIPPER. THE SHIPPER'S ATTENTION IS DRAWN TO THE NOTICE CONCERNING CARRIER'S LIMITATION OF LIABILITY. Shipper may increase such limitation of liability by declaring a higher value for carriage and paying a supplemental charge if required.

Issuing Carrier's Agent Name and City	Accounting Information

Agents IATA Code	Account No.	

Airport of Departure(Addr. of First Carrier) and Requested Routing	Reference number	Optional shipping information

To	By First Carrier	Routing and Destination	To	by	To	by	Currency	CHGS Code	WT/VAL		Other		Declared Value for Carriage	Declared Value for Customs
									PPD	COLL	PPD	COLL		

Airport of Destination	Flight/Date	For Carrier Use only	Flight/Date	Amount of Insurance	INSURANCE-If carrier offers insurance and such insurance is requested in accordance with the conditions thereof indicate amount to be insured in figures in box marked "Amount of Insurance".

Handling Information

SCI

No.of Pieces RCP	Gross Weight	Kg lb	Rate Class / Commodity Item No.	Chargeable Weight	Rate / Charge	Total	Nature and Quantity of Goods (incl. Dimensions or Volume)

Prepaid	Weight charge	Collect	Other Charges
	Valuation Charge		
	Tax		
	Total Other Charges Due Agent		Shipper certifies that the particulars on the face hereof are correct and that insofar as any part of the consignment contains dangerous goods, such part is properly described by name and is in proper condition for carriage by air according to the applicable Dangerous Goods Regulations Charges at Destination
	Total Other Charges Due Carrier		
			Signature of Shipper or his agent
Total Prepaid	Total Collect		
Currency Conversion	CC Charges in dest. Currency		Executed on(date) At(place) Signature of issuing Carrier or as Agent
For Carrier's Use Only at Destination	Charges at Destination	Total Collect Charges	AWB No.

§ 实训五

根据以下资料，审核并修改已填制的提单，在已填制的 20 个栏目（标号 1—20）中找出若干处填制错误，并说明原因。

（一）资料：国际货运委托书

国际货运委托书
Shipper's Letter of Instruction

Shipper（托运人） SHANGHAI MACHINE CO. , LTD. 1223 JIDI ROAD，MINGHANG， SHANGHAI 291197 CHINA		发票编号 06EX07	贸易方式 G. T.	收汇方式 L/C
		可否转船 否	运费方式 到付	提单份数 3
		可否分批 否	装运期限 2010-6-18	有效期限 2010-6-20
Consignee（收货人） TO ORDER OF HONGKONG&SHANGHAI BANK JAKARTA BRANCH		收货地点 MINGHANG	装货港 SHANGHAI	卸货港 JAKARTA
		目的地 Final destination for the merchant JAKARTA，INDONESIA		
Notified party（通知方） PT ANTA TIRTA KIRANA JI. GREEN GARDEN BLICK Z4 JAKARTA 11520 INDONESIA		交货地点 Place of delivery JAKARTA，INDONESIA		运输条款 CY/CY
		集装箱类别和数量	拼箱号	装箱方式 DOOR/DOOR
		20′ 40HT 40′×4 40HC 45′ 20HT		
Marks&Nos.	Kind of packages	Description of Goods	Gross Weight	Measurement
JAKARTA MADE IN CHINA	13 WOODEN CASES	CO-EXTRUSION FILM BLOWING LINE MODEL： SM-65-80-3E-1800	29900KGS	185M³

配载要求和备注：
1.6 月 16 日上门装箱并安排熏蒸
2.运费到付，杂费预付
3.指定货运代理公司 ABC COMPANY
所填全部属实并愿遵守承运人的一切载运章程。
WE CERTIFIES THAT THE PARTICULARS ON THE FACE HEREOF ARE CORRECT AND AGREES NDITIONS OF CARRIAGE OF THE CARRIER.

托运人（公章）：上海机械有限公司   托运日期：2010-06-09   经办人：王晓路

（二）配舱资料

船名及航次：KUO FU V.5065

提单号：CMAGLXFF98560

装船日：20 JUN 2010

开船日：21JUN 2010

起运港：SHANGHAI

卸货港：JAKARTA

（三）装箱资料

集装箱号、封号：CGMU4289466/2248269/40′

ECMU4143706/2248268/40′

FSCU4036720/2248364/40′

TGHU4532523/2257014/40′

件数：12PACKAGES

毛重：29100KGS

体积：175CBM

（四）已缮制的提单

Shipper(1) SHANGHAI　MACHINE CO.，LTD. 1223 JIDI ROAD，MINGHANG， SHANGHAI 291197 CHINA	**SINOTRANS**

	B/L NO.：CMAGLXFF98560（9）
Consignee or order(2) TO ORDER OF HONGKONG&SHANGHAI BANK JAKARTA BRANCH	中国对外贸易运输总公司 CHINA NATIONAL FOREIGN TRADE TRANSPORTATION CORP. 直运或转船提单 **BILL OF LADING** **DIRECT OR WITH TRANSSHIPMENT**

Notify address(3)
PT ANTA TIRTA KIRANA
JI. GREEN GARDEN BLICK Z4
JAKARTA 11520 INDONESIA

SHIPPED on board in apparent good order and condition（unless otherwise indicated）the goods or packages specified herein and to be discharged at the mentioned port of discharge or as near thereto as the vessel may safely get and be always afloat.

The weight, measure, marks and numbers, quality, contents and value, being particulars furnished by the Shipper, are not checked by the carrier on loading.

The Shipper, Consignee and the Holder of this Bill of Lading hereby expressly accept and agree to all printed, written or stamped provisions, exceptions and conditions of this Bill of Lading including those on the back hereof.

IN WITNESS Where of the number of original Bills of Lading stated below have been signed, one of which being accomplished, the other(s) to be void.

Pre-carriage by	Place of loading (5) SHANGHAI
Vessel (4) KUO FU V. 5065	Port of transshipment (7)
Port of discharge (6) JAKARTA	Final destination (8)

Container, Seal No. or Marks & Nos. (10)	Number & kind of packages (11)	Description of goods(12)	Gross weight (kgs) (13)	Measurement (m³) (14)
JAKARTA MADE IN CHINA 4×40′ FCL	13 WOODEN CASES	CO-EXTRUSION FILM BLOWING LINE MODEL： SM-65-80-3E-1800 CY/CY (15)	29900KGS	185CBM

ABOVE PARTICULARS FURNISHED BY SHIPPER	
Freight & charges OCEAN FREIGHT COLLECT (16) OTHER CHG COLLECT (17)	REGARDING TRANSSHIPMENT INFORMATION PLEASE CONTACT

Ex. rate	Prepaid at	Freight payable at	Place and date of issue SHANGHAI　20 JUN 2010 (19)
	Total Prepaid	Number of original B(s)/L THREE (18)	Signed for or on behalf of the master (20) CHINA NATIONAL FOREIGN TRADE TRANSPORTATION CORP. as Agents

实训指导

一、海运提单缮制说明

不同船公司签发的海运提单的正面格式有所不同,其正面需填制的栏目说明如下。

1. 托运人(Shipper)

托运人是委托运输的人,一般是合同的卖方。信用证方式下,托运人栏一般填写信用证中的受益人名址;在托收方式下,以托收的委托人为托运人。如果开证人为了贸易上的需要,要求做第三者提单(THIRD PARTY B/L),也可照办。

2. 收货人(Consignee)

又称为抬头栏,此栏应严格按照合同和信用证的有关规定填写。本栏有记名式收货人、不记名式收货人和指示式收货人三种填写方法。

(1)记名式收货人

在收货人栏内填写某人或某企业的具体名称,如信用证条款为"Full set of B/L consigned to D. E. company",则此栏填写"consigned to D. E. company"或"D. E. company"。

(2)不记名式收货人

即在本栏留空不填或仅填入"To Bearer"(给持有者)。这种提单谁持有都可以提货,转让时也不必背书,因而风险较大,目前国际上很少使用。

(3)指示式收货人

指示式的收货人又可分为不记名指示式(To order)和记名指示式(To order of...)两种。

①To order:凭指示或称空白抬头,常见信用证条款为"Full set of B/L made out to order",则收货人栏填写"To order"。这种提单须由托运人在提单背面背书,才可以转让。

②To order of...:凭×××指示,常见的有三种表达方法。

a. 凭开证行指示。常见信用证条款为"Full set of B/L made out to our order",our 指开证行,此种提单须经银行背书才可转让给买方,有利于开证银行在向买方收汇前牢牢掌握物权。

b. 凭开证申请人指示。常见信用证条款为"B/L issued to order of applicant",这种提单须经开证申请人背书才能转让,不利于银行掌握物权。

c. 凭托运人指示。常见信用证条款为"Full set of B/L made out to order of shipper",这种提单等同于凭提示(To order)提单,在国际贸易中使用非常普遍。

3. 被通知人(Notify Party)

该栏目填写船公司在货物到达目的港时发送到货通知的收件人。在信用证项下的提单,该栏必须严格按信用证要求填写。如果信用证没有规定被通知人,那么就应将L/C的开证申请人名称、地址填入副本提单的这一栏中,而正本的这一栏为空白。托收方式下,被通知方一般填托收的付款人。

4. 提单号码(B/L No.)

提单号码由承运人或其代理人提供。

5. 前段运输(Pre-carriage by)

如果货物需转运,此栏填写第一程船的船名;如果货物不需转运,此栏空白不填。

6. 收货地点(Place of Receipt)

如果货物需转运,此栏填写收货的港口名称;如果货物不需转运,此栏空白不填。

7. 船名航次(Vessel Voy. No.)

如果货物需转运,填写第二程船的船名和航次;如果货物不需转运,填写该批货物实际所装运的船名和航次号。

8. 装运港(Port of Loading)

填实际装船港口的具体名称。如果信用证中对装运港仅作笼统规定的(如 China Main Port)或同时列明几个装运港,应填写实际装运的港口名称。如果货物需转运,填写转运港的名称。

9. 卸货港(Port of Discharge)

填列货物实际卸下的港口名称,即目的港。

10. 最终目的地(Final Destination)

填写最终目的地的名称。如果货物的最终目的地是目的港,此栏空白。

11. 唛头、集装箱箱号与封号(Marks & Nos. ,Container,Seal No.)

填写唛头、集装箱箱号和封号。

信用证对唛头有规定的,则按信用证规定缮制;如信用证未作规定,可按卖方自己设计的唛头填写;如果货物包装上没有唛头,则填写"N/M"。唛头应与发票和装箱单完全一致。

12. 件数和包装种类(Number and Kind of Packages)

填写装入集装箱内货物的外包装件数或集装箱个数,分别用罗马数字小写和英文大写数字表示。

(1)对于包装货物,本栏应注明包装数量和单位,并加大写数量。如100纸箱,则此栏填写"100 CARTONS"和"SAY ONE HUNDRED CARTONS ONLY"。

(2)对于散装货物,例如煤炭、原油等,此栏可加"IN BULK",数量无须加大写。

(3)对于裸装货物,应加件数,如一台机器或一辆汽车,填"1 UNIT",100头猪则应填"100 HEADS"等,并加大写数量。

(4)如是集装箱运输,由托运人装箱的整箱货可只写集装箱数量,如2个集装箱,则此栏填"2 CONTAINERS"。只要海关已对集装箱封箱,承运人对箱内的内容和数量不负责任,提单内应加注"SHIPPER'S LOAD & COUNT"(托运人装货并计数)。如要注明集装箱箱内小件数量时,数量前应加"STC(SAID TO CONTAIN)",如"2 CONTAINER(STC 100 CARTONS)"。

(5)如是托盘装运,此栏应填托盘数量,同时用括号加注货物的包装件数,如"3 PAL-LETS(STC 45 CARTONS)"。提单内还应加注"SHIPPER'S LOAD & COUNT"。

(6)如是两种或多种包装,件数要显示数字相加的和,种类用"PACKAGE"表示,并在大写栏内写大写合计数量。

13. 货物名称或货物描述(Description of Goods)

货物名称应严格按照信用证或发票上的货名和文字填具。

14. 毛重(Gross Weight)

填报实际货物的毛重,一般以公斤为计量单位。

15. 尺码(Measurement)

填写实际货物的体积,一般以立方米为计量单位,小数点后保留 3 位数。

16. 特殊条款

(1)指定船名;

(2)强调运费的支付;

(3)不显示发票金额、单价、价格等的条款,或强调显示信用证号码、合同号码等的条款;

(4)限制使用班轮公会的条款或指定承运人的条款。

17. 运费条款(Freight and Charges)

此栏的填写应按信用证规定并根据成交的价格术语来确定。当使用 CIF 或 CFR 时,应填"Freight prepaid"(运费预付)或"Freight paid"(运费已付);当使用 FOB 时,应填"Freight collect"(运费待付)或"Freight payable at destination"(运费到付)。有时,信用证还要求注明运费的金额,则要填写实际运费支付额。

18. 正本提单份数(Number of Original B/L)

提单有正本副本之分。正本提单上印有"ORIGINAL"字样,并注明提单签发日期和签名。正本提单的份数必须符合信用证的要求。如,信用证规定"全套海运提单"(Full set or Complete set B/L),按惯例签发三份正本交银行议付。

19. 提单签发地点及日期(Place and Date of Issue)

提单签发地点一般为装运港所在城市。

提单签发日期表示货物实际装运的时间或已经接受船方、船代理等有关方面监管的时间。此时间应不迟于信用证或合同规定的最迟装运日期。已装船提单的签发日期视为装运日期。

20. 提单的签署(Signature)

提单必须经过签署手续后才能生效。有权签署提单的除了船长,还可以是承运人,或由他们授权的代理人。提单签署时应表明签署人的身份,代理人的任何签字必须标明其系代表承运人还是船长签字。

(1)承运人(CHINA OCEAN SHIPPING COMPANY)本人签字

提单签字处:CHINA OCEAN SHIPPING COMPANY AS CARRIER

(2)承运代理人(DEF SHIPPING CO.)签字

提单签字处:DEF SHIPPING CO. As agent for and/or on behalf of CHINA OCEAN SHIPPING COMPANY as Carrier (或 the master)

(3)船长(CAPTAIN Jame Brown)签字

提单签字处:CAPTAIN Jame Brown

　　　　　　　　As Master 或 The Master

(4)船长代理签字

提单签字处:DEF SHIPPING CO.

As agent for and /or on behalf of CAPTAIN Jame Brown as master(或 the master)

二、航空运单缮制说明

各航空公司所使用的航空运单大多借鉴 IATA 所推荐的标准格式,其主要栏目内容的填制说明如下。

1. 货运单号码(The Air Waybill Number)

货运单号码一般被印在货运单的左(右)上角及右下角。

2. 始发站机场(Airport of Departure)

需填写 IATA 统一制定的始发站机场三字代码(如果始发地机场名称不明确,可填制机场所在城市的 IATA 三字代码)。一般填在货运单的左上角,如 999/SHA/1234 5686。

3. 托运人姓名、住址(Shipper's Name and Address)

填写托运人姓名(名称)、地址、国家(或国家两字代号)以及托运人的电话、传真、电传号码等联络方法。信用证方式下必须与受益人名称地址一致。

4. 托运人账号(Shipper's Account Number)

此栏一般不需填写,除非承运人需要。

5. 收货人姓名、住址(Consignee's Name and Address)

应填写收货人姓名(名称)、地址、国家(或国家两字代号)以及收货人的电话、传真、电传号码等联络方法。航空运单不可转让,所以"凭指示"之类的字样不得出现。

6. 收货人账号(Consignee's Account Number)

同第 4 项一样只在必要时填写。

7. 签发运单的承运人代理的名称和所在城市(Issuing Carrier's Agent Name and City)

若航空运单由承运人的代理人签发时,本栏填写实际代理人的名称及城市名;如果运单直接由承运人本人签发时,此栏可空白不填。

8. 代理人的 IATA 代号(Agent's IATA Code)

代理人的国际航协代号,一般可不填。

9. 代理人账号(Account Number)

即代理人与航空公司运费结算账号。本栏一般不需填写,除非承运人需要。

10. 始发站机场及所要求的航线(Airport of Departure and Requested Routing)

填始发站机场或所在城市的全称,不得简写或使用代码。

11. 运输路线和目的站(Routing and Destination)

(1)至(第一承运人)To (by First Carrier)。如无转运,填制目的站机场的 IATA 代码;如需转运,填第一个中转机场的 IATA 代码。by First Carrier,填制第一承运人的全称或 IATA 代码。

(2)至(第二承运人)To (by Third Carrier)。填制目的站机场或第二个中转机场的 IATA 代码;by Second Carrier,填制第二承运人的 IATA 代码。

(3)至(第三承运人)To (by Third Carrier)。填制目的站机场或第三个中转机场的 IATA 代码;by Third Carrier,填制第三承运人的 IATA 代码。

12. 财务说明(Accounting Information)

填写与费用结算有关的事项,此栏只有在采用特殊付款方式时才填写。

13. 货币(Currency)

填制始发站所在国的 ISO(国际标准组织)货币代码。如,CNY—人民币;USD—美元。

14. 运费代号(Chgs Code)

运费的支付方式代码,一般不需填写,仅供电子传送货运单信息时用。

15. 运费/声明价值费(WT/VAL,weight charge/valuation charge)

该栏费用若是预付,则在 PPD(Prepaid)栏内打"×";若是待付,则在 COLL(collect)栏内打"×",此栏应注意与第 12 项保持一致。需要注意的是,航空货物运输中运费与声明价值费支付的方式必须一致,不能分别支付。

16. 其他费用(Other)

在始发站的其他费用,填法参考 15 栏。

17. 供运输用声明价值(Declared Value for Carriage)

此栏填入发货人要求的用于运输的声明价值,该价值即为承运人赔偿责任的限额,一般可按发票金额填列。如果发货人未办理货物声明价值,则填入"NVD(No value declared,无申报价值)"。空白不填,表示 NVD。

18. 海关声明价值(Declared Value for Customs)

此栏所填价值是提供给海关的征税依据。当以出口货物报关单或商业发票作为征税标准时,本栏可空白不填或填"AS PER INV.";如果货物系样品等数量少且无商业价值的,可填"NCV"(No customs valuation),表明没有商业价值。

19. 目的地机场(Airport of Destination)

填写最终目的地机场的全称。

20. 航班及日期(Flight/Date)

本栏由航空公司安排舱位后使用,填写航班号和日期。

21. 保险金额(Amount of Insurance)

只有在航空公司提供代理保险业务而客户也有此需要时才填写,如没有则打"×××"或"NIL"字样。中国民航不代理国际货物的保险业务。

22. 运输处理注意事项(Handling Information)

本栏填写承运人对货物处理的有关注意事项。

23. 海关信息(SCI)

填写海关信息,仅在欧盟国家之间运输货物时使用。

24. 货物件数和运价组合点(No. of Pieces,RCP,Rate Combination Point)

填入货物包装件数。如 10 包即填"10"。如果所使用的货物运价种类不同时,应分别填写。当需要组成比例运价或分段相加运价时,在此栏填入运价组成点机场的 IATA 代码。

25. 毛重(Gross Weight)

适用于运价的货物实际毛重(以公斤为单位时可保留至小数点后一位)。

26. 重量单位(Kg/Lb)

以公斤为单位用代号"K";以磅为单位用代号"L"。

27. 运价等级(Rate Class)

填写所采用的货物运价等级代码。

28. 商品代码(Commodity Item No.)

在使用特种运价时需要在此栏填写商品代码。使用指定商品运价时,此栏打印指定商品品名代号;使用等级货物运价时,此栏打印附加或附减的比例(百分比);如果是集装货物,打印集装货物运价等级。

29. 计费重量(Chargeable Weight)

此栏填入航空公司据以计算运费的计费重量,该重量可以与货物毛重相同也可以不同。

30. 运价(Rate/Charge)

填写该货物适用的费率。

31. 运费总额(Total)

填计收运费的总额,即计费重量与适用费率的乘积。

32. 货物的品名、数量(包括尺寸或体积)(Nature and Quantity of Goods incl. Dimensions or Volume)

填合同或信用证中规定的货物的名称、数量,包括填写货物的外包装尺寸或体积,计量单位为厘米或立方米。货物尺寸分别以货物最长、最宽、最高边为基础,按其外包装"长×宽×高×件数"的顺序填写。

33. 计重运费(Weight Charge)

在对应的"预付(Prepaid)"或"到付(Collect)"栏内填写按重量计算的运费额。

34. 声明价值费(Valuation Charge)

在对应的"预付"或"到付"栏内填写声明价值费。

35. 税费(Tax)

在对应的"预付"或"到付"栏内填写按规定收取的税款额。

36. 其他费用(Other Charges)

指除运费和声明价值附加费以外的其他费用。根据 IATA 规则各项费用分别用三个英文字母表示。其中前两个字母是某项费用的代码,如运单费就表示为 AW(Air Waybill Fee)。第三个字母是 C 或 A,分别表示费用应支付给承运人(Carrier)或货运代理人(Agent)。该栏是 37 栏代理人收取的其他费用、38 栏承运人收取的其他费用的金额的来源。

37. 代理人收取的其他费用(Total Other Charges Due Agent)

预付或到付由代理人收取的其他费用。

38. 承运人收取的其他费用(Total Other Charges Due Carrier)

预付或到付由承运人收取的其他费用。

39. 预付费用总额/到付费用总额(Total Prepaid/ Total Collect)

指预付或到付的运费及其他费用总额。即上述栏费用总额。

40. 货币兑换比价(Currency Conversion Rate)

打印目的站国家货币代号、兑换比率。如,USD7.00。

41. 用目的站国家货币支付的到付费(CC Charges in Destination Currency)

将到付总额,按兑换比率换算成目的站国家货币金额。

42.仅供承运人在目的站使用(For Carrier's Use Only at Destination)

43.在目的站的费用(Charges at Destination)

填写在目的地机场收取的各项费用的总额。

44.到付费用总额(Total Collect Charges)

该金额等于"用目的站国家货币支付的到付费"+"目的站费用",即41栏金额+43栏金额。

45.托运人或其代理人签名(Signature of Shipper or His Agent)

托运人或其代理人在本栏内签字、盖章。

46.承运人填写栏

(1)填开日期(Executed on Date)

本栏所表示的日期为签发本运单的日期,也就是本批货物的装运日期。如果信用证规定运单必须注明实际起飞日期,则以该所注的实际起飞日期作为装运日期。本栏的日期不得晚于信用证规定的装运日期。

(2)填开地点(At Place)

填写机场或城市的全称或缩写。

(3)承运人或代理人签字(Signature of Issuing Carrier or as Agent)

承运人或其代理人签字,和提单一样需表明签字人的身份。如果是承运人签字,需加注"AS CARRIER";如果是代理人签字,需加注"AS AGENT"。

项目六　保险单据缮制

实训目标

能够根据有关资料缮制保险单据。

实训任务

§ 实训一

根据下列资料缮制保险单据。

SOME MSG FROM L/C：

L/C NO. DATED：6104-309-2　　　NOV. 27,2009

ORDER ACCOUNT：…… MAHARASHTRA (INDIA)

IN FAVOUR OF：ZHEJIANG CATHAYA INTERNATIONAL CO. ,LTD

105 TIYUCHANG ROAD,HANGZHOU,CHINA

AMOUNT：USD 60000. 00

EVIDENCING SHIPMENT OF：

SILK WOVEN FABRICS NOT DYED AND NOT PRINTED

ART. NO. 10106	7510. 60M	USD2. 40/M
ART. NO. 10109	5056. 00M	USD3. 00/M
ART. NO. 11206	4925. 20M	USD2. 00/M
ART. NO. 11160	5466. 20M	USD2. 65/M

CIF CHENNAI BY SEA

SHIPMENT FROM CHINESE NINGBO PORT TO CHENNAI WITH PARTIAL SHIPMENTS AND TRANSHIPMENT ALLOWED ……

DOCUMENTS：

　……

INSURANCE POLICY OR CERTIFICATE IN DUPLICATE ISSUED IN AN IR-REVOCABLE FORM BLANK ENDORSED COVERING THE GOODS FOR INVOICE AMOUNT PLUS 10 PENCENT AGAINST THE FOLLOWING RISKS：ALL RISKS AND WAR RISKS AS PER OCEAN MARINE CARGO CLAUSES OF THE PICC DAT-ED 01. 01. 1981. AND INSURANCE POLICY OR CERTIFICATE MUST BE VALID FOR 60 DAYS AFTER THE DISCHARGE OF GOODS FROM THE VESSEL AT THE PORT OF DESTINATION CLAIMS,IF ANY,PAYABLE AT CHENNAI

　……

SOME MSG FROM S/O：

THE GOODS ARE PACKED IN 32 CARTONS. AND THE GOODS SHIPPED FROM NINGBO BY YUETKONG-542(S. S)ON　DEC. 30,2009

SHIPPING MARKS：KSSAR/CHENNAI/NOS. 1-UP

INVOICE NO：AG(29)88012

INVOICE DATE：DEC. 21,2009

中保财产保险有限公司

The People's Insurance (Property) Company of China, Ltd

发票号码　　　　　　　　　　　　　　　　　　　　　　　　保险单号次
Invoice No.　　　　　　　　　　　　　　　　　　　　　　　Policy No.

海 洋 货 物 运 输 保 险 单
MARINE CARGO TRANSPORTATION INSURANCE POLICY

被保险人：

Insured：

　　中保财产保险有限公司(以下简称本公司)根据被保险人的要求,及其所缴付约定的保险费,按照本保险单承担险别和背面所载条款与下列特别条款承保下列货物运输保险,特签发本保险单。

　　This policy of Insurance witnesses that the People's Insurance (Property) Company of China, Ltd. (hereinafter called "The Company"), at the request of the Insured and in consideration of the agreed premium paid by the Insured, undertakes to insure the undermentioned goods in transportation subject to conditions of the Policy as per the Clauses printed overleaf and other special clauses attached hereon.

保险货物项目 Descriptions of Goods	包装 Packing	单位 Unit	数量 Quantity	保险金额 Amount Insured

承保险别　　　　　　　　　　　　货物标记
Conditions　　　　　　　　　　　Marks of Goods

总保险金额：

Total Amount Insured：＿＿＿＿＿＿＿＿＿＿＿＿＿＿＿＿＿＿＿＿＿＿＿＿＿＿＿＿＿＿＿＿＿＿＿

保费　　　　　　　　载运输工具　　　　　　　　　　开航日期
Premium＿＿＿＿＿＿　Per Conveyance S. S＿＿＿＿＿＿＿　Slg. on or abt＿＿＿＿＿＿＿＿

起运港　　　　　　　目的港
Form ＿＿＿＿＿＿＿＿　To ＿＿＿＿＿＿＿＿＿＿＿＿＿＿＿＿＿＿＿＿＿＿＿＿＿＿＿＿＿＿

所保货物,如发生本保险单项下可能引起索赔的损失或损坏,应立即通知本公司下述代理人查勘。如有索赔,应向本公司提交保险单正本(本保险单共有　　　份正本)及有关文件。如一份正本已用于索赔,其余正本则自动失效。

In the event of loss or damage which may result in a claim under this Policy, immediate notice must be given to the Company's Agent as mentioned hereunder. Claims, if any, one of the Original Policy which has been issued in original (s) together with the relevant documents shall be surrendered to the Company. If one of the Original Policy has been accomplished, the others to be void.

赔款偿付地点

Claim payable at ＿＿＿＿＿＿＿＿＿＿

日期　　　　　　　　　在
Date ＿＿＿＿＿＿＿＿＿＿　at ＿＿＿＿＿＿＿＿＿＿＿＿

地址：

Address：＿＿＿＿＿＿＿＿＿＿＿＿＿＿＿＿＿＿＿＿＿＿＿＿＿

§ 实训二

根据下列资料缮制保险单据。

SOME MSG FROM L/C:

BENEFICIARY: ZHEJIANG RONGCHANG TRADING CO. ,LTD

　　　　　　NO. 222 HONGSHENG RODA,HANGZHOU,CHINA

APPLICANT: LUCKY VICTORY INTERNATIONAL

　　　　　　STUTTGART STIR. 5,

　　　　　　D-84618, SCHORNDORF, GERMANY

L/C NO. :LC06-4-1520

DATE OF ISSUE: 2009/11/18

LOADING IN CHARGE: NINGBO

FOR TRANSPORTATION TO: HAMBURG

LATEST DATE OF SHIPMENT 2010/01/03

DOCUMENTS REQUIRED:

　　+INSURANCE POLICY ISSUED TO THE APPLICANT, COVERING RISKS AS PER INSTITUTE CARGO CLAUSE (A) INCLUDING WAREHOUSE TO WAREHOUSE CLAUSE UP TO FINAL DESTINATION AT SCHORN-DORF, FOR AT LEAST 110 PCT OF THE CIF VALUE, MARKED PREMI-UM PAID, SHOWING CLAIM PAYABLE IN GERMANY

　　……

SOME MSG FROM S/C:

DESCRIPTION OF GOODS: MULBERRY RAW SILK

　　　　　　　　40/44　4/5A

SHIPPING MARKS: LUCKY/09HM23600256/HAMBURG/NO. 1-UP

PACKING: IN CARTONS OF 50 KGS EACH

QUANTITY: 3000KGS, 10% MORE OR LESS AT THE SELLER'S OPTION

UNIT PRICE :USD41. 3/KG CIF HAMBURG

SOME MSG FROM INVOICE:

INVOICE NO. :OC01A0120045

INVOICE DATE: NOV. 29,2009

INVOICE DATE: DEC. 25,2009

VESSEL: SENATOR V. 872W

SHIPMENT QUANTITY :3200KGS

中国人民保险公司××分公司

海洋货物运输保险单

发票号次   第一正本   保险单号次

INVOICE NO.   THE FIRST ORIGINAL   POLICY NO.

中 国 人 民 保 险 公 司 （ 以 下 简 称 本 公 司 ）

This Policy of Insurance witnesses that People's Insurance Company of China(hereinafter called "the

根 据

company") at the request of _____

（ 以 下 简 称 被 保 险 人 ） 的 要 求 ， 由 被 保 险 人 向 本 公 司 缴 付 约 定

(hereinafter called the "Insured") and in consideration of the agreed premium being paid to the Company by

的 保 险 费 ， 按 照 本 保 险 单 承 保 险 别 和 背 面 所 载 条 款 与 下 列

the Insured, undertakes to insure the undermentioned goods in transportation subject to the conditions of this

特 殊 条 款 承 保 下 述 货 物 运 输 保 险 ， 特 立 本 保 险 单 。

Policy as per the Clauses printed overleaf and other special clauses attached hereon.

标 记 MARKS. & NOS.	包装及数量 QUANTITY	保险货物项目 DESCRIPTION OF GOODS	保险金额 AMOUNT INSURED

总 保 险 金 额

Total Amount Insured _____

保费   费率   装载运输工具

Premium As Arranged   Rate As Arranged   Per Conveyance S. S. _____

开航日期   自   至

Slg on or abt. _____ From _____ To _____

承保险别：

Conditions

所 保 货 物 ， 如 遇 出 险 ， 本 公 司 凭 第 一 正 本 保 险 单 及 其 有 关 证 件 给

Claims, if any, payable on surrender of the first original of the Policy together with other relevant documents.

付 赔 款 。 所 保 货 物 ， 如 发 生 本 保 险 单 项 下 负 责 赔 偿 的 损 失 或 事

In the event of accident whereby loss or damage may result in a claim under this Policy immediate notice

故 ， 应 立 即 通 知 本 公 司 下 述 代 理 人 查 勘 。

applying for survey must be given to the Company's Agent as mentioned hereunder:

中国人民保险公司××分公司

THE PEOPLE'S INSURANCE CO. OF CHINA

×× BRANCH

赔款偿付地点

CLAIM PAYABLE AT _____

日期

DATE _____

§ 实训三

根据下列资料缮制保险单据。

SOME MSG FROM S/C:

DESCRIPTION OF GOODS:

        CARDBOARD BOX

        YL-256   2000PCS   USD4. 50/PC CIF ICD BANGALORE

        YL-258   2500PCS   USD4. 00/PC CIF ICD BANGALORE

SHIPPING MARKS: CTL/BANGALORE/NOS. 1-UP

PACKING: IN CARTONS OF 50 PCS EACH

INSURANCE: IS TO BE COVERED BY THE SELLERS FOR 120% OF THE INVOICE VALUE COVERING ALL RISKS AND WAR RISK AS PER CIC

SOME MSG FROM L/C:

BENEFICIARY: ZHEJIANG UNIK CO. ,LTD

              NO. 156 YILONG RODA,PINGHU,ZHEJIANG,CHINA

L/C NO. :LC09678

DATE OF ISSUE: 091015

LOADING IN CHARGE: SHANGHAI

FOR TRANSPORTATION TO: ICD BANGALORE

LATEST DATE OF SHIPMENT: 091130

DOCUMENTS REQUIRED:

      ……

+ INSURANCE POLICY OR CERTIFICATE ENDORSED IN BLANK FOR 110% OF CIF VALUE, COVERING WPA RISK AND WAR RISK AS PER CIC AND INDICATING L/C NO. AND INSURANCE CHARGES

其他资料:

INVOICE NO. :UNIK9810

INVOICE DATE: NOV. 10,2009

B/L DATE: NOV. 29,2009

VESSEL: HYUNDAI V. 526W

INSURANCE CHARGES: USD22. 00

INSURANCE AGENT: GLADSTONE AGENCIES LIMITED

        BANGALORE OFFICE

        CITY POINT(TF6 3RD FLOOR)

        INFANTRY ROAD BANGALORE 560001 INDIA

        TEL: 0091-80-2899272 FAX: 0091-80-2899273

        MOBILE: 0091-9844021011

中国人民保险公司××分公司
海洋货物运输保险单

发票号次   第一正本   保险单号次
INVOICE NO.   THE FIRST ORIGINAL   POLICY NO.

中 国 人 民 保 险 公 司 （ 以 下 简 称 本 公 司 ）
This Policy of Insurance witnesses that People's Insurance Company of China(hereinafter called "the
根 据
company") at the request of _____
（ 以 下 简 称 被 保 险 人 ） 的 要 求 ， 由 被 保 险 人 向 本 公 司 缴 付 约 定
(hereinafter called the "Insured") and in consideration of the agreed premium being paid to the Company by
的 保 险 费 ， 按 照 本 保 险 单 承 保 险 别 和 背 面 所 载 条 款 与 下 列
the Insured, undertakes to insure the undermentioned goods in transportation subject to the conditions of this
特 殊 条 款 承 保 下 述 货 物 运 输 保 险 ， 特 立 本 保 险 单 。
Policy as per the Clauses printed overleaf and other special clauses attached hereon。

标 记 MARKS. & NOS.	包装及数量 QUANTITY	保险货物项目 DESCRIPTION OF GOODS	保险金额 AMOUNT INSURED

总 保 险 金 额：
Total Amount Insured _____

保费   费率   装载运输工具
Premium As Arranged   Rate As Arranged   Per Conveyance S. S. _____

开航日期   自   至
Slg on or abt. _____ From _____ To _____

承保险别：
Conditions

所 保 货 物 ， 如 遇 出 险 ， 本 公 司 凭 第 一 正 本 保 险 单 及 其 有 关 证 件 给
Claims, if any, payable on surrender of the first original of the Policy together with other relevant documents。
付 赔 款 。 所 保 货 物 ， 如 发 生 本 保 险 单 项 下 负 责 赔 偿 的 损 失 或 事
In the event of accident whereby loss or damage may result in a claim under this Policy immediate notice
故 ， 应 立 即 通 知 本 公 司 下 述 代 理 人 查 勘 。
applying for survey must be given to the Company's Agent as mentioned hereunder:

中国人民保险公司××分公司
THE PEOPLE'S INSURANCE CO. OF CHINA
×× BRANCH

赔款偿付地点
CLAIM PAYABLE AT _____
日期
DATE _____

§实训四

根据以下资料,审核并修改已填制的保险单,在已填制的 17 个栏目(标号 1—17)中找出若干处填制错误,并说明原因。

(一)来自商业发票、装箱单的资料

EXPORT:SHANGHAI KOCI FRAGRANCE CO.,LTD.

NO. 559 XINLIN ROAD, XINSHEN ECONIMY AREA,

FENGXIAN DISTRICT, SHANGHAI CHINA

IMPORT:PT. MANE INDONESIA

INVOICE NO.:04-000005

L/C NO.:GDF205506

PORT OF LOADING:SHANGHAI

PORT OF DESTINATION:JAKARTA, INDONESIA

SHIPPING MARKS:PJF

MEANS OF TRANSPORT:BY SEA

TTL N. WEIGHT:1700KGS

TTL G. WEIGHT:1800KGS

TERMS OF PRICE:CIF JAKARTA

UNIT PRICE:USD3.7/KGS

TOTAL AMOUNT:USD6290.00

NOS. & KIND OF PACKAGE:10DRUMS

(二)来自信用证、提单的资料

CONDITIONS:INSURANCE POLICY COVERING MARINE TRANSPORTATION ALL RISKS AS PER ICC(A), INCLUDING WAREHOUSE TO WAREHOUSE RISKS INDICATING INSURANCE RATE AND PREMIUM

船名、航次:YM NAGOYA V. 11S

提单号:EURFL04N05345JAK

起运港:SHANGHAI

卸货港:JAKARTA, INDONESIA

件数及包装:10 DRUMS, TEN(10)DRUMS ONLY

毛重:1800KGS

货物描述:ALLYL HEXANOATE

开船日:20 NOV 2009

(三)合同、其他资料

保险费费率:2.5%

赔款偿付地点:JAKARTA, INDONESIA

保险经纪人:中国人民财产保险股份有限公司,徐浏

(四)已缮制的保险单

PICC 中国人民财产保险股份有限公司

PICC Property and Casualty Company Limited

货物运输保险单

CARGO TRANSPORTATION INSURANCE POLICY

发票号码（1）
INVOICE NO. 04-000005

保险单号次
POLICY NO. PYIE20043201930000142

被保险人：（2） SHANGHAI KOCI FRAGRANCE CO.，LTD.

中国人民财产保险股份有限公司（以下简称本公司）根据被保险人的要求，由被保险人向本公司缴付约定的保险费，按照本保险单承担险别和背面所载条款与下列特别条款承保下列货物运输保险，特立本保险单。

    This Policy of Insurance witnesses that the PICC Property and Casualty Company Ltd.（hereinafter called "The Company"）at the request of the Insured and in consideration of the agreed premium paid to the Company by the Insured，undertakes to insure the undermentioned goods in transportation subject to conditions of the Policy as per the Clauses printed overleaf and other special clauses attached hereon.

标 记（3） MARKS. & NOS.	包装及数量（4） QUANTITY	保险货物项目（5） DESCRIPTION OF GOODS	保险金额（6） AMOUNT INSURED
PJF	10 DRUMS	ALLYL HEXANOATE	USD6919.00

总保险金额：（7）
Total Amount Insured US DOLLARS SIX THOUSAND NINE HUNDRED AND NINETEEN ONLY

保费（8）
Premium USD172.98

费率（9）
Rate 2.5%

装载运输工具（10）
Per Conveyance S. S. YM NAGOYA V.11S

开航日期（13）
Slg on or abt. 20NOV. 2009

自（11）
From SHANGHAI

至（12）
To JAKARTA

承保险别：（14）
Conditions：ALL RISKS

所保货物，如发生本保险单项下可能引起索赔的损失或损坏，应立即通知本公司下述代理人查勘。如有索赔，应向本公司提交保险单正本（本保险单共有 2 份正本）及有关文件。如一份正本已用于索赔，其余正本则自动失效。

In the event of loss or damage which may result in a claim under this Policy，immediate notice must be given to the Company's Agent as mentioned here under. Claims, if any, one of the Original Policy which has been issued in **TWO** original（s）together with the relevant documents shall be surrendered to the Company. If one of the Original Policy has been accomplished，the others to be void.

PICC 中国人民财产保险股份有限公司
浙江分公司国际保险营业部
PICC Property and Casualty Company Ltd.
Zhejiang Branch Int'l Ins. Division

徐 浏
Authorized Signature（17）

赔款偿付地点：（15）
CLAIM PAYABLE AT HONGKONG

日期、地点：（16）
DATE NOV. 21,2009 SHANGHAI

实训指导

保险单缮制说明

各家保险公司根据自身印制的保险单固定格式和投保要求，制作保险单。保险单各栏目的内容缮制如下。

1. 保险公司名称(Name of Insurance Policy)

投保人应根据信用证和合同要求去相应的保险公司办理保险单据。如来证规定"Insurance Policy in Duplicant by PICC"，则保险单须由中国人民保险公司出具。

2. 保险单据名称(Name)

此栏按照信用证和合同要求填制。如来证规定"Insurance Policy in Duplicant"，即要求出具保险单而非保险凭证(Insurance Certificate)。

3. 发票号码(Invoice NO.)

填写投保货物发票的号码。

4. 保险单号码(Policy NO.)

填写保险公司的保险单号码。

5. 被保险人(Insured)

又称保险单的抬头人。一般填出口商的名称。若信用证要求保险单做成指示抬头，即"to order"，则在被保险人栏内填"to order"；若信用证要求以特定方(如开证行或开证申请人)为被保险人，则该栏内填特定方的名称。

6. 唛头(Marks & Nos.)

保险单上唛头应与发票、提单一致，也可简单填成"as per Invoice No. ×××"。

7. 包装及数量(Quantity)

包装货物填写最大包装件数；裸装货物要注明本身件数；煤炭、石油等散装货则注明"in bulk"，然后填写净重；有包装但以重量计价的，应把包装重量(数量)与计价重量(数量)都注上。

8. 货物名称(Description of Goods)

允许用统称，但不同类别的多种货物应注明不同类别的各自总称。这里与提单此栏目的填写一致。

9. 保险金额(Amount Insured)

保险金额的加成百分比应严格按信用证或合同规定掌握。如未规定，应按 CIF 或 CIP 发票价格的 110% 投保。保险金额不要小数，出现小数时采用"进一取整"的填法。所用币种应与发票一致。

10. 保险费及保险费率(Premium and Rate)

一般已由保险公司在保险单印刷时印上"As arranged"字样，出口公司在填写保险单时无需填写。若信用证要求具体列明此两栏，加盖校对章后可打上所需要的内容。如信用证要求"……Marked Premium Paid"，制单时应把原有的"as Arranged"删掉，加盖校对章后打上"Paid"字样。

11. 装载运输工具(Per Conveyance S. S)

该栏应填写装载的运输工具。海运方式下填写船名,最好再加航次。如需转船,应分别填写一程船名及二程船名,中间用"/"隔开;如果第二程船名未知,则只需打上"转船"字样。铁路运输则填 "by Railway(Train)",最好再加车号,即"by Railway(Train),Wagon No.×××";航空运输则填"by Air",邮包运输则填" by Parcel Post"。

12. 开航日期(Slg on or abt.)

应按 B/L 中的签发日期填,还可以简单地填作"AS PER B/L"。

13. 起讫地点(From. . . to. . .)

起点填装运港名称,讫点填目的港名称,中途需转船的应注明中转港。如,From Ningbo to Rotterdam W/T Hong Kong。若提单上目的港为美国长滩,来证规定投保至芝加哥,则起讫地点应填"From Ningbo to Long Beach and Thence to Chicago"。

14. 承保险别(Conditions)

应严格按照信用证规定的险别投保。如信用证没有具体规定险别,则可投保最低责任险别,即平安险"FPA"。

15. 赔款偿付地点(Claim Payable at)

严格按照信用证规定打制。若来证未规定,则应打目的港;如信用证规定不止一个目的港或赔付地,则应全部照打。有些信用证规定在偿付地点后注明偿付货币名称,应照办。

16. 日期(Date)

指填写保险单的日期。保险手续要求货物离开出口仓库前办理。保险单的日期不应迟于提单签发日、货物发运日或接受监管日。

17. 签字(Signature)

一般应包括保险公司名称和法人代表的签字或印章。保险单经保险公司签章后方有效。

18. 其他

根据信用证的要求在保险单上加注其他说明。如"所有单据注明信用证号码、开证日期和开证行名称"、"保险单上显示保险公司在目的地的保险代理人名称、地址、联系方法"等。

19. 份数

正本份数(NUMBER OF ORIGINAL POLICY)。根据《UCP600》规定,正本保险单必须有"正本"(ORIGINAL)字样,并显示该套保险单据正本的份数。如信用证没有特别说明保险单份数时,保险公司一般出具一套三份正本的保险单,每份正本上分别印有"第一正本"(THE FIRST ORIGINAL)、"第二正本"(THE SECOND ORIGINAL)及"第三正本"(THE THIRD ORIGINAL)以示区别。如信用证没有特别规定交几份正本的情况下,必须向银行提交全套正本。如果保险单据未注明正本份数,而信用证也没有特别规定,出口公司一般提交一套完整的保险单(一份正本 ORIGINAL,一份复本 DUPLICATE)。银行可以接受只提交一份正本的保险单据,但该保险单据必须注明是唯一正本。正本保险单可经背书转让。

项目七 原产地证书缮制

实训目标

能够根据有关资料缮制原产地证书。

实训任务

§ 实训一

根据下列资料缮制产地证。

信用证资料：

DOCUMENTS REQUIRED：

+CERTIFICATE OF ORIGIN REQUIRED FROM CHAMBER OF COMMERCE STATING MERCHANDISE TO BE OF CHINA ORIGIN.

……

其他内容：参考项目三（商业发票缮制）实训二资料

其他资料：出口公司于 2009 年 7 月 21 日向有关当局申请产地证，并当日获批。

1. Exporter (full name and address)		CERTIFICATE NO. BP18751		
		CERTIFICATE OF ORIGIN OF THE PEOPLE'S REPUBLIC OF CHINA		
2. Consignee (full name and address)				
3. Means of transport and route		5. For certifying authority use only		
4. Country/Region of Destination				
6. Marks and Numbers of Packages	7. Description of Goods; Number and Kind of Package	8. H. S. Code	9. Quantity or Weight	10. Number and Date of Invoices

11. Declaration by the exporter	12. Certification
The undersigned hereby declares that the above details and statements are correct; that all the goods were produced in China and that they comply with the Rules of Origin of the People's Republic of China.	It is hereby certified that the declaration by the exporter is correct.
Place and date, signature and stamp of authorized signatory	Place and date, signature and stamp of certifying authority

§ 实训二

根据下列资料缮制产地证。

信用证资料：

DOCUMENTS REQUIRED：

+CERFIFICATE OF ORIGIN FORM A ISSUED AND/OR VISAED BY COMPETENT AUTHORITIES：4 COPIES

其他内容：参考项目三（商业发票缮制）实训三资料

其他资料：货物完全中国原产。出口公司于 2009 年 12 月 22 日向有关当局申请产地证，当日获批。

1. Goods consigned from (Exporter's business name, address, country)	Reference No. GENERALIZED SYSTEM OF PREFERENCES **CERTIFICATE OF ORIGIN** （Combined declaration and certificate） **FORM　A** Issued in THE PEOPLE'S REPUBLIC OF CHINA （Country）
2. Goods consigned to (Consignee's name, address, country)	See Notes overleaf
3. Means of transport and route (as far as known)	4. For official use

5. Item Number	6. Marks and Nos. of Packages	7. Number and Kind of Package Description of Goods	8. Origin Criterion (See Notes Overleaf)	9. Gross Weight or Other Quantity	10. Number and Date of Invoices

11. Certification It is hereby certified, on the basis of control carried out, that the declaration by the exporter is correct.	12. Declaration by the exporter 　　The undersigned hereby declares that the above details and statements are correct; that all the goods were produced in CHINA 　　　　　　　　　（country） and that they comply with the origin requirements specified of those goods in the Generalized System of Preferences for goods exported to _____
.... Place and date, signature and stamp of certifying authority	.... Place and date, signature of authorized signatory

§ 实训三

根据下列资料缮制产地证。

信用证资料：

FORM OF DC	: IRREVOCABLE TRANSFERABLE
DC NO.	: DC HMN927739
DATE OF ISSUE	: 24SEP09
APPLICABLE RULES	: UCP LATEST VERSION
EXPIRY DATE AND PLACE	: 30DEC09 IN COUNTRY OF BENEFICIARIES
APPLICANT	: POINT ZERO GIRLS CLUB INC.
	1650 CHABANEL WEST
	MONTREAL QUEBEC
	CANADA H4N 3M8
BENEFICIARY	: ZHEJIANG CATHAYA INTERNATIONAL
	CO. ,LTD. 105 TIYU CHANG ROAD,
	HANGZHOU,ZHEJIANG,CHINA 310004
DC AMT	: USD 147600.00
PCT CR AMT TOLERANCE	: 05/05
PARTIAL SHIPMENTS	: SEE BELOW
TRANSHIPMENT	: ALLOWED
TAKE CHARGE/RECEIPT/DISP FM	: SHANGHAI CHINA
FINAL DEST/DELIVERY/TRNSP TO	: MONTREAL, QUEBEC, CANADA
LATEST DATE OF SHIPMENT	: 25DEC09

GOODS：LADY'S SWEATER

　　ALO099 50％RAYON,32％COTTON,2％SPANDEX

　　24000.00PCS AT USD6.15/PC FOB SHANGHAI,CHINA

　　DOCUMENTS REQUIRED：

　　＋CERTIFICATE OF ORIGIN SHOWING COUNTRY OF ORIGIN

　　……

ADDITIONAL CONDITIONS：

　　＋ALL DOCUMENTS SHOULD INDICATE L/C NO. L/C DATE AND NAME

　　OF ISSUING BANK.

其他资料：

本批出货数量:14400PCS　300CARTONS

INVOICE NO. ：BP919A530016

INVOICE DATE：DEC.11,2009

B/L DATE：DEC.19,2009

VESSEL/VOYAGE：HANJIN OTTAWA V.073E

H.S. CODE：6104

SHIPPING MARKS：
        POINT ZERO
        STYLE NO：ALO099
        QTY：
        N. W. ：
        G. W. ：
        MEAS. ：
        CARTON NO. ：

1. Exporter (full name and address)			**CERTIFICATE NO. BP**18751	
			CERTIFICATE OF ORIGIN	
2. Consignee (full name and address)			OF	
			THE PEOPLE'S REPUBLIC OF CHINA	
3. Means of transport and route			5. For certifying authority use only	
4. Country/Region of Destination				
6. Marks and Numbers of Packages	7. Description of Goods; Number and Kind of Package	8. H. S. Code	9. Quantity or Weight	10. Number and Date of Invoices
11. Declaration by the exporter The undersigned hereby declares that the above details and statements are correct; that all the goods were produced in China and that they comply with the Rules of Origin of the People's Republic of China.			12. Certification It is hereby certified that the declaration by the exporter is correct.	
----------------------------- Place and date, signature and stamp of authorized signatory			----------------------------- Place and date, signature and stamp of certifying authority	

§实训四

根据以下资料,审核并修改已填制的普惠制产地证明书 FORM A,在已填制的 16 个栏目(标号 1—16)中找出若干处填制错误,并说明原因。

(一)背景

上海某进出口公司 SHANGHAI ABC I/E CO. 接受服装厂 SHANGHAI SHENGDA GARMENT CO.，LTD 委托,代理出口货物 50000 件全棉男衬衫至日本东京。该产品的面料由日本进口商提供,款式也由日本设计师提供,上海工厂加工后返销日本。该外贸公司于 2010 年 3 月 5 日,持缮制完毕的《普惠制产地证明书申请书》一份,《普惠制产地证明书 FORM A》一份和商业发票一份,向出入境检验检疫局申请办理普惠制产地证。

(二)来自商业发票、装箱单的资料

INVOICE NO.：　01-00534

INVOICE DATE：5 MAR 2010

TO：　　DI　BAUE　JAPAN　INC.

　　　　7-1 IHONBASHI AKOZAKI-CHO

　　　　CHUO KU，TOKYO，JAPAN

ISSUED BY：SHANGHAI ABC I/E COMPANY，NO. 12345 WANPING ROAD，

　　　　　　　SHANGHAI, CHINA

SHIPPING MARKS：D. B. /TOKYO/NO. 1-1500

DESCRIPTIONS：MEN'S 100% COTTON WOVEN SHIRTS

QUANTITY：50000PCS /1500 CTNS/1500KGS/10CBM

(三)补充资料

装运港：SHANGHAI

目的港：TOKYO

船名航次：QIANZHENG HAO V. 00203

开船日：2010 年 3 月 9 日

签证机构:中华人民共和国上海出入境检验检疫局

贸易方式:来料加工

签证号码:SHZ/00033/0036

(四)已缮制的普惠制产地证

1. Goods consigned from (Exporter's business name, address, country) (1) SHANGHAI SHENGDA GARMENT CO. , LTD			Reference No. (4) SHZ/00033/0036 GENERALIZED SYSTEM OF PREFERENCES **CERTIFICATE OF ORIGIN** (Combined declaration and certificate) **FORM A**		
2. Goods consigned to (Consignee's name, address, country) (2) DI BAUE JAPAN INC. 7-1 IHONBASHI AKOZAKI-CHO CHUO KU，TOKYO, JAPAN			Issued in (5) THE PEOPLE'S REPUBLIC OF CHINA (Country)		
3. Means of transport and route (as far as known) (3) SHIPMENT BY VESSEL FROM SHANGHAI, CHINA TO TOKYO, JAPAN			4. For official use(6) See Notes overleaf		
5. Item Number (7)	6. Marks and Nos. of Packages(8) D. B. TOKYO NO. 1-1500	7. Number and Kind of Package Description of Goods(9) ONE THOUSAND FIVE HUNDRED CARTONS OF MEN'S 100% COTTON WOVEN SHIRTS	8. Origin Criterion (See Notes Overleaf) (10) P	9. Gross Weight or Other Quantity(11) 50000PCS	10. Number and Date of Invoices (12) 01-00543 5 MAR 2010
11. Certification(13) It is hereby certified, on the basis of control carried out, that the declaration by the exporter is correct. CIQ SHANGHAI 丁三 MAR. 09, 2010 ------------------------------------ Place and date, signature and stamp of certifying authority			12. Declaration by the exporter 　　The undersigned hereby declares that the above details and statements are correct; that all the goods were produced in CHINA(14) (country) and that they comply with the origin requirements specified of those goods in the Generalized System of Preferences for goods exported to ____(15) SHANGHAI ABC I/E COMPANY (16) SHANGHAI MAR. 09, 2010 韦明 ------------------------------------ Place and date, signature of authorized signatory		

实训指导

一、一般原产地证明书缮制说明

一般原产地证明书各栏目的内容缮制如下。

1. 出口方（Exporter）

填写出口方的名称、详细地址及国家（地区），一般填写有效外贸合同的卖方。

2. 收货方（Consignee）

应填写最终收货方的名称、详细地址及国家（地区），通常是外贸合同中的买方或信用证上规定的提单通知人。但由于贸易的需要，信用证会规定所有单证收货人一栏留空。在这种情况下，此栏应加注"TO WHOM IT MAY CONCERN"或"TO ORDER"，但不得留空。若需填写转口商名称时，可在收货人后面加填英文 VIA，然后填写转口商名称、地址、国家。

3. 运输方式和路线（Means of transport and route）

一般应填装货、到货地点（始运港、目的港）及运输方式（如海运、陆运、空运）。转运商品应加上转运港。该栏一般还要填明预计离开中国的日期。如，"ON JUL. 1, 2009 FROM SHANGHAI TO ROTTERDAM VIA HONGKONG BY VESSEL(BY SEA)"。

4. 目的国或地区（Country/region of destination）

指货物最终运抵目的地国家（地区），不能填写中间商国家（地区）名称。

5. 签证机构用栏（For certifying authority use only）

此栏为签证机构在签发证书后补发证书或加注其他声明时使用。证书申领单位应将此栏留空。

6. 运输标志（Marks and numbers）

应按照出口发票上所列唛头填写完整图案、文字标记及包装号码，不可简单地填写"按照发票（AS PER INVOICE NO. ×××）"，或者"按照提单（AS PER B/L NO. ×××）"。货物无唛头，应填写"N/M"。

7. 商品名称、包装数量及种类（Number and kind of packages; description of goods）

商品名称要填写具体名称。包装数量及种类要按具体单位填写，包装数量应在阿拉伯数字后加注英文表述。如：100 箱彩电，填写为"100 CARTONS(ONE HUNDRED CARTONS ONLY)OF COLOUR TV SET"。如货物系散装，在商品名称后加注"散装"（IN BULK），例如：1000 公吨生铁，填写为"1000M/T(ONE THOUSAND M/T ONLY)PIG IRON IN BULK"。有时信用证要求在所有单证上加注合同号、信用证号码等，可加在此栏。本栏的末行要打上表示结束的符号（＊＊＊＊＊＊），以防加添内容。

8. 商品 H.S 号税目号（H.S. Code）

此栏要求填写 8 位或 10 位 HS 编码。若同一证书包含几种商品，则应将相应的税目号全部填写。填报 10 位商品编码时，最后两位为补充编码。

9. 量值（数量或重量）（Quantity）

此栏应以商品的正常计量单位填写，如"只"、"件"、"双"、"台"、"打"等。以重量计算的则填毛重和/或净重。

10. 发票号码及日期(Number and date of invoices)

分两行写,第一行为发票号码,第二行为发票日期,月份一律用英文(可用缩写)表示。

11. 出口商的声明、签字、盖章(Declaration by the exporter)

出口商声明已印好,由出口公司填写申报地点和日期,并由公司盖章和专人签字。声明内容为:下列签署人在此声明,上述货物详细情况和声明是正确的,所有货物均在中国生产,完全符合中华人民共和国原产地规则。

申报日期不得早于发票日期(第十栏),同时不能迟于装运日期。手签人员应是本申请单位的法人代表或由法人代表指定的其他人员,并应保持相对稳定。手签人员的字迹必须清楚,印章使用中英文对照章。

12. 签证机构证明,签字盖章(Certification)

签证机构证明文句也是事先印好的。内容为:兹证明出口商声明是正确的。

所申请的证书,经签证机构审核人员审核无误后,由授权的签证人在此栏手签姓名并盖签证机构章,注明签署的时间和地点。盖章和签名不能重合。签发日期不得早于发票日期(第十栏)和申请日期(第十一栏)。

13. 其他

根据信用证要求加具的其他说明,如合同号、信用证号码等,可加在第七栏。

二、普惠制产地证明书缮制说明

普惠制产地证明书(格式 A)栏目的内容缮制如下。

1. 出口商名称、地址、国家(Goods consigned from)

填出口商名称、详细地址,包括街道名、门牌号码等。

2. 收货人的名称、地址、国家(Goods consigned to)

填给惠国最终收货人名称、地址、国家。如最终收货人不明确,则填发票抬头人或提单通知人,但不可填中间转口商的名称。

3. 运输方式及路线(就所知而言)(Means of transport and route)

填制方法与注意事项参见一般原产地证明书。

对输往内陆给惠国的商品,如瑞士、奥地利,如系海运,都须经第三国海岸,再转运至该国,填证时应注明:"从×××港口经转×××港口抵达×××给惠国"。如,"ON NOV. 6, 2009 BY VESSEL FROM GUANGZHOU TO HAMBURG W/T HONGKONG IN TRANSIT TO SWITZERLAND"。

4. 供官方使用(For official use)

此栏由签证当局填写,申请签证的单位应将此栏留空。正常情况下此栏空白。

5. 商品顺序号(Item number)

如同批出口货物有不同品种,则按不同品种、发票号等分列"1"、"2"、"3"……,以此类推。单项商品,此栏填"1"。

6. 唛头及包装号(Marks and numbers of packages)

填制方法与注意事项参见一般原产地证明书。

7. 包件数量及种类,商品的名称(Number and kind of packages;description of goods)

填制方法与注意事项参见一般原产地证明书。

8. 原产地标准(Origin criterion)

此栏用字最少,但却是国外海关审核的核心项目。现将填写该栏原产地标准符号的一般规定说明如下:

(1)完全原产品,不含任何进口成分,出口到所有给惠国,填"P"。

(2)含有进口成分的产品,出口到欧盟、挪威、瑞士和日本,填"W",其后加上出口产品的 HS 税目号,如"W"42.02。条件:

①产品列入了上述给惠国的"加工清单"符合其加工条件;

②产品未列入"加工清单",但产品生产过程中使用的进口原材料和零部件要经过充分的加工,产品的 HS 税目号不同于所用的原材料或零部件的 HS 税目号。

(3)含有进口成分的产品,出口到加拿大,填"F"。条件:进口成分的价值未超过产品出厂价的 40%。

(4)含有进口成分的产品,出口到波兰,填"W",其后加上出口产品的 HS 税目号,如"W"42.02。条件:进口成分的价值未超过产品离岸价的 50%。

(5)含有进口成分的产品,出口到俄罗斯、乌克兰、白俄罗斯、哈萨克斯坦、捷克、斯洛伐克六国,填"Y",其后加上进口成分价值占该产品离岸价格的百分比,如"Y"38%。条件:进口成分的价值未超过产品离岸价的 50%。

(6)输往澳大利亚、新西兰的商品,此栏可以留空。

9. 毛重或其他数量(Gross weight or other quantity)

此栏应以商品的正常计量单位填写,如"只"、"件"、"双"、"台"、"打"等。以重量计算的则填毛重,只有净重的填净重亦可,但要标上 N.W.。

10. 发票号码及日期(Number and date of invoices)

填制方法与注意事项参见一般原产地证明书。

11. 签证当局的证明(Certification)

签证机构的证明事先已印好。内容为:"兹证明出口商的声明是准确无误的,本批货物已由承运人运出。"签证机构批注四项内容包含:

(1)签证当局(出入境检验检疫局)公章。签证当局只签发正本,副本不予盖章。

(2)检验检疫局签证人经审核后在此栏(正本)签名。

(3)签证日期。此栏日期不得早于发票日期(第 10 栏)和申报日期 (第 12 栏),而且应早于货物的出运日期(第 3 栏)。

(4)签证地点。填具体的城市名。出证日期和地点由申报单位填写。

12. 出口商的声明(Declaration by the exporter)

在生产国横线上填英文的"中国"(CHINA)。进口国横线上填最终进口国,进口国必须与第三栏目的港的国别一致。凡货物运往欧盟十五国范围内,进口国不明确时,进口国可填 EU。

另外,申请单位应授权专人在此栏手签,标上申报地点、日期,并加盖申请单位中英文印章(正副本均须手签并盖章)。手签人手迹必须在检验检疫局注册备案,并保持相对稳定。

此栏日期不得早于发票日期(第 10 栏)。盖章时应避免覆盖进口国名称和手签人姓名。本证书一律不得涂改,证书不得加盖校对章。

13. 其他

根据信用证要求加具的其他说明,如合同号、信用证号码等,可加在第七栏。

项目八　汇票缮制

实训目标

能够根据有关资料缮制汇票。

实训任务

§ 实训一

根据下列资料缮制汇票。

来自信用证的资料：

ISSUING BANK：BANK OF CHINA，SEOUL BRANCH

ADVISING BANK：BANK OF CHINA，QINGDAO BRANCH

L/C NO.：810080000797 DATED NOV. 07，2009

EXPIRY DATE：JAN. 15，2010　　PLACE CHINA

BENEFICIARY：QINGHE LIGHT IND. PROD. IMP. & EXP. CORP

NO. 55 YINGBIN RD.，

QINGDAO，CHINA

APPLICANT：　SUNKUONG LIMITED

(HSRO) C. P. O. BOX 1780，

SEOUL，KOREA

L/C AMOUNT：USD AMOUNT 67050. 00

PLS. /NEG. TOL. (%)：05/05

AVAILABLE WITH/BY：ADVISING BANK

BY NEGOTIATION

DRAFTS AT：120 DAYS AFTER THE DATE OF SHIPMENT

FOR 100PCT OF THE INVOICE VALUE

DRAWEE：BKCHKRSE

* BANK OF CHINA SEOUL BRANCH

* SEOUL

QUANTITY 5 PCT MORE OR LESS ARE ALLOWED

LATEST DATE OF SHIPMENT：DEC. 31，2009

PRESENTATION PERIOD：DOCUMENTS TO BE PRESENTED WITHIN 15

DAYS AFTER THE DATE OF SHIPMENT, BUT

WITHIN THE VALIDITY OF THE CREDIT

来自发票的资料：

INVOICE NO.：81609D3030

INVOICE DATE：DEC. 19，2009

QUANTITY OF GOODS：9400DOZ

UNIT PRICE：USD7.45/DOZ CIFBUSAN

其他资料：

B/L DATE ：DEC.25，2009

凭

Drawn under ....

信用证或购买证第　　号

L/C or A/P No. ....

日期　　年　　月　　日

Dated ....

按　　息　　付　　款

Payable with interest@ _____ % per annum

号码	汇票金额	中国青岛	年　月　日
No.	Exchange for	Qingdao，China	200

见票　　　　　　　　日　后（本汇票之副本未付）付

At .... sight of this FIRST of Exchange (Second of exchange being unpaid)

Pay to the order of .... 或其指定人

金额

the sum of ....

此致

To ....

....

....

§ 实训二

根据下列资料缮制汇票。

ISSUING BANK：THE BANK OF TOKYO，LTD.，NAGOYA OFFICE　P.O. BOX 240，NAGOYA-NAKA，NAGOYA 460-91 JAPAN

PLACE AND DATE OF L/C：NAGOYA　OCT.6，2009

L/C NO.：123A-456

BENEFICIARY：ZHEJIANG KINGTEX TRADING CO.，LTD. NO.165 ZHONG-HE ZHONG ROAD HANGZHOU CHINA

ADVISING BANK：BANK OF CHINA，ZHEJIANG BRANCH

AMOUNT：USD13700.00

CREDIT AVAILABLE WITH FREELY NEGOTIABLE BY ANY BANK BY NE-GOTIATION AGAINST PRESENTATION OF THE DOCUMENTS DETAILED HEREIN AND OF YOUR DRAFTS AT SIGHT FOR 98% INVOICE COST DRAWN

ON THE BANK OF TOKYO, LTD. , NEW YORK AGENCY, NEW YORK, N. Y.
　　PARTIAL SHIPMENTS：ALLOWED
　　COVERING：T-SHIRTS
　　ITEM. 50402-A　　5,000PCS AT USD1. 60
　　ITEM. 50430-B　　3,000PCS AT USD1. 90
　　TRADE TERMS：FOBC2 KOBE
　　货物实际分三批装,第一批(ITEM. 50402-A　1000 件 ;ITEM. 50430-B 1000 件)于 2009 年 11 月 30 日装运完毕。出口方于 2009 年 12 月 5 日交单议付。发票号码为 ZJ200311。

凭
Drawn under _____

信用证或购买证第　　　号
L/C or A/P No. _____

日期　　年　　月　　日
Dated _____

按　　　息　　付　　款
Payable with interest@ _____ % per annum

号码	汇票金额		中国杭州	年　月　日
No.	Exchange for	**1**	Hangzhou, China	200

见票　　　　　日　后 （本 汇 票 之 副 本 未 付 ） 付
At _____ sight of this FIRST of Exchange (Second of exchange being unpaid)
Pay to the order of _____ 或其指定人

金额
the sum of _____

此致
To _____

§实训三

根据下列资料缮制汇票。

1. THE SELLER：SHANGHAI JINHAI IMP& EXP CORP. LTD.
2. THE BUYER：ANTAK DEVELOPMENT LTD.
3. TERMS OF PAYMENT：20% T/T BEFORE SHIPMENT AND 80% L/C AT SIGHT
4. DESCRIPTION OF GOODS：MEN'S COTTON WOVEN SHIRTS
　　3000DOZ　AT USD25. 00/DOZ CFR SINGAPORE
5. L/C NO. 123456 DATED AUG. 18，2009 ISSUED BY BANK OF CHINA SINGA-

PORE BRANCH

6. EXPIRY DATE AND PLACE：OCT. 15，2009 CHINA

7. ADVISING BANK：BANK OF CHINA，SHANGHAI

8. WE OPEN THIS IRREVOCABLE DOCUMENTARY CREDIT FAVOURING YOURSELVES AVAILABLE AGAINST YOUR DRAFT AT SIGHT BY NEGOTIATION WITH ADVISING BANK ON US

9. B/L DATED：SEP. 28，2009

10. INVOICE NO. SHGM70561

凭
Drawn under _____
信用证或购买证第　　　号
L/C or A/P No. _____
日期　　年　　月　　日
Dated _____
按　　　息　　　付　　　款
Payable with interest@ _____ % per annum

号码		汇票金额		中国上海	年　月　日
No. _____		Exchange for	**1**	Shanghai, China	_____ 200

见票　　　　　　　日　后（本　汇　票　之　副　本　未　付）付
At _____ sight of this FIRST of Exchange（Second of exchange being unpaid）
Pay to the order of _____ 或其指定人
金额
the sum of _____
_____

此致
To _____

§ **实训四**

根据下列资料缮制汇票。

信用证资料：

AVAILABLE WITH/BY：ANY BANK IN CHINA BY NEGOTIATION

DRAFTS AT：120 DAYS SIGHT

DRAWEE：OURSELVES

其他内容：参考项目三（商业发票缮制）实训二资料

凭

Drawn under ....

信用证或购买证第   号

L/C or A/P No. ....

日期   年   月   日

Dated ....

按   息   付   款

Payable with interest@ _____ % per annum

号码 No.	汇票金额 Exchange for	中国杭州 Hangzhou, China	年 月 日 200

见票   日 后（本 汇 票 之 副 本 未 付）付

At .... sight of this FIRST of Exchange (Second of exchange being unpaid)

Pay to the order of .... 或其指定人

金额

the sum of

此致

To ....

§ 实训五

根据以下资料,审核并修改已填制的汇票,在已填制的 11 个栏目(标号 1—11)中找出若干处填制错误,并说明原因。

(一)来自信用证的资料

BENEFICIARY：HAINING ABC LEATHER GOODS CO. ,LTD.

                 HUANGHE ROAD,HAINING, HAINING 314400,CHINA

APPLICANT：GRAPHIC IMAGE

                 305 SPAGNOLI ROAD, MELVILLE, NEW YORK 11747 USA

DRAFTS TO BE DRAWN AT 30 DAYS AFTER SIGHT ON ISSUING BANK FOR 90% OF INVOICE VALUE

YOU ARE AUTHORIZED TO DRAWN UNDER ROYAL BANK OF NEW YORK FOR DOCUMENTARY IRREVOCABLE CREDIT NO. 742863 DATED JAN. 15TH,2010

EXPRITY DATE 20100205 FOR NEGOTIATION

ISSUING BANK：CITIBANK OF NEW YORK，NEW YORK BRANCH

(二)来自提单、商业发票的资料

发票号：IN34567

发票金额：USD108,0000 FOB SHANGHAI

起运地：SHANGHAI，CHINA
目的地：NEW YORK，USA
装船日期：JAN.26TH，2010
开船日期：JAN.26TH，2010
发票签发人：HAINING ABC LEATHER GOODS CO.，LTD
         姚小兵

（三）已缮制的汇票

凭
Drawn under   ROYAL BANK OF NEW YORK（1）

信用证或购买证第   号
L/C or A/P No.   742863   （2）

日期   年   月   日
Dated   JAN.15，2010 （3）

按   息   付   款
Payable with interest@ _____ % per annum

号码   汇票金额   中国海宁   年   月   日
No. IN34567（4） Exchange for（5）USD108000.00 Haining，China JAN 25 （6） 2010
见票   日   后   （本 汇 票 之 副 本 未 付 ）付
At   ×××（7）   sight of this FIRST of Exchange（Second of exchange being unpaid）
Pay to the order of   BANK OF CHINA，ZHEJIANG BRANCH（8）   或其指定人

金额
the sum of   UNITED STATES DOLLARS ONE HUNDRED AND EIGHT THOUSAND
ONLY（9）

此致
To（10）ROYAL BANK OF NEW YORK

                    （11）HAINING ABC LEATHER GOODS CO.，LTD
                        姚小兵

✿ **实训指导**

商业汇票缮制说明

商业汇票各栏目的内容缮制如下。

1. 出票条款

又称出票依据。信用证业务中,如信用证有具体规定的,则必须按信用证规定填写;如信用证没有规定的,则填开证行名称与地址、信用证号码、开证日期。

在托收业务中,一般应加具货物的名称、数量、启运港、目的港及合同号码等,并注明"for Collection",如"DRAWN UNDER CONTRACT NO. 123 AGAINST SHIPMENT OF 200M/T PEANUT FROM XINGGANG TO SYDNEY"。

2. 年息

这一栏由结汇银行填写,用以清算企业与银行间利息费用。出口公司不必填写此栏目。

3. 号码

即汇票号码,一般都以相应的发票号码兼作汇票号码。

4. 汇票金额

汇票上应填上小写金额和大写金额。汇票小写金额填在"Exchange for"后,金额数保留两位小数。汇票大写金额填在"The Sum of"后,要求顶格写,以防有人故意在汇票金额上做手脚。

在填制汇票金额时,应注意以下几点:

(1)除非信用证另有规定,汇票金额应与发票金额一致。

(2)如信用证规定汇票金额为发票金额的百分之几,例如97%,那么发票金额应为100%,汇票金额为97%,其差额3%一般为应付的佣金。这种做法通常用于中间商代开信用证的场合。

(3)如信用证规定部分信用证付款,部分托收,则分做两套汇票:信用证项下支款的按信用证允许的金额填制,以银行为付款人;其余部分为托收项下汇票的金额,以客户为付款人;两者之和等于发票金额。

(4)如信用证要求两张汇票分别支付一笔交易额,则在两张汇票上打上信用证所要求的金额。

(5)如信用证规定以《贷记通知单》(Credit Note)扣应付佣金的,那么发票金额开100%,而汇票金额应按发票金额减去贷记通知单上的金额后的余额开立。

(6)汇票上的金额大小写必须一致。

5. 出票日期和出票地点

出票地点一般是出口商所在地,一般事先已印好,无需现填。

出票地点后的横线填出票日期。信用证方式下,一般以议付日期作为出票日期;托收方式下,该日期按托收行寄单日期填写。该日期一般由银行代填,需用英文,不能全部用阿拉伯数字。

6. 汇票付款期限

汇票付款期限分即期和远期两种。按不同的付款期限缮制:

(1)即期付款,只需在横线上用"＊＊＊"或"---"或"×××"表示,也可直接打上"AT SIGHT",但不能留空。

(2)远期付款,按信用证的规定填入相应的付款期限。

托收方式下的汇票付款期限,除表明即期或远期的期限外,还要在期限前注明具体的托收种类,如"D/P AT SIGHT"或"D/P AT ××× DAYS AFTER SIGHT"或"D/A AT ××× DAYS AFTER SIGHT"。

7. 受款人

又称收款人,也称汇票抬头人。具体写法有三种:

(1)限制性抬头

例如,"仅付给甲公司（Pay A Co. Only)"或"付给甲公司,不准转让(Pay A Co., Not Transferable)"。这种汇票不能经背书进行转让。

(2)指示式抬头

例如,"付给甲公司或其指定人(Pay A Co. or Order;Pay to the Order of A Co.)"。这种载有指示性抬头的汇票可以经过背书转让。

(3)来人抬头

即在汇票上不指定收款人名称,而只写明"付给持票人(Pay holder)"或"付给来人(Pay bearer)"字样。这种汇票不经过背书就可转让。

我国《票据法》这种汇票不经过背书就可转让。规定不记载收款人名称的汇票是无效的。目前出口业务中使用最广泛的是指示式抬头,汇票的格式上也基本印好"Pay to the order of ×××",×××是汇票的记名收款人,通过他的背书,汇票可以转让。

在信用证方式下,汇票中受款人这一栏目中填写的应是银行名称和地址,一般都是议付行的名称和地址。究竟要哪家银行作为受款人,这要看信用证中是否有具体的规定。

在托收方式下,一般以托收行(出口地银行)作为收款人。

8. 付款人

又称受票人。在信用证方式下,汇票的付款人应按照信用证的规定填写;若信用证中未规定付款人,则填写开证行。托收方式下,一般以进口商作为汇票的付款人。

9. 出票人

一般填出口企业,包括企业全称和负责人的签字或盖章。在可转让信用证情况下,也有可能为信用证的第二受益人。

10. 汇票份数

汇票在没有特殊规定时,都打两张,一式两份。汇票一般都在醒目的位置上印着"1"、"2"字样,表示第一联和第二联。汇票的第一联和第二联在法律效力上无区别。第一联生效则第二联自动作废,第二联生效则第一联自动作废,即付一不付二,付二不付一。

项目九　其他常用结汇单据缮制

实训目标

能够根据有关资料缮制检验证书、装船通知、受益人证明、船公司证明等单据。

实训任务

§ 实训一

根据下列资料缮制装船通知、受益人证明。

信用证资料：

DOCUMENTS REQUIRED：

＋BENEFICIARY'S CERTIFICATE ATTESTINGTHAT：

1/3 ORIGINAL BILL OF LADING，ORIGINAL CERTIFICATE OF ORIGIN，ORIGINAL CERTIFICATE OF ORIGIN FORM A AND ONE COPY OF ALL OTHER DOCUMENTS WERE SENT DIRECTLY TO：CALZDDONIA S. P. A. ，VIA SPINETTI 1，37050 VALLESE DI OPPEANO C/A SIG. RA FRANCESCA ROTONDI C/O UFFICIO IMPORT-EXPORT.

＋COPY OF FAX SENT BY BENEFICIARY TO APPLICANT WITHIN SHIPMENT DATE SHOWING ALL DETAILS OF DELIVERY FOR INSURANCE PURPOSES. (FAX REPORT MUST BE INCLUDED)

……

其他内容：参考项目三(商业发票缮制)实训三资料

1. 受益人证明

浙江楚帛贸易有限公司

ZHEJIANG CHUBO TRADING CO. , LTD.

NO. 35 HUSHU ROAD, HANGZHOU, CHINA

BENEFICIARY'S CERTIFICATE

TO：   DATE：

RE：L/C NO.   INVOICE NO.

WE HEREBY CERTIFY THAT …

2. 装船通知

浙江楚帛贸易有限公司
ZHEJIANG CHUBO TRADING CO., LTD.
NO. 35 HUSHU ROAD, HANGZHOU, CHINA
SHIPPING ADVICE

TO: DATE:

RE: L/C NO.   INVOICE NO.
WE HEREBY INFORMED YOU THAT THE GOODS UNDER THE ABOVE MENTIONED CREDIT HAVE BEEN SHIPPED. THE DETAILS OF SHIPMENT ARE STATED BELOW.

COMMODITY:

QUANTITY:

INVOICE VALUE:

OCEAN VESSEL/ SHIPPED PER S. S. :

ETD DATE:

ETA DATE:

PORT OF LOADING:

PORT OF DESTINATION:

MARKS:

Signature

§ 实训二

根据下列资料缮制预装船检验证书、装船通知、受益人证明、船公司证明。

信用证资料：

DOCUMENTS REQUIRED

+SHIPMENT UNDER THIS CREDIT MUST BE ADVISED BY BENEFICIARY DIRECT TO M/S PRAGATI INSURANCE LTD, BANGABANDHU AVENUE BRANCH 13, B.B. AVENUE, DHAKA-1000, BANGLADESH QUOTING THEIR COVER NOTE NO. PIL/BBA/MC-0164/07/2009 DTD 16JUL09 GIVING FULL DETAILS OF SHIPMENT. A COPY OF THIS ADVICE MUST ACCOMPANY EACH SET OF SHIPPING DOCS.

......

ADDITIONAL CONDITIONS：

01-SHIPMENT /TRANSHIPMENT ON FLAG VESSEL OF IRAQ/LIBYA/ISRA-EL/CUBA PROHIBITED.

02-ONE SET OF NON-NEGOTIABLE COPY OF DOCS TO BE SENT THE APPLICANT WITHIN 7 DAYS AFTER SHIPMENT BY COURIER, COURIER RECEIPT MUST ACCOMPANY WITH SHIPPING DOCS.

03-PRE-SHIPMENT INSPECTION CERTIFICATE ISSUED BY SGS/LLOYDS/OR ANY INTERNATIONAL REPUTED ORGANISATION/BENE-FICIARY/ MANUFACTURER ACCEPTABLE.

04-CONTINUOUS LENGTH OF FABRICS MUST NOT BE LESS THAN 20 YDS. A CERTIFICATE TO THIS EFFECT SHOULD ACCOMPANY SHIP-PING DOCS.

其他内容：参考项目三（商业发票缮制）实训二资料

1. 预装船检验证书

浙江纺大贸易有限公司

ZHEJIANG FANTA TRADING CO., LTD.

NO. 158 ZHONGSHAN ZHONG ROAD, HANGZHOU, CHINA

PRE-SHIPMENT INSPECTION CERTIFICATE

2. 装船通知

浙江纺大贸易有限公司

ZHEJIANG FANTA TRADING CO., LTD.

NO. 158 ZHONGSHAN ZHONG ROAD, HANGZHOU, CHINA

SHIPPING ADVICE

TO: DATE:

RE: L/C NO.   INVOICE NO.

COVER NOTE NO.

WE HEREBY INFORMED YOU THAT THE GOODS UNDER THE ABOVE MENTIONED CREDIT HAVE BEEN SHIPPED. THE DETAILS OF SHIPMENT ARE STATED BELOW.

COMMODITY:

QUANTITY:

INVOICE VALUE:

OCEAN VESSEL/ SHIPPED PER S. S. :

DATE OF SHIPMENT:

PORT OF LOADING:

PORT OF DESTINATION:

MARKS:

Signature

3.受益人证明(1)

浙江纺大贸易有限公司

ZHEJIANG FANTA TRADING CO.，LTD.

NO.158 ZHONGSHAN ZHONG ROAD，HANGZHOU，CHINA

BENEFICIARY'S CERTIFICATE

TO：   DATE：

RE：L/C NO.   INVOICE NO.

WE HEREBY CERTIFY THAT...

4.受益人证明(2)

浙江纺大贸易有限公司

ZHEJIANG FANTA TRADING CO.，LTD.

NO.158 ZHONGSHAN ZHONG ROAD，HANGZHOU，CHINA

BENEFICIARY'S CERTIFICATE

TO：   DATE：

RE：L/C NO.   INVOICE NO.

WE HEREBY CERTIFY THAT...

5.船公司证明

§ 实训三

根据下列资料缮制检验证书、装船通知、受益人证明。

信用证资料：

APPLICANT：CHAMUNDI TEXTILES(SILK MILLS) LTD, 56 OHTEMACHI, 1-CHOME，CHIIYADA-KU，YOKOHAMA

BENEFICIARY：ZHEJIANG RAIN TEXTILES CO. ,LTD.

　　　　　　RM1808，WEST LAKE INTERNATION MANSION，

　　　　　　NO. 235 WENER ROAD, HANGZHOU,CHINA

MERCHANDISE：MULBERRY RAW SILK 80 CARTONS

COUNRTY OF ORIGIN：CHINA

CIFVALUE：USD99,033. 68

PACKED IN SEAWORTHY CARTONS

DOCUMENTS REQUIRED：

　　＋INSPECTION CERTIFICATE OF QUALITY ISSUED BY THE ENTRY-EXIT INSPECTION AND QUARANTINE OF THE PEOPLE'S REPUBLIC OF CHINA EVIDENCING THAT THE GOODS HAVE BEEN INSPECTED AND FOUND TO BE IN COMPLIANCE WITH THE CONTRACT.

　　＋BENEFICIARY'S STATEMENT STATING THAT THEY HAVE SENT ONE FULL SET OF N/N DOCUMENTS REQUIRED BY L/C TO THE APPLICANT VIA DHL WITHIN 2 DAYS AFTER SHIPMENT.

+BENEFICIARY'S CERTIFIED COPY OF FAX TO THE APPLICANT(FAX NO. 0098-2-23456) ADVISING MERCHANDISE, SHIPMENT DATE, GROSS INVOICE VALUE, NAME AND VOYAGE OF VESSEL, CARRIER'S NAME, PORT OF LOADING AND PORT OF DISCHARGE IMMEDIATELY ON THE DATE OF SHIPMENT.

......

ADDITIONAL CONDITIONS:

+ALL DOCUMENTS MUST BE MADE OUT IN THE NAME OF THE AP-PLICANT UNLESS OTHERWISE STIPULATED BY THE L/C

+ALL DOCUMENTS MUST INDICATE OUR L/C NUMBER 789DC AND ISSUING BANK NAME: THE BANK OF TOKYO-MITSUBISHI UFJ, LTD. 2-7-1, MARUNOUCHI, CHIYODA-KU, TOKYO, JAPAN

其他资料：

S/C NO. :SC 9802

N. W. : 2397. 91KGS

G. W. :2640. 00KGS

MEASUREMENT: 8. 240CBM

DATE OF INSPECTION: JAN. 10, 2010

DATE OF SHIPMENT: JAN. 12, 2010

CARRIER: AHEAD LOGISTICS CO. , LTD

PORT OF LOADING: SHANGHAI

PORT OF DESTINATION: YOKOHAMA

NAME AND VOYAGE OF VESSEL: HYUNDAI VLADIVOSTOK 526W

INVOICE NO. :0C01A0120045

INVOICE DATE: JAN. 3, 2010

SHIPPING MARKS: CTL/YOKAHAMA/NO. 1-80

1. 检验证书

中华人民共和国出入境检验检疫
ENTRY-EXIT INSPECTION AND QUARANTINE
OF THE PEOPLE'S REPUBLIC OF CHINA

INSPECTION CERTIFICATE OF QUALITY

发货人
Consignor _____

收货人
Consignee _____

品名
Commodity _____

报检数量/重量
Quantity/Weight Declared _____

包装种类及数量
Number and Type of Package _____

运输工具
Means of Conveyance _____

标记及号码
Marks & Nos. _____

检验结果
Results of Inspection _____

印章   签证地点   签证日期
Official Stamp   Place of Issue   Date of Issue

                         授权签字人   签名
                         Authorized Officer   Signature

我们已尽所知和最大能力实施上述检验，不能因我们签发本证书而免除卖方或其他方面根据合同和法律所承担的产品种类责任和其他责任。All inspections are carried out conscientiously to the best of our knowledge and ability. This certificate does not in any respect absolve the seller and other related parties from his contractual and legal obligations especially when product quality is concerned.

2. 装船通知

ZHEJIANG RAIN TEXTILES CO. ,LTD.

RM1808，WEST LAKE INTERNATION MANSION，

NO. 235 WENER ROAD，HANGZHOU，CHINA

SHIPPING ADVICE

TO：   DATE：

RE：L/C NO.   INVOICE NO.

WE HEREBY INFORMED YOU THAT THE GOODS UNDER THE ABOVE MENTIONED CREDIT HAVE BEEN SHIPPED. THE DETAILS OF SHIPMENT ARE STATED BELOW.

COMMODITY：

QUANTITY：

INVOICE VALUE：

OCEAN VESSEL/ SHIPPED PER S. S. ：

DATE OF SHIPMENT：

PORT OF LOADING：

PORT OF DESTINATION：

MARKS：

                                                         Signature

3. 受益人证明

ZHEJIANG RAIN TEXTILES CO. ,LTD.

RM1808,WEST LAKE INTERNATION MANSION,

NO. 235 WENER ROAD, HANGZHOU,CHINA

BENEFICIARY'S STATEMENT

TO：   DATE：

RE：L/C NO.   INVOICE NO.

WE HEREBY CERTIFY THAT...

....

§ 实训四

根据下列资料缮制出口许可证。

信用证资料：

NATIONAL PARIS BANK

24 MARSHALL AVE DONCASTER MONTREAL，CANADA

WE ISSUE OUR IRREVOCABLE DOCUMENTARY CREDIT NUMBER：TH2003
IN FAVOUR OF：PINGHU KNITWEAR AND MANUFACTURED GOODS IM-
PORT AND EXPORT TRADE CORPORATION

321，ZHOUGSHAN ROAD, PINGHU, CHINA

BY ORDER OF：YI YANG TRADING CORPORATION

88 MARSHALL AVE

DONCASTER VIC 3108

CANADA

FOR AN AMOUNT OF USD 89705. 50

DATE OF EXPIRY：15NOV09

PALCE：IN BENEFICIARY'S COUNRTY

AVAILABLE WITH ANY BANK BY NEGOTIATION OF BENEFICIARY'S

DRAFT DRAWN ON US AT SIGHT IN MONTREAL AGAINST DELIVERY OF
THE FOLLOWING DOCUMENTS:
+EXPORT LICENSE OF THE PEOPLE'S REPUBLIC OF CHINA
......
COVERING SHIPMENT OF COTTON TEATOWELS AS PER S/C ST303
FOR 1-300 SIZE 10 INCHES ＊ 10 INCHES 16000 DOZ. AT USD 1. 31/DOZ
301-600 SIZE 20 INCHES ＊ 20 INCHES 6000 DOZ. AT USD 2. 51/DOZ
AND 601-900 SIZE 30 INCHES ＊ 30 INCHES 11350 DOZ. AT USD 4. 73/DOZ
CIF MONTREAL
FROM SHANGHAI PORT TO MONTREAL PORT
NOT LETER THAN 31OCT09
PARTIAL SHIPMENTS: ALLOWED
TRANSHIPMENT: ALLOWED
SPECIAL INSTRUCTIONS:
+ALL CHARGES IF ANY RELATED TO SETTLEMENTS ARE FOR ACCOUNT
OF BENEFICIARY
+IN CASE OF PRESENTATION OF DOCUMENTS WITH DISCREPANCY (IES)
A CHARGE OF USD 55. 00 WILL BE DEDUCTED
+THIS CREDIT IS TRANSFERABLE
THIS CREDIT IS SUBJECT TO UCP FOR DOCUMENTARY CREDITS 2007 RE-
VISION ICC PUBLICATION 600 AND IS THE OPERATIVE INSTRUMENT
其他资料:
有关唛头、件数等内容应与该信用证的要求相符
单位中文名称:苏州毛织品进出口贸易公司
单位编码:195762654
出口许可证编码:2002122433
商品中文名称:全棉抹布
商品编码:888. 666

中华人民共和国出口许可证

EXPORT LICENSE OF THE PEOPLE'S REPUBLIC OF CHINA

1. 出口商 Exporter　　　编码	3. 出口许可证号 Export License No.
2. 发货人 Consignor	4. 许可证有效截止日期 Export License Expiry Date
5. 贸易方式 Terms of Trade	8. 进口国（地区）Country /Region of Purchase
6. 合同号码 Contract No.	9. 支付方式 Payment
7. 报关口岸 Place of Clearnce	10. 运输方式 Means of Transport

11. 商品名称 Descriptions of Goods			商品编码 H. S. Code		
12. 规格等级 Specification	13. 单位 Unit	14. 数量 Quantity	15. 单价（$） Unit Price	16. 总值（$） Amount	17. 总值折美元 Amount in USD
18. 总计 Total					

19. 备注 Supplementary Details	20. 发证机关签章 Issuing Authority's Stamp & Signature
	21. 发证日期 License Date

商务部监制　　　　　　　　　　　　　　　　　　本证不得涂改，不得转让

§ 实训五

阅读下列信用证并指出制作相应单据时应注意的问题。

```
2010JAN31 15：23：46                                    LOGICAL TERMINAL E102
MT S700        ISSUE OF A DOCUMENTARY CREDIT
                                                       PAGE 00001
                                                       FUNCMSG700
                                                       UMR   06607642
```

MSGACK DWS765I AUTH OK, KEY B110106173BAOC53B, BKCHCNBJ BNP＊＊＊RE-CORD

BASIC HEADER F 01 BKCHCNBJA940 0542 725524

APPLICATION HEADER 0 700 1122 100129 BNPACAMMAXXX 4968 839712 100130 0028 N

　　　　　　　　　　　　　　＊BNP PARIBAS（CANADA）

　　　　　　　　　　　　　　＊MONTREAL

USER HEADER	SERVICE CODE	103：	
	BANK. PRIORITY	113：	
	MSG USER REF.	108：	（银行盖信用证通知专用章）
	INFO. FROM CI	115：	

SEQUENCE OF TOTAL　　　＊27:1 / 1

FORM OF DOC. CREDIT　　＊40 A:IRREVOCABLE

DOC. CREDIT NUMBER　　　＊20:63211020049

DATE OF ISSUE　　　　　31 C:100129

EXPIRY　　　＊31 D:　　DATE 100410 PLACE IN BENEFICIARY'S COUNTRY

APPLICANT　　　　　　　＊50:FASHION FORCE CO. , LTD

　　　　　　　　　　　　240 ST. GEORGE STREET, OTTAWA , CANADA

BENEFICIARY　＊59:HANGZHOU SICODA TEXTILE GARMENT CO. , LTD.

　　　　　　　RM2901, YELLOW DRAGON MANSION,

　　　　　　　NO.85 SHUGUANG ROAD, HANGZHOU,310016, CHINA

AMOUNT　　　　　　　　＊32 B:CURRENCY USD AMOUNT 32640,

AVAILABLE WITH/BY　　＊41 D:ANY BANK BY NEGOTIATION

DRAFTS AT...　　　　　42 C:SIGHT

DRAWEE　　　　　　　　42 A:BNPACAMMXXX

　　　　　　　　　　　＊BNP PARIBAS（CANADA）

　　　　　　　　　　　＊MONTREAL

PARTIAL SHIPMTS　　　43 P:NOT ALLOWED

TRANSSHIPMENT　　　　43 T:ALLOWED

LOADING ON CHARGE　　44 A:CHINA

FOR TRANSPORT TO...　44 B:MONTREAL

LATEST DATE OF SHIP.　44 C:100325

DESCRIPT OF GOODS　　　　　45 A:

　　SALES CONDITIONS: CIF MONTREAL/CANADA

　　SALES CONTRACT NO. F01LCB05127

　　LADIES COTTON BLAZER (100% COTTON, 40S×20/140×60)

　　STYLE NO.　　PO NO.　　QTY/PCS　　USD/PC

　　46-301A　　10337　　2550　　12.80

DOCUMENTS REQUIRED　　　　46 A:

　　+ COMMERCIAL INVOICES IN 3 COPIES SIGNED BY BENEFICIARY'S REPRESENTATIVE.

　　+ CANADA CUSTOMS INVOICES IN 4 COPIES.

　　+ FULL SET OF ORIGINAL MARINE BILLS OF LADING CLEAN ON BOARD FLUS 2 NON NEGOTIABLE COPIES MADE OUT OR ENDORSED TO ORDER OF BNP PARIBAS (CANADA) MARKED FREIGHT PREPAID AND NOTIFY APPLICANT'S FULL NAME AND ADDRESS.

　　+ DETAILED PACKING LISTS IN 3 COPIES.

　　+ COPY OF CERTIFICATE OF ORIGIN FORM A.

　　+ COPY OF EXPORT LICENCE.

　　+ BENEFICIARY'S LETTER STATING THAT ORIGINAL CERTIFICATE OF ORIGIN FORM A, ORIGINAL EXPORT LICENCE, COPY OF COMMERCIAL INVOICE, DETAILED PACKING LISTS AND A COPY OF BILL OF LADING WERE SENT DIRECT TO APPLICANT BY COURIER WITHIN 5 DAYS AFTER SHIPMENT. THE RELATIVE COURIER RECEIPT IS ALSO REQUIRED FOR PRESENTATION.

　　+ COPY OF APPLICANT'S FAX APPROVING PRODUCTION SAMPLES BEFORE SHIPMENT.

　　+ LETTER FROM SHIPPER ON THEIR LETTERHEAD INDICATING THEIR NAME OF COMPANY AND ADDRESS, BILL OF LADING NUMBER, CONTAINER NUMBER AND THAT THIS SHIPMENT, INCLUDING ITS CONTAINER, DOES NOT CONTAIN ANY NON-MANUFACTURED WOODEN MATERIAL, DUNNAGE, BRACING MATERIAL, PALLETS, CRATING OR OTHER NON-MANUFACTURED WOODEN PACKING MATERIAL.

　　+ INSPECTION CERTIFICATE ORIGINAL SINGED AND ISSUED BY FASHION FORCE CO., LTD STATING THE SAMPLES OF FOUR STYLE GARMENTS HAS BEEN APPROVED, WHICH SEND THROUGH DHL BEFORE 15 DAYS OF SHIPMENT.

　　+ INSURANCE POLICY OR CERTIFICATE IN 1 ORIGINAL AND 1 COPY ISSUED OR ENDORSED TO THE ORDER OF BNP PARIBAS (CANADA) FOR THE CIF INVOICE PLUS 10 PERCENT COVERING ALL RISKS, INSTITUTE STRIKES, INSTITUTE WAR CLAUSES AND CIVIL COMMO-

TIONS CLAUSES.

ADDITIONAL COND.　　　47 A:

+IF DOCUMENTS PRESENTED ARE FOUND BY US NOT TO BE FULL COMPLIANCE WITH CREDIT TERMS, WE WILL ASSESS A CHARGE OF USD 55.00 PER SET OF DOCUMENTS.

+ALL CHARGES IF ANY RELATED TO SETTLEMENTS ARE FOR AC-COUNT OF BENEFICIARY.

+3 PCT MORE OR LESS IN AMOUNT AND QUANTITY IS ALLOWED.

+ALL CERTIFICATES/LETTERS/STATEMENTS MUST BE SIGNED AND DATED.

+FOR INFORMATION ONLY, PLEASE NOTE AS OF JANUARY 4, 1999 THAT ALL SHIPMENTS FROM CHINA THAT ARE PACKED WITH UN-TREATED WOOD WILL BE BANNED FROM CANADA DUE TO THE THREAT POSED BY THE ASIAN LONGNORNED BEETLE.

+THE CANADIAN GOVERNMENT NOW INSIST THAT EVERY SHIP-MENT ENTERING CANADA MUST HAVE THE ABOVE DOCUMENTA-TION WITH THE SHIPMENT.

+BILL OF LADING AND COMMERCIAL INVOICE MUST CERTIFY THE FOLLOWING: THIS SHIPMENT, INCLUDING ITS CONTAINER DOES NOT CONTAIN ANY NON-MANUFACTURED WOODEN MATERIAL, DUNNAGE, BRACING MATERIAL PALLETS, CRATING OR OTHER NON-MANUFACTURED WOODEN PACKING MATERIAL.

+BENEFICIARY'S BANK ACCOUNT NO. 07773108201140121

CHARGES　　　71 B:

+OUTSIDE COUNTRY BANK CHARGES TO BE BORNE BY THE BENEFI-CIARY

+OPENING BANK CHARGES TO BE BORNE BY THE APPLICANT

CONFIRMATION　　*　49　:　WITHOUT

INSTRUCTIONS　　　78　:

+WE SHALL COVER THE NEGOTIATING BANK AS PER THEIR IN-STRUCTIONS

+FORWARD DOCUMENTS IN ONE LOT BY SPECIAL COURIER PRE-PAID TO BNP PARIBAS (CANADA) 1981 MCGILL COLLECE AVE. MONTREAL QC H3A 2W8 CANADA.

SEND. TO REC. INFO.　　72　:

THIS CREDIT IS SUBJECT TO UCP FOR DOCUMENTARY CREDIT 2007 REVI-SION ICC PUBLICATION 600 AND IS THE OPERATIVE INSTRUMENT

TRAILER　ORDER IS <MAC:> <PAC:> <ENC:> <CHK:> <TNG:> <PDE:>

MAC: F344CA36

CHK: AA6204FFDFC2

实训指导

一、检验证书缮制说明

1. 外贸企业或生产企业出具的检验检疫证书缮制

外贸企业或生产企业出具的检验检疫证书样式及其各栏目填写如下。

第1栏：填写出口公司或生产企业名称和地址。

第2栏：填写检验证书名称，如品质检验证书、数量检验证书。证件的名称视检验检疫的内容而定。但应注意的是，证件名称及所列项目和检验检疫结果应与出口合同和信用证规定相符。

第3栏：填写发票号码。

第4栏：填写检验证书的日期。该日期不能迟于装运日期，即提单日。

第5栏：填写商品名称。

第6栏：填写唛头；如无唛头，填"N/M"。

第7栏：填写计算单价时使用的计量单位的数量和/或提单或其他运输单据相同栏目中最大包装的件数。

第8栏：填写净重和/或毛重。

第9栏：填写检验结果。

第10栏：出口公司或生产企业经办人签字并加盖公章。

2. 出入境检验检疫局出具的检验检疫证书缮制

出入境检验检疫局出具的检验检疫证书大部分栏目的填写方法和外贸企业或生产企业出具的检验检疫证书基本一致，不同点有以下几个方面：

(1)编号由检验机构编制，不填发票号码。

(2)增加发货人和收货人两个栏目。发货人(Consignor)：一般为出口人，即信用证受益人。受货人(Consignee)：一般为进口人，即信用证开证申请人；也可只填"TO WHOM IT MAY CONCERN"（致有关当事人/敬启者）。

(3)由检验机构经办人签字并加盖公章。

二、装船通知缮制说明

装船通知缮制一般包括以下内容：

1. 单据名称

有关装船通知性质的单据名称常见的有 Shipping/Shipment Advice、Advice of Shipment、Insurance Declaration、Beneficiary's Certified Copy of Fax 以及 Declaration of Shipment。不同名称的装船通知，内容上也有所不同。名称如信用证有具体规定的，从其规定。

2. 通知对象

应按信用证规定，可以是开证申请人、申请人的指定人或保险公司等。若抬头为买方指定的保险公司，则应同时注明预约保险单号码。

3.参考号码

参考号码包括信用证号码、发票号码,尤其是预约保险单的号码。

4.制作和发出时间

日期不能超过信用证规定的时限,常见的有以小时为准(within 24/48 hour)和以天为准(within 2 days after shipment date)两种情形。若信用证未对装船通知的出单日期作出明确规定,或要求装船后立即通知(immediately after shipment),一般要求出口商在货物离开起运地后三个工作日内向进口商发出装船通知,即提单日后三个工作日内。

5.通知内容

通知内容主要包括所发运货物的品名、数量、金额、运输工具名称、开行日期、起运地和目的地、提运单号、运输标志等。如信用证提出具体项目要求,应严格按规定出单。此外,通知中还可能出现包装说明、ETD(船舶预计离港时间)、ETA(船舶预计抵港时间)、ETC(预计开始装船时间)等内容。

6.特殊要求

根据信用证要求加具一些特殊说明。

7.证明真实性的语句(可以选择是否需要写)

8.签署

一般可以不签署,但如果信用证要求"CERTIFIED COPY OF SHIPPING ADVICE",则受益人必须在该装船通知上进行签字盖章。

三、受益人证明缮制说明

受益人证明缮制一般包括以下内容。

第1栏:填写出口公司名称和地址。

第2栏:填写单据名称,按 L/C 规定填,如 BENEFICIARY'S CERTIFICATE 、BENEFICIARY'S STATEMENT 、BENEFICIARY'S DECLARATION。

第3栏:抬头栏,类似这样的公开证明或声明,抬头可采用笼统填法,即"致有关当事人(TO:WHOM IT MAY CONCERN)"。

第4栏:日期,应与证明的内容符合。如证明副本单据必须在装船后×××天内寄给开证申请人,那么受益人证明的签发日期最好在这段时间内。

第5栏:参考号码,填写 L/C 号码和发票号码。

第6栏:证明内容,按照信用证要求填写。

第7栏:签署,受益人证明必须要由出口公司签署才能生效,填写受益人名称和签字。

四、船公司证明缮制说明

各家船公司出具的船公司证明的格式虽不一样,但通常包括以下主要内容:

1.出证日期和地址:一般为签发提单的日期和地址。

2.船名和提单号:表明本次运输的运载船舶及其提单号。

3.单据名称:按信用证规定填写。

4.抬头人:一般都笼统打印"TO:WHOME IT MAY CONCERN"。

5.证明内容:按照信用证要求,根据实际作出相应证明。

6.出证人签章：应与提单签单人一致，通常为承运货物的船公司或其代理人、外轮代理公司或承担联运业务的外运公司等。

五、其他附属单据缮制说明

受益人证明、船公司证明、预装船检验证书等附属单据名称多样，内容、制作格式五花八门。制作附属单据时，出单者可采用自己设计的单据格式，也允许用白纸或印有出单者英文信头的信纸打印，显示对应的发票编号和进口商要求的单据名称。

六、出口许可证缮制说明

出口许可证申请表各栏目的内容缮制如下。

1. 出口商（Exporter）

指出口合同签订单位，应与出口批准文件一致。出口商代码为《对外贸易经营者备案登记表》、《中华人民共和国进出口企业资格证书》或者《中华人民共和国外商投资企业批准证书》中的13位企业代码。

2. 发货人（Consignor）

指具体执行合同发货报关的单位。

3. 出口许可证号（Export License No.）

填出口许可证号码。

4. 出口许可证有效截止日期（Export License Expiry Date）

按《货物出口许可证管理办法》确定的有效期，由发证系统自动生成。

5. 贸易方式（Terms of Trade）

指该项出口货物的贸易性质。包括：一般贸易、进料加工、来料加工、出料加工、外资企业出口、捐赠、赠送等。只能填报一种。

6. 合同号（Contract No.）

指申请出口许可证时提交的出口合同的编号。一份出口许可证只能填报一个合同号。

7. 报关口岸（Place of Clearnce）

指出口口岸，只允许填报一个关区。出口许可证实行"一证一关"制。对指定口岸的出口商品，按国家有关规定执行。

8. 进口国（地区）（Country /Region of Purchase）

指合同目的地。只能填报一个国家（地区）。不能使用地区名，如欧盟等。如对中国保税区出口，进口国（地区）应打印"中国"。

9. 付款方式（Payment）

包括：信用证、托收、汇付等。只能填报一种。

10. 运输方式（Means of Transport）

指货物离境时的运输方式。包括：海上运输、铁路运输、公路运输、航空运输等。只能填报一种。如对远洋出口冷冻商品，运输方式不得打印陆运，包括铁路运输、公路运输。

11. 商品名称、商品编码（Descriptions of Goods H. S. Code）

按商务部公布的年度《出口许可证管理货物目录》中的10位商品编码填报，商品名称由发证系统自动生成。只能填报一个商品编码并应与出口批准文件一致。

12. 规格、等级(Specification)

只能填报同一商品编码下的 4 种不同规格等级,超过 4 种规格等级的,另行申请许可证。

13. 单位(Unit)

指计量单位。按商务部公布的年度《出口许可证管理货物目录》中的计量单位执行,发证系统自动生成。如合同使用的计量单位与规定的计量单位不一致,应换算成规定的计量单位。无法换算的,可在备注栏注明。

14. 数量(Quantity)

指申请出口商品数量。最大位数为 9 位阿拉伯数字,最小保留小数点后 1 位。如数量过大,可分证办理;如数量过小,可在备注栏内注明。计量单位为"批"的,此栏均为"1"。

15. 单价(币别)(Unit Price)

指与第 13 项"单位"所使用的计量单位相应的单价和货币种类。计量单位为"1"批的,此栏为总金额。

16. 总值(Amount)

17. 总值折美元(Amount in USD)

18. 总计(Total)

第 16、17、18 项:由发证系统自动计算。

19. 备注(Supplementary Details)

用于注明其他需要说明的情况。如不是一批一证报关的出口许可证,在此栏注明"非一批一证"。

20. 发证机关签章(Issuing Authority's Stamp & Signature)

发证机构发放出口许可证前在此栏加盖《中华人民共和国出口许可证专用章》。

21. 发证日期(License Date)

由发证系统自动生成。

模块二

综合能力训练

≫ ≫ ≫ ≫

实训一　电汇方式下出口单据缮制

实训目标

能够根据相关资料缮制电汇方式下的出口单据。

实训任务

一、训练资料

(一)销售合同

SHANGHAI TENGXUN TOOLS IMP. & EXP. CO., LTD.

280 NANJING ROAD, SHANGHAI, CHINA

SALES CONTRACT

TO: ETI COMPANY

300 VTRA SEMARANG INDONESIA

NO. 20100501

DATE: MAY 01, 2010

P/I NO: 20100201

Dear Sirs,

We hereby confirm having sold to you the following goods on terms and conditions as specified bellow:

Shipping mark	Descriptions of goods	quantity	Unit price	Amount
N/M	TOOLS Double Open End Spanner 8×10mm(MTM) 10×12mm(MTM)	60000PCS 80000PCS	CPT SEMARANG USD0.50/PC USD0.40/PC	USD30000.00 USD32000.00
TOTAL:		140000PCS		USD62000.00

1. Terms of Payment: 30% T/T IN ADVANCE, THE OTHERS 70% T/T BEFORE SHIPMENT.

2. Airport of Departure: PUDONG AIRPORT SHANGHAI, CHINA

3. Airport of Destination: SEMARANG AIRPORT INDONESIA

4. Latest Date of Shipment：JUL．10，2010

Our bank information is as follows：

    Beneficiary：SHANGHAI TENGXUN TOOLS IMP．＆ EXP．CO．，LTD．

        280 NANJING ROAD, SHANGHAI, CHINA

    Bank Name：BANK OF CHINA SHANGHAI BRANCH

    Bank Address：NO.98 NANJING ROAD, SHANGHAI, CHINA

    ACCOUNT NO：RMB80456860

THE BUYER：　　　　　　　　　　　　　　THE SELLER：

ETI COMPANY　　　　　　　SHANGHAI TENGXUN TOOLS IMP．＆ EXP．CO．，LTD．

PETER　　　　　　　　　　　　　　　　　*DONG LI*

（二）补充资料

1. INVOICE NO.：STT20100501

2. PACKING

Double Open End Spanner	G. W.	N. W.	MEAS.
8x10mm（MTM）	2KGS/CTN	1.8KGS/CTN	0.02CBM/CTN

PACKED IN CARTONS OF 100 PCS EACH

10x12mm（MTM）	2.5KGS/CTN	2.2KGS/CTN	0.01CBM/CTN

PACKED IN CARTONS OF 100 PCS EACH

TRANSPORTED IN ONE 20'CONTAINER NO. TEX212111

3. H.S. CODE：82041100

4. CERTIFICATE NO.：010512345

5. FREIGHT：USD2400.00

6. AIR WAYBILL NO：B050577777

7. AIR WAY BILL DATE：JULY01，2010

8. 报检单位登记号：1318775561

9. 报检单编号：780055756

10. 生产单位注册号：SH1887056

11. 申请单位注册号：YT781120

12. 发货人账号：089877

13. 外币账号：MY567890012

14. 海关编号：1234567890

15. 境内货源地：上海

16. 生产厂家：上海腾讯工具制造有限公司（3105726445）

17. 报关员：张琴 电话：87865544

18. 随附单据：出口货物通关单（5566447856）

二、训练要求

请以"单证员"身份，根据销售合同和补充资料缮制下列单据。

1.商业发票

SHANGHAI TENGXUN TOOLS IMP. & EXP. CO., LTD.

280 NANJING ROAD, SHANGHAI, CHINA

Commercial Invoice

TO：   INV. NO. :＿＿＿＿＿＿＿

DATE：＿＿＿＿＿＿＿＿

P/I NO. :＿＿＿＿＿＿＿

FROM ＿＿＿＿＿＿＿ TO ＿＿＿＿＿＿＿

MARKS & NOS.	DESCRIPTION OF GOODS	QUANTITY	UNIT PRICE	AMOUNT

TOTAL AMOUNT：

WE HEREBY CERTIFY THAT THE ABOVE MENTIONED
GOODS ARE OF CHINESE ORIGIN.

＿＿＿＿＿＿＿＿＿＿

2. 装箱单

SHANGHAI TENGXUN TOOLS IMP. & EXP. CO., LTD.
280 NANJING ROAD, SHANGHAI, CHINA

Packing List

TO:

INV. NO. : _____

DATE: _____

P/I NO. : _____

MARKS & NOS.	DESCRIPTION OF GOODS	QTY (PCS)	CTNS	G. W. (KGS)	N. W. (KGS)	MEAS. (CBM)
TOTAL:						

3.原产地证书申请书和原产地证书

(1)原产地证书申请书

中华人民共和国出口货物
一般原产地证明书/加工装配证明书申请书

企业名称：_____ 证书号：_____

申请人郑重声明：

本人被正式授权代表本企业办理和签署本申请书。

本申请书及《中华人民共和国出口货物原产地证明书/加工装配证明书申请书》所列内容正确无误,如发现弄虚作假,冒充证书所列货物,擅改证书,本人愿按《中华人民共和国出口货物原产地规则》的有关规定接受处罚并承担法律责任,现将有关情况申报如下:

商品名称(中英文)		H.S.编码(六位数)		
商品 FOB 总值(以美元计)		最终目的国/地区		
转口国/地区		拟出运日期	发票号	
贸易方式和企业性质(请在适用处画"√")				
一般贸易		灵活贸易		其他贸易
中资企业	外资企业	中资企业	外资企业	中资企业 外资企业
数量或总量		是否含有进口成分:是( )否( )		
证书种类(画"√")	一般原产地		加工装配证	
该批货物实际生产企业				

现提交中国出口货物商业发票副本一本,《中华人民共和国货物原产地证明书/加工装配证明书》一正三副,以及其他附件_____份,请予审核签证。

申领人(签名)：

申请单位盖章：

电话：

日期：   年   月   日

注:1.灵活贸易包括:来料加工、补偿贸易、进料加工贸易。

2.外资企业指所有含有外资的企业。

3.其他贸易指一般贸易和灵活贸易以外的贸易,如展卖、易货、租赁等贸易方式。

（2）原产地证书

1. Exporter (Full Name and Address)	CERTIFICATE NO.
	CERTIFICATE OF ORIGIN
	OF
2. Consignee (Full Name and Address)	**THE PEOPLE'S REPUBLIC OF CHINA**
3. Means of Transport and Route	5. For Certifying Authority Use Only
4. Country/Region of Destination	

6. Marks and Numbers of Packages	7. Description of Goods; Number and Kind of Package	8. H. S. Code	9. Quantity or Weight	10. Number and Date of Invoices

11. Declaration by the Exporter

The undersigned hereby declares that the above details and statements are correct; that all the goods were produced in China and that they comply with the Rules of Origin of the People's Republic of China.

Place and date, signature and stamp of authorized signatory

12. Certification

It is hereby certified that the declaration by the exporter is correct.

Place and date, signature and stamp of certifying authority

4. 出境货物报检单

中华人民共和国出入境检验检疫

出境货物报检单

报检单位(加盖公章):　　　　　　　　　　　　　　　　* 编号:＿＿＿＿＿＿＿＿＿

报检单位登记号:　　　　　联系人:　　　电话:　　　　报检日期:　　年　月　日

发货人	(中文)					
	(外文)					
收货人	(中文)					
	(外文)					
货物名称(中/外文)	H. S. 编码	产地	数/重量	货物总值	包装种类及数量	

运输工具名称号码		贸易方式		货物存放地点	
合同号		信用证号		用途	
发货日期		输往国家(地区)		许可证/审批证	
起运地		到达口岸		生产单位注册号	
集装箱规格、数量及号码					

合同、信用证订立的检验检疫条款或特殊要求	标记及号码	随附单据(画"√"或补填)	
		□合同 □信用证 □发票 □换证凭单 □装箱单 □厂检单	□包装性能结果单 □许可/审批文件 □ □ □

需要证单名称(画"√"或补填)			* 检验检疫费	
□品质证书　　＿＿正＿＿副	□植物检疫证书　＿＿正＿＿副		总金额	
□重量证书　　＿＿正＿＿副	□熏蒸/消毒证书　＿＿正＿＿副		(元人民币)	
□数量证书　　＿＿正＿＿副	□出境货物换证凭单			
□兽医卫生证书　＿＿正＿＿副	□		计费人	
□健康证书　　＿＿正＿＿副	□			
□卫生证书　　＿＿正＿＿副	□		收费人	
□动物卫生证书　＿＿正＿＿副	□			

报检人郑重声明:	领取证单	
1. 本人被授权报检。 2. 上列填写内容正确属实,货物无伪造或冒用他人的厂名、标志、认证标志,并承担货物质量责任。	日期	
签名:＿＿＿＿＿	签名	

注:有"*"号栏由出入境检验检疫机关填写　　　　　　◆国家出入境检验检疫局制

5.国际货物托运书

上海客货运输服务有限公司

SHANGHAI EXPRESS SERVICE CO.，LTD.

国际货物托运书

SHIPPER'S LETTER OF INSTRUCTIONS

托运人姓名及地址 Shipper's Name and Address	托运人账号 Shipper's Account Number	供承运人用 For Carrier Use Only	
		班期/日期 Flight/Day	航班/日期 Flight/Day
收货人姓名及地址 Consignee's Name and Address	收货人账号 Consignee's Account Number	已预留吨位 Booked	
		运费 Charges PP（　　）	CC（　　）
代理人的名称和城市 Issuing Carrier's Agent Name and City		ALSO notify：	
始发站 Airport of Departure			
到达站 Airport of Destination			
托运人声明价值 Shipper's Declared Value	保险金额 Amount of Insurance	所附文件 Document to Accompany Air Waybill	
供运输用 For Carriage　供海关用 For Customs			

处理情况（包括包装方式、货物标志及号码等）

Handling Information (Incl Method of Packing Identifying Marks and Numbers Etc)

件数 No. of Packages	实际毛重 Actual Gross Weight(Kg)	运价类别 Rate Class	收费重量 Chargeable Weight	费率 Rate/ Charge	货物品名及数量（包括体积或 尺寸） Nature and Quantity of Goods (Incl. Dimension or Volume)

托运人证实以上所填全部属实并遵守承运人的一切载运章程。

The shipper certifies that the particulars on the face hereof are correct and agrees to the conditions of carriage of the carrier.

托运人签字 Signature shipper	日期 Date	经手人 Agent	日期 Date

6. 空运单

Shipper's name and address	Shipper's Account Number	Not negotiable

Air Waybill 中国东方航空公司

ISSUED BY CHINA EASTERN AIRLINES

Copies 1、2 and 3 of this Air Waybill are originals and have the same validity

Consignee's name and address	Consignee's Account Number	It is agreed that the goods described herein are accepted in apparent good order and condition (except as noted) for carriage SUBJECT TO THE CONDITIONS OF CONTRACT ON THE REVERSE HEREOF, ALL GOODS MAY BE CARRIED BY ANY OTHER MEANS. INCLUDING ROAD OR ANY OTHER CARRIER UNLESS SPECIFIC CONTRARY INSTRUCTIONS ARE GIVEN HEREON BY THE SHIPPER. THE SHIPPER'S ATTENTION IS DRAWN TO THE NOTICE CONCERNING CARRIER'S LIMITATION OF LIABILITY. Shipper may increase such limitation of liability by declaring a higher value for carriage and paying a supplemental charge if required.

Issuing Carrier's Agent Name and City	Accounting Information

Agents IATA Code	Account No.	

Airport of Departure(Addr. of First Carrier) and Requested Routing	Reference number	Optional shipping information

To	By First Carrier	Routing and Destination	To	by	To	by	Currency	CHGS Code	WT/VAL		Other		Declared Value for Carriage	Declared Value for Customs
									PPD	COLL	PPD	COLL		

Airport of Destination	Flight/Date	For Carrier Use only	Flight/Date	Amount of Insurance	INSURANCE-If carrier offers insurance and such insurance is requested in accordance with the conditions thereof indicate amount to be insured in figures in box marked "Amount of Insurance".

Handling Information

						SCI

No.of Pieces RCP	Gross Weight	Kg lb	Rate Class / Commodity Item No.	Chargeable Weight	Rate / Charge	Total	Nature and Quantity of Goods (incl. Dimensions or Volume)

Prepaid	Weight charge	Collect	Other Charges
	Valuation Charge		
	Tax		
	Total Other Charges Due Agent		Shipper certifies that the particulars on the face hereof are correct and that insofar as any part of the consignment contains dangerous goods, such part is properly described by name and is in proper condition for carriage by air according to the applicable Dangerous Goods Regulations Charges at Destination
	Total Other Charges Due Carrier		

Signature of Shipper or his agent

Total Prepaid	Total Collect	
Currency Conversion	CC Charges in dest Currency	Executed on(date) At(place) Signature of issuing Carrier or as Agent
For Carrier's Use Only at Destination	Charges at Destination	Total Collect Charges

AWB No.

7. 出口货物报关单

中华人民共和国海关出口货物报关单

预录入编号： 　　　　　　　　　　　　　海关编号：

出口口岸	备案号		出口日期		申报日期
经营单位	运输方式		运输工具名称		提/运单号
发货单位	贸易方式		征免性质		结汇方式
许可证号	运抵国（地区）		指运港		境内货源地
批准文号	成交方式	运费	保费		杂费
合同协议号	件数	包装种类	毛重（千克）		净重（千克）
集装箱号		随附单据		生产厂家	
标记唛码及备注					

项号	商品编号	商品名称、规格型号	数量及单位	最终目的地国（地区）	单价	总价	币制	征免

税费征收情况

录入员	录入单位	兹声明以上申报无讹并承担法律责任	海关审单批注及放行日期（签单）	
			审单	审价
报关员 单位地址		申报单位（签章）	征税	统计
邮编　　电话　　填制日期			查验	放行

未 经 核 销 此 联 不 得 撕 开

8. 出口收汇核销单

出口收汇核销单
存根
（浙）编号：

出口单位：	
单位编码：	
出口币种总价：	
收汇方式：	
预计收款日期：	
报关日期：	
备注：	
此出口报关单有效期截止到	

（出口单位盖章）

出口收汇核销单
（浙）编号：

出口单位：

单位编码：

类别	币种金额	日期	盖章

签注栏

海关签注栏：

外汇局签注栏

年 月 日（盖章）

（出口单位盖章）

出口收汇核销单
出口退税专用
（浙）编号：

出口单位：

单位编码：

货物名称	数量	币种总价

报关单编号：

外汇局签注栏

年 月 日（盖章）

实训指导

一、一般原产地证明书申请书缮制

一般原产地证明书/加工装配证明书申请书是申请单位向贸促会办理一般原产地证明书/加工装配证明书签证时需填写的专用申请表,其各栏目的内容缮制如下。

1.企业名称

填写申请企业全称。

2.证书号

企业根据贸促会的编号规则按顺序编号,不得重号或跳号。网上申请系统会自动生成的。

3.商品名称

填写商品品名的中、英文,并且与发票的商品名称一致。

4.H.S 税目号(六位数)

填写海关《商品编码协调制度》商品 H.S.税目号(前六位)。

5.商品 FOB 总值(以美元计)

根据申报的出口货物发票上所列的金额以 FOB 价格填写(以美元计),如出口货物不是以 FOB 价格成交,应换算成 FOB 价格。

6.最终目的国/地区

据实填写货物即将运抵的最终目的国/地区。

7.转口国/地区

如货物运输过程中有中转的,此栏填写转口国/地区。

8.拟出运日期

填写货物离开启运口岸的当天日期(年月日)。

9.发票号

填商业发票号码。

10.贸易方式和企业性质(请在适用处画"√")

根据实际情况选择画"√"即行。

11.数量或总量

填写该批出口货物箱数、毛重或个数。

12.是否含有进口成分

根据实际情况选择画"√"即行。

13.证书种类(画"√")

根据实际情况选择画"√"即行。

14.该批货物实际生产企业

填写该批出口货物的生产企业全称及地点。

15."提交单据"栏

如有提供其他相关单据,一并补填。

16.申请单位盖章

填写申请单位全称并盖章。

17.申领员

申领员签字并填写联系电话和申报日期。

二、航空运输托运书缮制

航空货物运输托运书是托运人用于委托承运人或其代理人填开航空货运单的一种表单,上面列有填制货运单所需各项内容,其各栏目填制如下。

1.托运人(Shipper's Name and Address)

填列托运人的全称、街名、城市名称、国家名称以及便于联系的电话、电传或传真号码。

注意:

①集中托运方式时托运人:货运代理人;直接托运方式时的托运人:货主。

②有时承运人要求托运人提供账号,以便在收货人拒付运费时向托运人索偿。

③在信用证结汇方式下,托运人一般按信用证的受益人内容填写。

④托运危险货物时,托运人必须填写实际托运人,航空公司不接受货运代理人托运。

2.收货人(Consignee's Name and Address)

填列收货人的全称、街名、城市名称、国家名称(特别是在不同国家内有相同城市名称时,更应注意填上国名)以及电话、电传或传真号码。

注意:

①本栏不得填写"To Order"或"To Order of Shipper"等字样。因为航空运单不能转让。

②集中托运方式时收货人:货运代理人海外代理;直接托运方式时收货人:实际收货人。

③承运人一般不接受一票货物有两个或两个以上收货人。如果实际上有两个以上收货人,本栏填第一收货人,通知栏填第二收货人。

3.始发站机场(Airport of Departure)

填写始发站机场的全称。

注意:

①在始发站机场的全称不清楚的情况下,允许填写始发站所在城市名称。

②与不同国家的其他城市同名的,还需要填写国家名称。

③同一城市的不同机场,需要填写机场名称。

4.目的地机场(Airport of Destination)

填写最后目的地机场名称或三字代码。

注意:

①按国际航空运输协会 IATA 规范的机场代码填报。

②机场名称不明确时,可填城市名称。如果某一城市名称用于一个以上国家时,应加上国名。

③标签上的卸货港机场代码与托运单上目的地机场代码必须一致。

④如果有"转运路线"要求,可以填在专门栏目内。

5.要求的路线/申请订舱(Requested Routing/Requested Booking)

本栏用于航空公司安排运输路线时使用,但如果托运人有特别要求时,也可填入本栏。

6.供运输用的声明价值(Declared Value for Carriage)

填列供运输用的托运人向承运人声明的货物价值,该价值即为承运人赔偿责任的限额。如果发货人未办理货物声明价值,则填入"NVD(No value declared,无声明价值)"。空白不填,表示"NVD"。

7.供海关用的声明价值(Declared Value for Customs)

填列托运人向海关申报的货物价值金额,该价值是提供给海关的征税依据。当以出口货物报关单或商业发票作为征税标准时,本栏可空白不填或填"AS PER INV.";如果货物系样品等数量少且无商业价值,可填"NCV"(No customs valuation),表明没有商业价值。

8.保险金额(Insurance Amount Requested)

中国民航各空运企业暂未开展国际航空运输代保险业务,本栏可空白不填。

9.处理事项(Handling Information)

填列附加的处理要求。

10.货运单所附文件(Document to Accompany Air Waybail)

填列随附在货运单上运往目的地的文件,应填上所附文件的名称。

11.件数和包装方式(Number and Kind of Packages)

填列该批货物的总件数,并注明其包装方法。如货物没有包装时,就注明为散装(Loose)。如货物运价种类不同时,应分别填写,并将总件数相加,包装种类用"Packages"。

12.实际毛重(Actual Gross Weight)

本栏内的重量应由承运人或其代理人在称重后填入。如托运人已填上重量,承运人或其代理人必须进行复核。

13.运价类别(Rate Class)

填写所采用的货物运价种类的代号。

M—最低运价

N—45公斤以下普通货物运价

Q—45公斤以上普通货物运价

C—指定商品运价

14.计费重量(公斤)(Chargeable Weight)(KGS)

本栏内的计费重量应由承运人或其代理人在量过货物的尺寸(以厘米为单位)后,由承运人或其代理人算出计费重量后填入,如托运人已经填上,承运人或其代理人必须进行复核。

15.费率(Rate/Charge)

填写所适用的货物运价。

①使用最低运费时,填写与运价代号M相对应的最低运费。

②使用代号N、Q、C、S、R运价时,填写相对应的运价。本栏可空白不填。

16.货物的品名及数量(包括体积及尺寸)

[Nature and Quantity of Goods(Incl. Dimensions or Volume)]

填列货物的品名和数量(包括尺寸或体积)。

注意:

①不得填写表示货物类别的名称,应填货物品名、数量、体积、产地等细节。

②危险品、鲜活易腐货,应分别填写其标准的学术名称。

③按货物外包装"最长×最宽×最高×件数"顺序或总计体积填写。

17.运费(Charges)

在 PP 后打(×)表示预付;CC 后打(×)表示到付。

18.要求预订吨位(Booked)

此栏用于航空公司安排舱位时使用,但如果托运人有要求时,也可以按计费吨位填入。

19.托运人签字(Signature of Shipper)

托运人必须在本栏内签字。

20.日期(Date)

填托运人或其代理人交货的日期。

三、出境货物报检单缮制说明

出境货物报检单由各口岸出入境检验检疫局统一印刷,除编号由检验检疫机构指定外,其余各栏由报检单位填制并盖章确认。对无法填写的栏目或无此内容的栏目,统一填写"＊＊＊",不得留空。

1.报检单位

报检单位指向检验检疫机构申报检验、检疫、鉴定业务的单位。本栏填写报检单位的中文名称,并加盖报检单位公章。可以用"报检专用章"。

2.报检单位登记号

报检单位登记号指报检单位在检验检疫机构的登记或注册号码。

3.联系人、电话

要详细填写报检人姓名和联系电话。

4.报检日期

报检日期按检验检疫机构受理的报检日期用数字填写。出境货物最迟应于报关或装运前 7 天报检,对于个别检验检疫周期较长的货物,应留有相应的检验检疫时间。

5.发货人

发货人指本批货物贸易合同中卖方或信用证中受益人名称,如需要出具英文证书的,填写中英文。如检验检疫证书对发货人有特殊要求的,应在备注栏声明。

6.收货人

收货人指本批出境货物贸易合同中或信用证中买方名称,如需要出具英文证书的,填写中英文。如检验检疫证书对收货人有特殊要求的,应在备注栏声明。

7.货物名称

货物名称按贸易合同或发票或信用证所列货物名称填写,根据需要可填写型号、规格或牌号。

8.H.S.编码

H.S.编码指货物对应的海关商品代码,填写 8 位数或 10 位数。一般填写 8 位数商品编码,有些商品有最后两位补充编码时,则填写 10 位数编码。

9. 产地

产地指货物生产/加工的省(自治区、直辖市)以及地区(市)名称。

10. 数/重量

填写报检货物的数/重量,重量一般填写净重,如填写毛重,或以毛重作净重则需注明。

11. 货物的总值

货物的总值按本批货物合同或发票上所列的总值填写。如同一报检单报检多批货物,需列明每批货物的总值。填写时应注意币种,不需填写贸易术语,如 CIF。

12. 包装件数及种类

包装件数及种类指本批货物运输包装的件数及种类。

13. 运输工具名称号码

填写货物实际装载的运输工具类别名称(如船、飞机、货柜车、火车等)及运输工具编号(船名、飞机航班号、车牌号码、火车车次)。报检时,未能确定运输工具名称和编号的,可只填写运输工具类别,如"船舶"或"飞机"。

14. 贸易方式

贸易方式根据实际情况填写。常见的贸易方式有:一般贸易、来料加工、进料加工、补偿贸易、边境贸易、易货贸易等。

15. 货物存放的地点

货物存放的地点指本批货物存放的地点,如××仓库、××码头等。

16. 合同号

合同号指本批货物贸易合同编号。

17. 信用证号

以信用证结汇的,填信用证号;不是信用证方式结汇的,须注明结汇方式。

18. 用途

指本批出境货物用途。自以下 9 个选项中选择:Ⅰ种用或繁殖、Ⅱ食用、Ⅲ奶用、Ⅳ观赏或演艺、Ⅴ伴侣动物、Ⅵ试验、Ⅶ药用、Ⅷ饲用、Ⅸ其他。

19. 发货日期

按本批货物信用证或合同上所列的出境日期填写。填写实际开船日或起飞日,以年月日的顺序填报。

20. 输往国家(地区)

输往国家(地区)填写贸易合同中买方(进口方)所在的国家或地区的中文名称。

21. 许可证/审批号

对实施许可证制度或者审批制度管理的货物,报检时填写许可证编号或审批单编号。

22. 启运地

填写装运本批货物离境的交通工具的启运口岸/地区城市的中文名称。

23. 到达口岸

指装运本批货物的交通工具最终抵达目的地停靠的口岸的中文名称。

24. 生产单位注册号

指生产/加工本批货物的单位在检验检疫机构的注册登记编号。

25. 集装箱规格、数量及号码

填写装载本批货物的集装箱规格（如 40 英尺、20 英尺等）以及分别对应的数量和集装箱号码。集装箱数量指实际集装箱个数，不需要换算成标准箱。本栏按"实际集装箱个数×规格/箱号"形式填写，如 1x20′/TGHU8491952。

26. 合同、信用证订立的检验检疫条款或特殊要求

合同、信用证订立的检验检疫条款或特殊要求指贸易合同或信用证中贸易双方对本批货物特别约定而订立的质量、卫生等条款和报检单位对本批货物检验检疫的特别要求。

27. 标记及号码

标记及号码按出境货物实际运输包装标记填写，如没有标记，填写"N/M"。

28. 随附单据

随附单据按实际提供的单据，在对应的"□"打内"√"。

29. 需要证单名称

按需要检验检疫机构出具的证单，在对应的"□"打内"√"或补充填写需要单据，并注明所需证单的正副本的数量。检验证书一般一正二副，如对证书的正、副本数量或语种有特殊要求的，请在备注栏声明。

30. 报检人郑重声明

报检人郑重声明由持有《报检员》证的报检员签名。

31. 检验检疫费用

检验检疫费用由检验检疫机构计费人员核定费用后填写，如熏蒸费、消毒费等。

32. 领取证单

报检人在领取证单时填写领证日期和领证人签名。

四、进（出）口货物报关单缮制说明

根据《中华人民共和国海关进（出）口货物报关单填制规范》（海关总署公告 2008 年第 52 号），进（出）口货物报关单各栏目的填制规范如下。

1. 预录入编号

本栏目填报预录入报关单的编号。预录入编号规则由接受申报的海关决定。

2. 海关编号

本栏目填报海关接受申报时给予报关单的编号，一份报关单对应一个海关编号。

3. 进口口岸/出口口岸

本栏目应根据货物实际进出境的口岸海关，填报海关规定的《关区代码表》中相应口岸海关的名称及代码。

4. 备案号

本栏目填报进出口货物收发货人在海关办理加工贸易合同备案或征、减、免税备案审批等手续时，海关核发的各种加工贸易手册、征免税证明等备案审批文件的编号。

一份报关单只允许填报一个备案号。

备案号标记代码含义（部分）

第一位字母	含　义	例　如
B	中华人民共和国加工贸易手册（来料加工）	B57704150022
C	中华人民共和国加工贸易手册（进料加工）	C57205711700
D	中华人民共和国加工贸易设备登记手册	D57200100609
Y	原产地证书	Y3M03A000001
Z	进出口货物征免税证明	Z22004A50142

5. 进口日期/出口日期

进口日期填报运载进口货物的运输工具申报进境的日期。

出口日期指运载出口货物的运输工具办结出境手续的日期。

"出口日期"栏供海关签发打印报关单证明联用,在申报时免予填报。

无实际进出境的报关单填报海关接受申报的日期。

本栏目填制格式为8位数字,顺序为年（4位）、月（2位）、日（2位）。

6. 申报日期

申报日期指海关接受进出口货物收发货人或受委托的报关企业申报数据的日期。

进口货物申报日期不得早于进口日期（进口后再申报）,出口货物申报日期不得晚于出口日期（申报、放行后才能出口）。

本栏目填制格式为8位数字,顺序为年（4位）、月（2位）、日（2位）。

7. 经营单位

本栏目填报在海关注册登记的对外签订并执行进出口贸易合同的中国境内法人、其他组织或个人的名称及海关注册编码。

特殊情况下填制要求如下:

（1）进出口货物合同的签订者和执行者非同一企业的,填报执行合同的企业。

（2）外商投资企业委托进出口企业进口投资设备、物品的,填报外商投资企业,并在标记唛码及备注栏注明"委托某进出口企业进口"。

（3）国内的企业委托有进出口经营权的企业进出口,经营单位应填代理方,也就是有进出口经营权的企业。

8. 运输方式

本栏目应根据货物实际进出境的运输方式,按照海关规定的《运输方式代码表》选择填报相应的运输方式或代码。

如,1/监管仓库;2/江海运输;3/铁路运输;4/汽车运输;5/航空运输等。

9. 运输工具名称

本栏目填报载运货物进出境的运输工具名称和航次编号。一份报关单只允许填报一个运输工具名称。

直接在进出境地或采用"属地申报,口岸验放"通关模式办理报关手续的报关单,该栏填报要求如下:

（1）水路运输:填报船舶编号（来往港澳小型船舶为监管簿编号）或者船舶英文名称/船舶的航次号。

(2)公路运输:填报该跨境运输车辆的国内行驶车牌号/运输车辆的8位进出境日期〔顺序为年(4位)、月(2位)、日(2位),下同〕。

(3)铁路运输:填报车厢编号或交接单号/列车的进出境日期。

(4)航空运输:填报航班号。

(5)邮件运输:填报邮政包裹单号/运输工具的进出境日期。

(6)其他运输:填报具体运输方式名称,例如:管道、驮畜等。

10. 提运单号

本栏目填报进出口货物提单或运单的编号。一份报关单只允许填报一个提单或运单号。具体填报要求如下:

(1)水路运输:填报进出口提单号。如有分提单的,填报进出口提单号+"*"+分提单号。

(2)公路运输:免予填报。

(3)铁路运输:填报运单号。

(4)航空运输:填报总运单号+"-"+分运单号,无分运单的填报总运单号。

(5)邮件运输:填报邮运包裹单号。

11. 收货单位/发货单位

收货单位填报已知的进口货物在境内的最终消费、使用单位的名称,包括:(1)自行从境外进口货物的单位;(2)委托进出口企业进口货物的单位。

发货单位填报出口货物在境内的生产或销售单位的名称,包括:(1)自行出口货物的单位;(2)委托进出口企业出口货物的单位。

有海关注册编码或加工企业编码的收、发货单位,本栏目应填报其中文名称及编码;没有编码的应填报其中文名称。

12. 贸易方式(监管方式)

本栏目应根据实际对外贸易情况按海关规定的《监管方式代码表》选择填报相应的监管方式简称或代码。一份报关单只允许填报一种监管方式。

贸易方式、征免性质、用途、征免四个栏目协调(部分)

贸易方式	备案号第一字母	征免性质	用　途	征　免
一般贸易 0110	空	一般征税 101	外贸自营内销 01	照章征税 1
	Z 征免税证明	鼓励项目 789	企业自用 04	全免 3
		自有资金 799		
		科教用品 401		
来料加工 0214	B 登记手册	来料加工 502	加工返销 05	全免 3
进料对口 0615	C 登记手册	进料加工 503	加工返销 05	全免 3
合资合作设备 2025	Z	鼓励项目 789	企业自用 04	全免 3
外资设备物品 2225	Z	鼓励项目 789	企业自用 04	全免 3

13.征免性质

本栏目应根据实际情况按海关规定的《征免性质代码表》选择填报相应的征免性质简称或代码。一份报关单只允许填报一种征免性质。

14.征税比例/结汇方式

进口报关单本栏目免予填报。

出口报关单填报结汇方式,按海关规定的《结汇方式代码表》选择填报相应的结汇方式名称或代码。如,1/信汇(MT)、2/电汇(TT)、3/票汇(DD)、4/付款交单(DP)、5/承兑交单(DA)、6/信用证(L/C)。

15.许可证号

本栏目填报许可证的编号。一份报关单只允许填报一个许可证号。

16.启运国(地区)/运抵国(地区)

启运国(地区)填报进口货物启始发出直接运抵我国或者在运输中转国(地区)未发生任何商业性交易的情况下运抵我国的国家(地区)。

运抵国(地区)填报出口货物离开我国关境直接运抵或者在运输中转国(地区)未发生任何商业性交易的情况下最后运抵的国家(地区)。

经过第三国(地区)转运的进出口货物,如在中转国(地区)发生商业性交易,则以中转国(地区)作为启运/运抵国(地区)。

本栏目应按海关规定的《国别(地区)代码表》选择填报相应的启运国(地区)或运抵国(地区)中文名称或代码。如,中国香港/110,日本/116,韩国/133,美国/502,德国/304,澳大利亚/601,中国澳门/121,中国/142,台澎金马关税区/143。

无实际进出境的,填报"中国"(代码142)。

17.装货港/指运港

装货港填报进口货物在运抵我国关境前的最后一个境外装运港。

指运港填报出口货物运往境外的最终目的港。

本栏目应根据实际情况按海关规定的《港口航线代码表》选择填报相应的港口中文名称或代码。如,香港/1039,新加坡/0132,洛杉矶/3154。

无实际进出境的,本栏目填报"中国境内"(代码0142)。

18.境内目的地/境内货源地

境内目的地填报已知的进口货物在国内的消费、使用地或最终运抵地,其中最终运抵地为最终使用单位所在的地区。

境内货源地填报出口货物在国内的产地或原始发货地。

本栏目按海关规定的《国内地区代码表》选择填报相应的国内地区名称或代码。代码含义与经营单位代码的前5位定义相同。

19.批准文号

进口报关单中本栏目免予填报。出口报关单中本栏目填报出口收汇核销单编号。

20.成交方式

本栏目应根据进出口货物实际成交价格条款,按海关规定的《成交方式代码表》选择填报相应的成交方式或代码。如,CIF/1,CFR/C&F/CNF/2,FOB/3,C&I/4。

无实际进出境的报关单,进口填报CIF/1,出口填报FOB/3。

发票中的贸易术语	报关单中应填写的成交方式	成交方式代码
CIF、CIP 以及 D 组的 5 个贸易术语填	CIF	1
CFR(CNF、C&F)、CPT 填	CFR(CNF、C&F)	2
FCA、FAS、EXW、FOB 填	FOB	3

21.运费

本栏目填报进口货物运抵我国境内输入地点起卸前的运输费用,出口货物运至我国境内输出地点装载后的运输费用。

进口货物成交价格包含前述运输费用或者出口货物成交价格不包含前述运输费用的,本栏目免于填报。

运费可按运费单价、总价或运费率三种方式之一填报,注明运费标记(运费标记"1"表示运费率,"2"表示每吨货物的运费单价,"3"表示运费总价),并按海关规定的《货币代码表》选择填报相应的币种代码。

运保费合并计算的,填报在本栏目。

常见币种代码:港元/110,日元/116,人民币/142,欧元/300,美元/502,加拿大元/501,英镑/303。

例如:

A.10%运费率填报为 10;

B.50 英镑的运费单价填报为 303/50/2;

C.9000 日元的运输总价填报为 116/9000/3。

22.保费

本栏目填报进口货物运抵我国境内输入地点起卸前的保险费用,出口货物运至我国境内输出地点装载后的保险费用。

进口货物成交价格包含前述保险费用或者出口货物成交价格不包含前述保险费用的,本栏目免于填报。

保费可按保险费总价或保险费率两种方式之一填报,注明保险费标记(保险费标记"1"表示保险费率,"3"表示保险费总价),并按海关规定的《货币代码表》选择填报相应的币种代码。

运保费合并计算的,本栏目免予填报。

	成交方式	运费	保费
进口	CIF	不填	不填
	CFR	不填	填
	FOB	填	填
出口	FOB	不填	不填
	CFR	填	不填
	CIF	填	填

23.杂费

本栏目填报成交价格以外的、按照《中华人民共和国进出口关税条例》相关规定应计入完税价格或应从完税价格中扣除的费用,如手续费、佣金、回扣等。

可按杂费总价或杂费率两种方式之一填报,注明杂费标记(杂费标记"1"表示杂费率,"3"表示杂费总价),并按海关规定的《货币代码表》选择填报相应的币种代码。

应计入完税价格的杂费填报为正值或正率,应从完税价格中扣除的杂费填报为负值或负率。

24.合同协议号

本栏目填报进出口货物合同(包括协议或订单)编号。

25.件数

(1)本栏目填报有外包装的进出口货物的实际件数。

(2)散装、裸装货物填报为"1",相应的包装种类填报"裸装"或"散装"。

(3)如果有关单据列明托盘件数的;或者既有托盘数又有单件件数的填"托盘数"。

(4)如果有关单据有集装箱个数,又列明托盘件数、单件包装件数的填"托盘数"。

(5)如仅列明集装箱个数,未列明托盘或者单件包装件数的,则填"集装箱个数"。

26.包装种类

本栏目应根据进出口货物的实际外包装种类,按海关规定的《包装种类代码表》选择填报相应的包装种类或代码。

如果包装种类有多种,则填报"件/PKGS"。

27.毛重(千克)

本栏目填报进出口货物的实际毛重,计量单位为千克,不足一千克的填报为"1"。

28.净重(千克)

本栏目填报进出口货物的实际净重,计量单位为千克,不足一千克的填报为"1"。

29.集装箱号

专指海运集装箱。

本栏填制规则为:一个集装箱号/集装箱规格/集装箱的自重。

如,COSU4243123/20/2275,表示这是一个20英尺的集装箱,箱号为COSU4243123,自重2275公斤。

多个集装箱的,任选一个填报该栏,其余依次填在"备注"栏。

非集装箱货物填报为"0"。

30.随附单证

本栏目根据海关规定的《监管证件代码表》选择填报除本规范第十八条规定的许可证件以外的其他进出口许可证件或监管证件代码及编号。

本栏目分为随附单证代码和随附单证编号两栏,其中代码栏应按海关规定的《监管证件代码表》选择填报相应证件代码;编号栏应填报证件编号。

合同、发票、装箱单、许可证等必备的随附单证不在本栏目填报。

格式为:"监管证件代码:监管证件编号"。如,"Y:03"。

多个监管证件的,第一个监管证件代码和编号填在此栏,其余监管证件代码和编号填在"备注"栏。

31.用途/生产厂家

进口货物本栏目填报用途,应根据进口货物的实际用途按海关规定的《用途代码表》选择填报相应的用途或代码。

出口货物本栏目填报其境内生产企业。

32.标记唛码及备注

本栏目填报要求如下：

(1)标记唛码中除图形以外的文字、数字。

(2)受外商投资企业委托代理其进口投资设备、物品的进出口企业名称。

(3)多个集装箱的,填其余的集装箱号;多个监管证件的,填其余监管证件代码及编号。

33.项号

本栏目分两行填报及打印。

第一行填报报关单中的商品顺序编号;第二行专用于加工贸易、减免税等已备案、审批的货物,填报和打印该项货物在《加工贸易手册》或《征免税证明》等备案、审批单证中的顺序编号。

34.商品编号

本栏目应填报由《中华人民共和国进出口税则》确定的进出口货物的税则号列和《中华人民共和国海关统计商品目录》确定的商品编码,以及符合海关监管要求的附加编号组成的10位商品编号。

35.商品名称、规格型号

本栏目分两行填报及打印。

第一行填报进出口货物规范的中文商品名称,第二行填报规格型号。

36.数量及单位

本栏目分三行填报及打印。

(一)第一行应按进出口货物的法定第一计量单位填报数量及单位,法定计量单位以《中华人民共和国海关统计商品目录》中的计量单位为准。

(二)凡列明有法定第二计量单位的,应在第二行按照法定第二计量单位填报数量及单位。无法定第二计量单位的,本栏目第二行为空白。

(三)成交计量单位及数量应填报并打印在第三行。

37.原产国(地区)/最终目的国(地区)

原产国(地区)指进口货物的生产、开采或加工制造国家(地区)。

进口货物原产国(地区)无法确定的,填报"国别不详"(代码701)。

最终目的国(地区)填报已知的出口货物的最终实际消费、使用或进一步加工制造国家(地区)。

本栏目应按海关规定的《国别(地区)代码表》选择填报相应的国家(地区)名称或代码。

38.单价

本栏目填报同一项号下进出口货物实际成交的商品单位价格。

金额非整数的,保留4位数,第5位及以后略去。

39.总价

本栏目填报同一项号下进出口货物实际成交的商品总价格。

金额非整数的,保留4位数,第5位及以后略去。

40. 币制

币制指进（出）口货物实际成交价格的币种。

本栏目应按海关规定的《货币代码表》选择相应的货币名称或代码或符号填报。如，港元/110/HKD，日元/116/JPY，人民币/142/CNY，欧元/300/EUR，美元/502/USD，英镑/303/GBP。

41. 征免

本栏目应按照海关核发的《征免税证明》或有关政策规定，对报关单所列每项商品选择海关规定的《征减免税方式代码表》中相应的征减免税方式填报。如，照章征税/1，折半征税/2，全免/3等。

42. 税费征收情况

本栏目供海关批注进（出）口货物税费征收及减免情况。

43. 录入员

本栏目用于记录预录入操作人员的姓名。

44. 录入单位

本栏目用于记录预录入单位名称。

45. 申报单位

自理报关的，本栏目填报进出口企业的名称及海关注册编码；委托代理报关的，本栏目填报经海关批准的报关企业名称及海关注册编码。

本栏目还包括报关单左下方用于填报申报单位有关情况的相关栏目，包括报关员、报关单位地址、邮政编码和电话号码等栏目。

46. 填制日期

本栏目填报申报单位填制报关单的日期。本栏目为8位数字，顺序为年（4位）、月（2位）、日（2位）。

47. 海关审单批注及放行日期（签章）

本栏目供海关作业时签注。

注：规范所述尖括号（<>）、逗号（,）、连接符（一）、冒号（:）等标点符号及数字，填报时都必须使用非中文状态下的半角字符。

五、出口收汇核销单缮制说明

出口收汇核销单一式三联：第一联为出口企业存根联；第二联正文部分，为外汇管理局留存；第三联为出口退税专用。出口收汇核销单各栏目填写如下。

1. 存根（第一联）

（1）编号。应与出口报关单的编号一致。由发放机关事先印好，无须出口商填写。

（2）出口单位。此栏填签订并执行合同的有出口经营权的外贸单位（包括外商投资企业）的全称。委托报关时，填委托单位名称；委托出口并以代理出口单位名义签订出口合同并负责收汇时，填代理出口单位名称；两个或两个以上单位联合出口时，填负责报关的出口单位的名称。

（3）单位代码。填写领取核销单的单位在外汇管理局备案的号码。

（4）出口币种总价。此栏填写出口成交货物总价及使用币种。

（5）收汇方式。按实际情况填信用证、托收、T/T 等收汇方式中的一种，并列明即期或远期，如远期收汇还须列明相应的远期收汇天数。

（6）预计收款日期。

该栏目一般情况下不填，只有当收汇日期超过报关日期后 180 天需要办理远期备案时，该栏目内容才由外汇局进行变更。

（7）报关日期。填海关放行日期，同出口报关单右上角的出单日期。

（8）备注。填写出口单位就该核销单项下需说明的事项。如已发生变更的出口商品项下的原核销单的编号等情况。

（9）有效期。

2．正联（第二联）

（1）编号。同存根。由外汇管理部门事先印好。

（2）出口单位。同存根。

（3）单位代码。同存根。

（4）银行签注栏（类别、币种金额、日期、公章）。由银行填写结算业务的类别（即收汇方式）、实际收汇金额币种、收汇日期及银行盖章。现在一般不填。

（5）海关签注栏。海关验放该核销单项下的出口货物后，在该栏目内加盖"放行"或"验讫"章，并填写放行日期。如遇退关，海关需在该栏目加盖有关更正章。

（6）外汇管理局签注栏。由外汇管理部门将核销单、报关单、发票等配对审核无误后，在该栏内签注意见，并由核销人员签字，加盖"已核销"章。

3．出口退税专用联（第三联）

（1）编号。同存根。

（2）出口单位。同存根。

（3）单位代码。同存根。

（4）货物名称。按实际出口品名填写，同发票、报关单。

（5）出口数量。按外包装数或件数填写，同发票、报关单。

（6）币种总价。按发票、报关单上总金额和币种填写，同存根。

（7）报关单编号。按实际情况填写。

（8）外汇局签注栏。同正联。

另外，需要注意的是：

①在存根联和正文连接处、正文和出口退税专用联连接处需要分别加盖出口企业公章（用于报关时）。

②在正文和出口退税专用联连接处需要盖海关验讫章（报关后）。

实训二　托收方式下出口单据缮制

实训目标

能够根据相关资料缮制托收方式下的出口单据。

实训任务

一、训练资料

(一)销售合同

ZHEJIANG TEXTILES IMP. & EXP. GROUPS
165 MIDDLE OF ZHONGHE ROAD, HANGZHOU, ZHEJIANG, CHINA

SALES CONTRACT

TO：JEVAN TRADING CO. ,　　　　　　　　　　　　　　　　NO. JT001
　　15 MARAHALL AVE　　　　　　　　　　　　DATE：JULY. 01, 2010
　　MONTREAL CANADA

Dear Sirs,

　　We hereby confirm having sold to you the following goods on terms and conditions as specified bellow：

Shipping mark	Descriptions of goods	quantity	Unit price	Amount
J T C MONTREAL C/NO. 1-260	TEATOWELS 100％COTTON 10″×10″ 20″×20″ 30″×30″	10,000DOZ 6,000 DOZ 10,000 DOZ	CIF MONTREAL USD1. 30/DOZ USD2. 50/DOZ USD4. 70/DOZ	USD13,000. 00 USD15,000. 00 USD47,000. 00
TOTAL：		26,000DOZ		USD75,000. 00

1. Terms of Payment：50％ L/C at Sight, 50％ D/P at Sight

2. Port of Loading：Shanghai, China

3. Port of Destination：Montreal

4. Latest Date of Shipment：Sep. 30, 2010

5. Partial Shipments and Transshipment：Allowed

6. Insurance：to be Covered by the Sellers for 110％ of Invoice Value Covering All Risks.

7. Certificate of Origin GSP China Form A, Issued by Entry-Exit Inspection and Quarantine Bureau.

THE BUYER：　　　　　　　　　　　　　　　　　　THE SELLER：
JEVAN TRADING CO.　　　　　　　ZHEJIANG TEXTILES IMP. & EXP. GROUPS

(二)补充资料

1. INVOICE NO.：HH1001，DATE：2010.09.05

2. PACKING

　　G.W.：2.5KGS/CTN

　　N.W.：2.0KGS/CTN

　　0.02CBM/CTN

　　PACKED IN CARTONS OF 100 DOZ EACH

　　TRANSPORTED IN ONE 20' CONTAINER NO. COSU112244

3. H.S. CODE：6302.5900

4. CERTIFICATE NO.：580511478

5. FREIGHT：USD1100.00

6. INSURANCE PREMIUM：USD900.00

7. VESSEL：HONGXING V.231

　　B/L NO.：COSCO1122

　　B/L DATE：SEP. 20，2010

8. 报检单位登记号：WE5566

9. 报检单编号：75861

10. 生产单位注册号：1223418056

11. 投保单编号：TB567

12. 发货人人民币账号：089877

13. 外币账号：MY567890012

14. 海关编号：23456

15. 境内货源地：浙江杭州

16. 生产厂家：浙江纺织品厂

二、训练要求

请以"单证员"身份,根据销售合同和补充资料缮制下列单据。

1.商业发票

ZHEJIANG TEXTILES IMP. & EXP. GROUPS
165 MIDDLE OF ZHONGHE ROAD, HANGZHOU, ZHEJIANG, CHINA

Commercial Invoice

TO:

INV. NO. : _____

DATE: _____

S/C NO. : _____

L/C NO. : _____

FROM _____ TO _____

MARKS & NOS.	DESCRIPTION OF GOODS	QUANTITY	UNIT PRICE	AMOUNT

TOTAL AMOUNT:

WE HEREBY CERTIFY THAT THE ABOVE MENTIONED
GOODS ARE OF CHINESE ORIGIN.

_____

2.装箱单

ZHEJIANG TEXTILES IMP. & EXP. GROUPS
165 MIDDLE OF ZHONGHE ROAD，HANGZHOU，ZHEJIANG，CHINA

Packing List

TO：

INV. NO. :＿＿＿＿＿＿＿＿

DATE：＿＿＿＿＿＿＿＿

S/C NO. :＿＿＿＿＿＿＿＿

L/C NO. :＿＿＿＿＿＿＿＿

CASE NOS.	MARKS & NOS.	QUANTITY & DESCRIPTION OF GOODS	G. W. (KGS)	N. W. (KGS)	MEAS. (CBM)
TOTAL:					

TOTAL：

＿＿＿＿＿＿＿＿＿＿

3. 汇票

凭
Drawn under ....

信用证
L/C No. ....

日 期　　　年　　月　　日
Dated ....

按　　　息　　付　　款
Payable with interest@ _____ % per annum

号码　　　　汇票金额　　　　　中国杭州　　　　　年　月　日
No. .... Exchange for ▓▓▓▓ Hangzhou, China 2010

见票　　　　　　　日　后　　（本 汇 票 之 副 本 未 付 ） 付
At .... sight of this FIRST of Exchange (Second of exchange being unpaid)

Pay to the order of ....

金额
The sum of ▓▓▓▓▓▓▓▓▓▓▓▓▓▓▓▓▓▓▓▓▓▓▓▓▓▓▓▓▓▓▓▓

此致
To ....

....

....

4.普惠制产地证明书申请书和普惠制产地证

(1)普惠制产地证明书申请书

普惠制产地证明书申请书

申请单位(盖章)　　　　　　　　　　　　　　　　　　　证书号：

注　册　号：

申请人郑重声明：

　　本人是被正式授权代表出口单位办理和签署本申请书的。

　　本申请书及普惠制产地证格式 A 所列内容正确无误,如发现弄虚作假,冒充格式 A 所列货物,擅改证书,自愿接受签证机关的处罚并负法律责任。现把有关情况申报如下：

生产单位		生产单位联系人电话		
商品名称 (中英文)		HS税目号 (以六位数码计)		
商品(FOB)总值(以美元计)	发票号	最终销售国	证书种类"√"	
			加急证书 (　　)	普通证书 (　　)

货物拟出运日期(以提单日期为准)

贸易方式和企业性质(请在适用处画"√")

正常贸易 C.	来料加工 L.	补偿贸易 B.	中外合资 H.	中外合作 Z.	外商独资 D.	零售 Y.	展卖 M.

毛重、包装数量或其他数量	

原产地标准：

本项商品系在中国生产,完全符合该给惠国方案规定,其原产地情况符合以下第 ＿＿＿＿ 条：

　　(1)"P"(完全国产,未使用任何进口原料)；

　　(2)"W"其 HS CODE 号为 ＿＿＿＿＿＿＿＿＿＿＿＿＿＿＿(含进口成份)；

　　(3)"F"(对加拿大出口产品,其进口成份不超过产品出厂价值的 40%)。

　　(4)"Y"　　　%

ZQ＊2 本批产品系:1.直接运输从 ＿＿＿＿＿＿ 到 ＿＿＿＿＿＿＿＿＿＿ ；

　　　　　　　　2.转口运输从 ＿＿＿＿＿＿ 中转国地区 ＿＿＿＿ 到 ＿＿＿＿＿＿ 。

申请人说明：	申请人(签名)： 电话： 日期：　　　年　　　月　　　日

　　现提交中国出口商业发票副本一份,普惠制产地证明书格式 A(FORM A)一正二副,以及其他附件＿＿＿＿份,请给予审核签证。

　　注:凡含有进口成份的商品,必须按要求提交《含进口成份受惠商品成本明细单》。

证书号：		申请单位：		领证人签收	
以下由商检填写：					
接单日期：		备注：			

(请凭此单领取证书,取证日期一般为本局接单之日后两天。)

（2）普惠制产地证

1. Goods consigned from (Exporter's business name,address,country)	Reference No. GENERALIZED SYSTEM OF PREFERENCES **CERTIFICATE OF ORIGIN** (Combined declaration and certificate) **FORM　A** Issued in THE PEOPLE'S REPUBLIC OF CHINA (Country)
2. Goods consigned to（Consignee's name, address,country)	
	See Notes overleaf
3. Means of transport and route (as far as known)	4. For official use

5. Item Number NOS.	6. Marks and NO. of Packages	7. Number and Kind of Package;Description of Goods	8. Origin Criterion (See Notes Overleaf)	9. Gross Weight or Other Quantity	10. Number and Date of Invoices

11. Certification It is hereby certified,on the basis of control carried out,that the declaration by the exporter is correct.	12.　Declaration by the exporter 　　The undersigned hereby declares that the above details and statements are correct; that all the goods were produced in CHINA 　　　　　　(country) and that they comply with the origin requirements specified of those goods in the Generalized System of Preferences for goods exported to ＿＿＿＿＿＿
⋯⋯⋯⋯⋯⋯⋯⋯⋯⋯⋯⋯ Place and date,signature and stamp of certifying authority	⋯⋯⋯⋯⋯⋯⋯⋯⋯⋯⋯⋯ Place and date, signature of authorized signatory

5.出境货物报检单

中华人民共和国出入境检验检疫

出境货物报检单

报检单位(加盖公章):   * 编号：_____

报检单位登记号：   联系人：   电话：   报检日期：   年   月   日

发货人	（中文）					
	（外文）					
收货人	（中文）					
	（外文）					
货物名称(中/外文)	H.S.编码		产地	数/重量	货物总值	包装种类及数量

运输工具名称号码		贸易方式		货物存放地点	
合同号		信用证号		用途	
发货日期		输往国家(地区)		许可证/审批证	
起运地		到达口岸		生产单位注册号	
集装箱规格、数量及号码					

合同、信用证订立的检验检疫条款或特殊要求	标记及号码	随附单据(画"√"或补填)	
		□合同	□包装性能结果单
		□信用证	□许可/审批文件
		□发票	□
		□换证凭单	□
		□装箱单	
		□厂检单	

需要证单名称(画"√"或补填)		* 检验检疫费	
□品质证书 ____正____副	□植物检疫证书 ____正____副	总金额	
□重量证书 ____正____副	□熏蒸/消毒证书 ____正____副	（元人民币）	
□数量证书 ____正____副	□出境货物换证凭单		
□兽医卫生证书 ____正____副	□	计费人	
□健康证书 ____正____副	□		
□卫生证书 ____正____副	□	收费人	
□动物卫生证书 ____正____副	□		

报检人郑重声明：	领取证单	
1.本人被授权报检。	日期	
2.上列填写内容正确属实,货物无伪造或冒用他人的厂名、标志、认证标志,并承担货物质量责任。		
签名：_____	签名	

注:有"*"号栏由出入境检验检疫机关填写   ◆国家出入境检验检疫局制

6.投保单和保险单

(1)投保单

中保财产保险有限公司浙江分公司

THE PEOPLE'S INSURANCE (PROPERTY) COMPANY OF CHINA, LTD. ZHEJIANG BRANCH

进出口货物运输保险投保单
APPLICATION FORM FOR I/E MARINE CARGO INSURANCE

被保险人 ASSURED'S NAME			
发票号码(出口用)或合同号码(进口用) INVOICE NO. OR CONTRACT NO.	包装数量 QUANTITY	保险货物项目 DESCRIPTION OF GOODS	保险金额 AMOUNT INSURED

装载运输工具　　　　　　　　航次、航班或车号　　　　　　开航日期
PER CONVEYANCE _____ VOY. NO. _____ SLG. DATE _____
自　　　　　至　　　　　转运地　　　　赔款地
FROM _____ TO _____ VIA _____ CLAIM PAYABLE AT _____

承保险别:
CONDITIONS &/OR
SPECIAL COVERAGE

投保人签章及公司名称、电话、地址
APPLICANT'S SIGNATURE AND CO.'S NAME, ADD. AND TEL. NO

备注:　　　　　　　　　投保日期
　　　　　　　　　　　　DATE

保险公司填写　　报单号:　　　　　费率:　　　　　核保人:

（2）保险单

中保财产保险有限公司

海洋货物运输保险单

发票号次	第一正本	保险单号次
INVOICE NO.	THE FIRST ORIGINAL	POLICY NO.

中 保 财 产 保 险 有 限 公 司 （ 以 下 简 称 本 公 司 ）
This Policy Of Insurance witnesses that People's Insurance Company of China(hereinafter called "the company")根据
At the request of _____
（ 以 下 简 称 被 保 险 人 ） 的 要 求 ， 由 被 保 险 人 向 本 公 司 缴 付 约 定
(hereinafter called the "Insured") and in consideration of the agreed premium being paid to the Company by
的 保 险 费 ， 按 照 本 保 险 单 承 保 险 别 和 背 面 所 载 条 款 与 下 列
the Insured, undertakes to insure the undermentioned goods in transportation subject to the conditions of this
特 殊 条 款 承 保 下 述 货 物 运 输 保 险 ， 特 立 本 保 险 单 。
Policy as per the Clauses printed overleaf and other special clauses attached hereon.

标 记 MARKS. & NOS.	包装及数量 QUANTITY	保险货物项目 DESCRIPTION OF GOODS	保险金额 AMOUNT INSURED

总 保 险 金 额：
Total Amount Insured _____

保费 _____ 费率 _____ 装载运输工具
Premium _____ Rate _____ Per Conveyance S. S. _____

开航日期 自 至
Slg on or abt. _____ From _____ To _____

承保险别：
Conditions

所 保 货 物 ， 如 遇 出 险 ， 本 公 司 凭 第 一 正 本 保 险 单 及 其 有 关 证 件 给
Claims, if any, payable on surrender of the first original of the Policy together with other relevant
付 赔 款 。 所 保 货 物 ， 如 发 生 本 保 险 单 项 下 负 责 赔 偿 的 损 失 或 事
Documents. In the event of accident whereby loss or damage may result in a claim under this Policy
故 ， 应 立 即 通 知 本 公 司 下 述 代 理 人 查 勘 。
Immediate notice applying for survey must be given to the Company's Agent as mentioned hereunder:

中保财产保险有限公司浙江分公司
The People'S Insurance(property) Company of China
Zhejiang Branch

赔款偿付地点
CLAIM PAYABLE AT _____
日期
DATE _____ × ×

7. 海运货物委托书和海运提单

(1)海运货物委托书

海运出口托运单

托运人 Shipper					
编号 No.			船名 S/S		
目的港 For					
唛头 Marks & Nos.	件数 Quantity	货名 Description of Goods	重量(千克)Weight(kilos)		
			净 Net	毛 Gross	
共计件数(大写) Total Number of Packages in Writing			运费付款方式 Mode of Freight Payment		
运费计算 Freight Charges			尺码 Measurement		
备注 Remarks					
抬头 Order of		可否转船 Transshipment		可否分批 Partial Shipment	
通知 Notify		装运期 Time of Shipment	有效期 Expiry Date		提单张数 Copies of B/L
		金额 Amount			
收货人 Consignee		银行编号 Bank No.		信用证号 L/C No.	

制单　　　　月　　　　日

（2）海运提单

Shipper		SINOTRANS B/L No.
Consignee or order		中国对外贸易运输总公司 CHINA NATIONAL FOREIGN TRADE TRANSPORTATION CORP. 直运或转船提单 **BILL OF LADING** **DIRECT OR WITH TRANSSHIPMENT**
Notify address		SHIPPED on board in apparent good order and condition（unless otherwise indicated）the goods or packages specified herein and to be discharged at the mentioned port of discharge or as near thereto as the vessel may safely get and be always afloat.
Pre-carriage by	Place of loading	The weight, measure, marks and numbers, quality, contents and value, being particulars furnished by the Shipper, are not checked by the carrier on loading.
Vessel	Port of transshipment	The Shipper, Consignee and the Holder of this Bill of Lading hereby expressly accept and agree to all printed, written or stamped provisions, exceptions and conditions of this Bill of Lading including those on the back hereof.
Port of discharge	Final destination	IN WITNESS Where of the number of original Bills of Lading stated below have been signed, one of which being accomplished, the other(s) to be void.

Container, seal No. or marks & Nos.	Number & kind of packages	Description of goods	Gross weight (kgs)	Measurement (m³)

ABOVE PARTICULARS FURNISHED BY SHIPPER

Freight & charges		Regarding transshipment information please contact

Ex. rate	Prepaid at	Freight payable at	Place and date of issue
	Total Prepaid	Number of original B(s)/L	Signed for or on behalf of the master as Agents

8. 出口货物报关单

中华人民共和国海关出口货物报关单

预录入编号： 海关编号：

出口口岸	备案号		出口日期		申报日期
经营单位	运输方式		运输工具名称		提/运单号
发货单位	贸易方式		征免性质		结汇方式
许可证号	运抵国(地区)		指运港		境内货源地
批准文号	成交方式	运费		保费	杂费
合同协议号	件数	包装种类		毛重(千克)	净重(千克)
集装箱号		随附单据		生产厂家	
标记唛码及备注					

项号	商品编号	商品名称、规格型号	数量及单位	最终目的地国(地区)	单价	总价	币制	征免

税费征收情况				
录入员	录入单位	兹声明以上申报无讹并承担法律责任	海关审单批注及放行日期(签单)	
			审单	审价
报关员 单位地址		申报单位(签章)	征税	统计
			查验	放行
邮编　　电话		填制日期		

未 经 核 销 此 联 不 得 撕 开

出口收汇核销单　出口退税专用

（浙）编号：

出口单位：

出口单位：

单位编码：

货物名称	数量	币种总价

报关单编号：

外汇局签注栏

年　月　日（盖章）

（出口单位盖章）

出口收汇核销单

（浙）编号：

出口单位：

单位编码：

	类别	币种金额	日期	盖章
签注栏				

海关签注栏：

外汇局签注栏

年　月　日（盖章）

（出口单位盖章）

9. 出口收汇核销单

出口收汇核销单　存根

（浙）编号：

出口单位：

单位编码：

出口币种总价：

收汇方式：

预计收款日期：

报关日期：

备注：

此单报关有效期截止到

❋ **实训指导**

一、普惠制产地证明书申请书缮制说明

普惠制产地证明书申请书是申请单位向检验检疫机构办理普惠制原产地证明书时需填写的专用申请表,其各栏目填制如下。

1. 申请单位(盖章)

填写申请单位全称并盖章。

2. 注册号

填写申请单位在当地检验检疫局产地证签证部门注册的编号。

3. 证书号

企业根据检验检疫局的编号规则,按顺序编号,不得重号或跳号。通常由出入境检验检疫局受理后填写。

4. 生产单位/联系人电话

填写这批出口商品的生产企业全称及联系人电话。

5. 商品名称

填写商品品名的中、英文,并且与发票的商品名称及 H. S. 税目号一致。

6. H. S 税目号(以六位数码计)

填写海关《商品编码协调制度》商品 H. S. 税目号(前六位数字)。

7. 商品(FOB)总值(以美元计)

根据申报的出口货物发票上所列的金额以 FOB 价格填写(以美元计),如出口货物不是以 FOB 价格成交,应换算成 FOB 价格。

8. 发票号

填所附发票的号码。

9. 最终销售国

填写出口商品的最终销售国家。

10. 证书种类画"√"

根据需要在"加急证书"和"普通证书"处画"√"即行。

11. 货物拟出运日期

填写货物离开启运口岸的当天日期(年月日)。

12. 贸易方式和企业性质(请在适用处画"√")

根据实际情况选择画"√"即行。

13. 包装数量、毛重或其他数量

填写该批出口货物的箱数、毛重或个数。

14. 原产地标准

根据提示及货物实际情况选择 1－4 项如实填写。符合"W"的,加填 H. S. 的税目号(前四位数字)。

15. "本批商品系"栏

填写本批货物的运输路线,如直接运输,填起运地到目的地;如为转运,则需加填中转

国家(地区)。

16. 提供单据

申请单位根据所提供单证画"√",如有提供其他相关单据,一并补填。

17. 申领员

由已在检验检疫局产地证部门注册备案的申领员签名,并填写申请单位的联系电话和申报日期。

二、海运出口托运单缮制说明

海运出口托运单各栏目的内容缮制如下。

1. 托运人(SHIPPER /CONSIGNOR)

一般情况下,填写出口公司的名称和地址。

2. 托运单编号(NO.)

一般填写商业发票的号码。

3. 目的港(FOR)

由出口企业按信用证的目的港填写。

4. 标记及号码(MARKS & NUMBERS)

信用证或买卖合同都规定了唛头,要求填写内容和形式与所规定的完全一致。

如果信用证和买卖合同中没有规定唛头,可填写"N/M"(无唛头),也可自行选择一个合适的唛头。

5. 件数(QUANTITY)

托运单的件数指最大包装的件数。

例如出口 5 万码布,分别捆成 50 捆,填写这一栏目时应是 50 捆而不是 5 万码。

如果出口货物有若干种,包装方式和材料完全不同,则应填写每种货物的最大包装件数。例如:20 个托盘,20 捆布匹,合计数量:40 件。

6. 货名(DESCRIPTION OF GOODS)

对这一栏目的填写允许只写大类名称或统称,应和信用证的要求一致。

如果同时出口几种不同的商品,应分别填写,而不允许只填写其中一种数量较多或金额较大的商品。

7. 重量(GROSS WEIGHT/NET WEIGHT)

重量应分别计算毛重和净重。计量单位是公吨或千克。

8. 运费付款方式

托运单上一般不显示具体运费,只填写"运费待付"或"运费预付/已付"。

9. 尺码(MEASUREMENT)

该栏目填写一批货的尺码总数,一般单位是立方米。

10. 收货人(CONSIGNEE)

按信用证要求填制,具体参考海运提单该栏目的填制方法。

11. 通知(NOTIFY)

填写接受船方所发货到通知的人的名称与地址。

具体参考海运提单该栏目的填制方法。

12. 可否分批(PARTIAL SHIPMENTS)

应严格按照合同或信用证条款填写。填写的内容限在"允许"、"不允许"两者中取一。

如果合同或信用证规定分若干批,或对分批有进一步说明,不要将这些说明填入本栏目,而应将这些说明填入"备注"类的栏目中。

13. 可否转船(TRANSHIPMENT)

填写要求与分批一致,只能在"允许"和"不允许"两者中取一。

14. 装运期(TIME OF SHIPMENT)

装运期的表示可以全部使用阿拉伯数字,也可以使用英文与阿拉伯数字一起表示。

15. 有效期(EXPIRY DATE)

按信用证规定填写。

16. 提单份数

需要船公司提供的提单份数应考虑信用证和合同的要求以及自己的需要,包括正本提单份数和副本提单份数。

如要求"3 ORIGINAL BILLS OF LADING",指 3 份正本提单;

"ORIGINAL BILL OF LADING IN 3",指 3 份正本提单;

"FULL SET OF BILL OF LADING",指全套提单。可以是 2 份,也可以是 3 份。

提单副本份数＝出口企业留底份数＋寄单所需份数＋信用证对副本提单要求的份数。

17. 信用证号

填写信用证号码。

18. 备注

填写信用证或合同中有关运输方面的特殊要求。

三、投保单缮制说明

投保单一般是保险人根据不同险种事先设计的。各保险公司投保单格式不完全一致,其各栏目的内容缮制如下。

1. 被保险人(Insured)

一般填出口商的名称。若信用证要求保险单做成指示抬头,即"to order",则在被保险人栏内填"to order";若信用证要求以特定方(如开证行或开证申请人)为被保险人,则该栏内填特定方的名称。

2. 唛头(Marks & Nos.)

保险单上标记应与发票、提单上一致,也可简单填成"as per Invoice No. ×××"。

3. 包装及数量(Quantity)

有包装的填写最大包装件数;裸装货物要注明本身件数;煤炭、石油等散装货则注明"in bulk",然后填写净重;有包装但以重量计价的,应把包装重量(数量)与计价重量都注上。

4. 货物名称(Description of Goods)

允许用统称,但不同类别的多种货物应注明不同类别的各自总称。这里与提单此栏目的填写一致。

5. 保险金额(Amount Insured)

保险金额的加成百分比应严格按信用证或合同规定掌握。如未规定,应按 CIF 或 CIP

发票价格的 110% 投保。保险金额不要小数，出现小数时采用"进一取整"的填法。所用币种应与发票一致。

6. 装载运输工具(Per Conveyance S. S)

该栏应填写装载的运输工具。海运方式下填写船名，最好再加航次。如需转船，应分别填写一程船名及二程船名，中间用"/"隔开；如果第二程船名未知，则只需打上"转船"字样。铁路运输则填"By railway(Train)"，最好再加车号，即"By railway(Train)，Wagon No.×××"；航空运输则填"By air"，邮包运输则填"By parcel post"。

7. 开航日期(Slg on or abt.)

应按 B/L 中的签发日期填写，还可以简单地填作"AS PER B/L"。

8. 发票或提单号(Invoice No. or B/L No.)

填写相应的发票号码或提单号码。

9. 赔款偿付地点(Claim Payable at)

严格按照信用证规定打制；若来证未规定，则应打目的港。如信用证规定不止一个目的港或赔付地，则应全部照打。有些信用证规定在偿付地点后注明偿付货币名称，如"AT NEW YORK IN USD"。若信用证要求，如发生货损，赔款给某某公司，则在赔款地点后加注"PAY TO ×××CO."。赔款货币一般为投保额相同的货币。

10. 起讫地点或装运港、目的港(From. . . to. . .)

起点填装运港名称，讫点填目的港名称，中途需转船的应注明中转港。如，"From Ningbo to Rotterdam W/T Hong Kong"。若提单上目的港为美国长滩，来证规定投保至芝加哥，则起讫地点应填"From Ningbo to Long Beach and Thence to Chicago"。

11. 承保险别(Conditions)

应严格按照信用证规定的险别投保。如信用证没有具体规定险别，则可投保最低险别平安险"FPA"。

12. 投保人签字(Signature)

一般应包括投保人名称和法人代表的签字或印章。

13. 投保日期(Applicant's Date)

指填写投保单的日期。保险手续要求货物离开出口仓库前办理。投保单的日期不应迟于提单签发日、货物发运日或接受监管日。

14. 其他

根据信用证的要求在保险单上加注其他说明。如"所有单据注明信用证号码、开证日期和开证行名称"、"保险单上显示保险公司在目的地的保险代理人名称、地址、联系方法"等。

赔付代理人(Claim Settling Agent)：一般选择在目的港或目的港附近有关机构为货损检验、理赔代理人，并详细注明代理人的地址。如果保险单上注明保险责任终止是在内地而非港口，则应填列内地代理人名址。如当地无中国人民保险公司的代理机构，可以注明由当地法定检验机构代为检验。如果信用证自行指定买方选择的代理人，则不应接受。

实训三　信用证方式 FOB 下出口单据缮制

🌣 实训目标

能够根据相关资料缮制信用证方式 FOB 下的出口单据。

🌣 实训任务

一、训练资料

(一)销售合同

ZHEJIANG　COCO　CO.，LTD.

110 TIYU CHANG ROAD HANGZHOU CHINA

SALES CONTRACT

TO：YAGI AND CO.，LTD. TOKYO BRANCH.　　　　　NO.：20100001

SEC：417 SUMISEI NIHONBASHI　　　　　　　　DATE：APRIL 24,2010

KOAMICHO BLDG. 14-1 KOAMICHO　　　　　　Tel：78556431

NIHONBASHI CHUO-KU TOKYO JAPAN

Dear Sirs,

We hereby confirm having sold to you the following goods on terms and conditions as specified bellow：

Shipping mark	Descriptions of goods	quantity	Unit price	Amount
N/M	T-SHIRTS 504002-A 504002-B	 5000PCS 3000PCS	FOB SHANGHAI USD1.34/PC USD1.34/PC	 USD6,700.00 USD4,020.00
TOTAL：		8000PCS		USD10,720.00

1. Terms of Payment：L/C AT SIGHT，PAYABLE BY NEGOTIATION WITH ANY BANK

2. Port of Loading：SHANGHAI, CHINA

3. Port of Destination：JAPANESE PORT

4. Latest Date of Shipment：MAY. 25，2010

5. Partial Shipment：ALLOWED　　　　　Transshipment：NOT ALLOWED

6. Insurance：TO BE COVERED BY THE BUYERS.

7. 5PCT More or Less in Quantity and Amount is Allowed.

THE BUYER：　　　　　　　　　　　　　　　THE SELLER：

YAGI AND CO.，LTD. TOKYO BRANCH.　　　　ZHEJIANG COCO CO.，LTD.

JOHN　　　　　　　　　　　　　　　　　　　王斌

（二）信用证

APPLICATION HEADER： MIZUHO BANK LTD.
                    TOKYO
SEQUENCE OF CREDIT： 1/1
FORM OF DOC. CREDIT： IRREVOCABLE
DOC. CREDIT NUMBER： 30-0031-152303
DATE OF ISSUE： 100428
EXPIRY： DATE100601 PLACE NEGOTIATING BANK
APPLICANT： YAGI AND CO., LTD. TOKYO BRANCH.
          SEC：417 SUMISEI NIHONBASHI
          KOAMICHO BLDG. 14-1 KOAMICHO
          NIHONBASHI CHUO-KU TOKYO JAPAN
BENEFICIARY： ZHEJIANG COCO CO., LTD.
            110 TIYU CHANG ROAD HANGZHOU CHINA
AMOUNT： CURRENCY USD AMOUNT 10,836.58
POS./NEG. TOL.(%)： 05/05
AVAILABLE WITH/BY： ANY BANK
                  BY NEGOTIATION
DRAFTS AT...： BENEFICIARY'S DRAFT(S)
             AT SIGHT
             FOR FULL INVOICE COST
DRAWEE： MIZUHO BANK LTD.
        TOKYO
PARTIAL SHIPMENTS： ALLOWED
TRANSSHIPMENT： PROHIBITED
LOADING IN CHARGE：
        SHIPMENT FROM SHANGHAI PORT
FOR TRANSPORT TO...：
        FOR TRANSPORTATION TO JAPANESE PORT
LATEST DATE OF SHIP.： 100525
DESCRIPT. OF GOODS： T-SHIRTS

CONTRACT NO.	ITEM	QUANTITY	UNIT PRICE
20100001	504002-A	5000PCS	USD1.34
20100001	504002-B	3000PCS	USD1.34

        FOB SHANGHAI PORT
DOCUMENTS REQUIRED：
    +SIGNED COMMERCIAL INVOICE IN 2 COPIES, STATING APPLICANT'S RE-
    FER NO. IM417H1533
    +3/3 SET OF CLEAN ON BOARD MARINE BILLS OF LADING AND/OR

COMBINED TRANSPORT B/L MADE OUT TO ORDER OF YAGI AND CO., LTD., NOTIFY APPLICANT, INDICATING CREDIT NUMBER, EACH MARKED FREIGHT COLLECT

+PACKING LIST IN 2 COPIES

+BENEFICIARY'S CERTIFICATE IN 2 COPIES WITH RELATIVE COURIER RECEIPT STATING THAT: 2 SETS OF TYPED AND SIGNED NON-NEGOTIABLE SHIPPING DOCUMENTS HAVE BEEN SENT TO ACCOUNTEE BY COURIER WITHIN 2 DAYS AFTER SHIPMENT

ADDITIONAL COND. :

1) 5PCT MORE OR LESS IN QUANTITY AND AMOUNT IS ALLOWED

2) INVOICE TO BE SPECIFIED COUNTRY OF ORIGIN

3) INVOICE TO BE STATED FOLLOWS:

　BREAKDOWN FOR EACH ITEM

　TOTAL NET/GROSS WEIGHT

4) PACKING LIST TO BE STATED FOLLOWS:

　QUANTITY FOR EACH ITEM IN EACH CARTON

5) OCEAN B/L INDICATING L/C NO.

6) SHIPPING ADVICE SHOULD BE SENT BEFORE TYPED INVOICE AND PACKING LIST, B/L DIRECTLY TO ACCOUNTEE BY FAX(NO. 813-3667-4130)(ATTN. MR. INAGAKI SEC. 382) WITHIN 24 HOURS AFTER SHIPMENT ADVISING L/C NO. / VESSEL NO. / OPEN COVER NO. / QUANTITY /AMOUNT/ B/L NO. BY SHIPPER

7) SHIPMENT SHOULD BE EFFECTED BY CONTAINER VESSEL.

8) SHIPMENT MUST BE EFFECTED THRU AIT CORP., SHANGHAI OFFICE(ATTN: MR. ZHOU JIE TEL: 021-5356-0651) AND CLEAN ON BOARD MULTIMODAL TRANSPORT B/L OF AIT CORP IS ALSO ACCEPTABLE

9) INSURANCE HAS BEEN EFFECTED BY APPLICANT

10) INSTRUCTION TO THE NEGOTIATING BANK:

NEGOTIATING BANK MUST FORWARD NEGOTIATED DOCUMENTS TO MIZUHO BANK, LTD., HEAD OFFICE(ADDRESS: UCHISAIWAICHO, CHOME, CHIYODA-KU, TOKYO, JAPAN)

DETAILS OF CHARGES:　ALL BANK CHARGES OUTSIDE JAPAN

　　　　　　　　　　ARE FOR THE BENEFICIARY'S ACCOUNT

PRESENTATION PERIOD: DOCUMENT MUST BE PRESENTED WITHIN 15

　　　　　　　　　　DAYS AFTER THE DATE OF SHIPMENT BUT

　　　　　　　　　　WITHIN THE VALIDITY OF THIS CREDIT

CONFIRMATION:　　　WITHOUT

INSTRUCTIONS:　　　INSTRUCTIONS TO THE NEGOTIATING BANK:

　UPON RECEIPT OF THE ORIGINAL DOCUMENTS IN ORDER, WE

SHALL REIMBURSE YOU BY REMITTING THE AMOUNT CLAIMED TO YOUR DESIGNATED ACCOUNT.

ALL DOCUMENTS MUST BE AIRMAILED TO US IN ONE LOT BY REGISTERED MAIL.

A DISCREPANCY FEE WILL BE DEDUCTED/CHARGED IF DOCUMENTS ARE PRESENTED WITH DISCREPANCIES

(三)补充资料

1. 商业发票号码为:IVO 346

2. 商业发票的日期:2010 年 5 月 8 日

3. 合同日期:2010 年 4 月 24 日

4. 船名:XINGXING V. 123

　装船日期:2010 年 5 月 15 日

　目的港:东京(TOKYO)

　提单号码:AIT123

5. 预约保险单号码:OC123

6. 商品:T-SHIRT 504002A　5000PCS 装成 50 个纸箱,每箱 100 件,每箱净重 5.5KGS,毛重 5.6KGS,箱子的规格为 30×40×50CM,单价 USD 1.34。

　T-SHIRT 504002B　3000PCS 装成 30 个纸箱,每箱 100 件,每箱净重 5.8KGS,毛重 5.9KGS,箱子的规格为 30×40×50CM,单价 USD 1.34。

　拼箱,装入 20 英尺集装箱,集装箱号码为 COSCO771120

7. H. S. CODE:6206.4000

8. 报检单位登记号:125566

9. 报检单编号:1234

10. 生产单位注册号:3452338654

11. 发货人人民币账号:089877

12. 外币账号:MY567890012

13. 海关编号:12445667

14. 境内货源地:浙江杭州

15. 生产厂家:浙江纺织品厂

二、训练要求

根据上述信用证和合同资料缮制下列有关单据。

1. 商业发票

ZHEJIANG COCO CO. ,LTD.

110 TIYU CHANG ROAD HANGZHOU CHINA

Commercial Invoice

TO：

INV. NO. :＿＿＿＿＿＿＿＿

DATE：＿＿＿＿＿＿＿＿

S/C NO. :＿＿＿＿＿＿＿＿

L/C NO. :＿＿＿＿＿＿＿＿

FROM ＿＿＿＿＿＿＿＿ TO ＿＿＿＿＿＿＿＿

MARKS & NOS.	DESCRIPTION OF GOODS	QUANTITY	UNIT PRICE	AMOUNT

TOTAL AMOUNT：

2.装箱单

ZHEJIANG COCO CO. ,LTD.

110 TIYU CHANG ROAD HANGZHOU CHINA

Packing List

TO：

INV. NO. : _____

DATE：_____

S/C NO. : _____

L/C NO. : _____

CASE NOS.	MARKS & NOS.	QUANTITY & DESCRIPTION OF GOODS	G. W. (KGS)	N. W. (KGS)	MEAS. (CBM)
TOTAL：					

TOTAL：

3. 汇票

凭
Drawn under ....
信用证
L/C No. ....
日期　　年　月　日
Dated ....
按　　　息　　付　　款
Payable with interest@ _____ % per annum

号码	汇票金额	中国杭州		年　月　日
No.	Exchange for ▓▓▓▓	Hangzhou，China		2010 ....

见票　　　　　　日　后　　　（本　汇　票　之　副　本　未　付）　付
At .... sight of this FIRST of Exchange (Second of exchange being unpaid)

Pay to the order of ....
金额
The sum of ▓▓▓▓▓▓▓▓▓▓▓▓▓▓▓▓▓▓▓▓▓▓
此致
To ....

....

....

4. 海运提单

Shipper	SINOTRANS B/L No.
Consignee or order	中国对外贸易运输总公司 CHINA NATIONAL FOREIGN TRADE TRANSPORTATION CORP. 直运或转船提单 **BILL OF LADING** **DIRECT OR WITH TRANSSHIPMENT**
Notify address	SHIPPED on board in apparent good order and condition (unless otherwise indicated) the goods or packages specified herein and to be discharged at the mentioned port of discharge or as near thereto as the vessel may safely get and be always afloat.

SHIPPED on board in apparent good order and condition (unless otherwise indicated) the goods or packages specified herein and to be discharged at the mentioned port of discharge or as near thereto as the vessel may safely get and be always afloat.

The weight, measure, marks and numbers, quality, contents and value, being particulars furnished by the Shipper, are not checked by the carrier on loading.

The Shipper, Consignee and the Holder of this Bill of Lading hereby expressly accept and agree to all printed, written or stamped provisions, exceptions and conditions of this Bill of Lading including those on the back hereof.

IN WITNESS Where of the number of original Bills of Lading stated below have been signed, one of which being accomplished, the other(s) to be void.

Pre-carriage by	Place of loading
Vessel	Port of transshipment
Port of discharge	Final destination

Container, seal No. or marks & Nos.	Number & kind of packages	Description of goods	Gross weight (kgs)	Measurement (m³)

ABOVE PARTICULARS FURNISHED BY SHIPPER

Freight & charges	Regarding transshipment information please contact

Ex. rate	Prepaid at	Freight payable at	Place and date of issue
	Total Prepaid	Number of original B(s)/L	Signed for or on behalf of the master as Agents

5.装船通知

ZHEJIANG COCO CO. ,LTD.

110 TIYU CHANG ROAD HANGZHOU CHINA

SHIPPING ADVICE

TO：   DATE：

RE：L/C NO.   INVOICE NO.

WE HEREBY INFORMED YOU THAT THE GOODS UNDER THE ABOVE MENTIONED
CREDIT HAVE BEEN SHIPPED. THE DETAILS OF SHIPMENT ARE STATED BELOW.

COMMODITY：

QUANTITY：

INVOICE VALUE：

OCEAN VESSEL/ SHIPPED PER S. S. ：

DATE OF SHIPMENT：

PORT OF LOADING：

PORT OF DESTINATION：

MARKS：

                                                                      Signature

6. 受益人证明

ZHEJIANG COCO CO. ,LTD.

110 TIYU CHANG ROAD HANGZHOU CHINA

BENEFICIARY'S STATEMENT

TO：   DATE：

            RE：L/C NO.   INVOICE NO.

WE HEREBY CERTIFY THAT...

                                                  ....

7. 出境货物报检单

中华人民共和国出入境检验检疫

出境货物报检单

报检单位(加盖公章):　　　　　　　　　　　　　　　　* 编号:＿＿＿＿＿＿＿＿

报检单位登记号:　　　联系人:　　　电话:　　　　报检日期:　　年　月　日

发货人	(中文)				
	(外文)				
收货人	(中文)				
	(外文)				
货物名称(中/外文)	H.S. 编码	产地	数/重量	货物总值	包装种类及数量

运输工具名称号码		贸易方式		货物存放地点	
合同号		信用证号		用途	
发货日期		输往国家(地区)		许可证/审批证	
起运地		到达口岸		生产单位注册号	

集装箱规格、数量及号码

合同、信用证订立的检验检疫条款或特殊要求	标记及号码	随附单据(画"√"或补填)
		□合同　　　　　　□包装性能结果单 □信用证　　　　　□许可/审批文件 □发票　　　　　　□ □换证凭单　　　　□ □装箱单　　　　　□ □厂检单

需要证单名称(画"√"或补填)		* 检验检疫费
□品质证书　　＿＿正＿＿副　□植物检疫证书　　＿＿正＿＿副 □重量证书　　＿＿正＿＿副　□熏蒸/消毒证书　＿＿正＿＿副 □数量证书　　＿＿正＿＿副　□出境货物换证凭单 □兽医卫生证书　＿＿正＿＿副　□ □健康证书　　＿＿正＿＿副　□ □卫生证书　　＿＿正＿＿副　□ □动物卫生证书　＿＿正＿＿副　□		总金额 (元人民币) 计费人 收费人

报检人郑重声明:	领取证单
1.本人被授权报检。 2.上列填写内容正确属实,货物无伪造或冒用他人的厂名、标志、认证标志,并承担货物质量责任。 　　　　　　　　　签名:＿＿＿＿＿＿	日期 签名

注:有"＊"号栏由出入境检验检疫机关填写　　　　　　◆国家出入境检验检疫局制

8. 出口货物报关单

中华人民共和国海关出口货物报关单

预录入编号：   海关编号：

出口口岸	备案号		出口日期		申报日期
经营单位	运输方式		运输工具名称		提/运单号
发货单位	贸易方式		征免性质		结汇方式
许可证号	运抵国（地区）		指运港		境内货源地
批准文号	成交方式	运费		保费	杂费
合同协议号	件数	包装种类		毛重（千克）	净重（千克）
集装箱号		随附单据		生产厂家	
标记唛码及备注					

项号	商品编号	商品名称、规格型号	数量及单位	最终目的地国（地区）	单价	总价	币制	征免

税费征收情况

录入员	录入单位	兹声明以上申报无讹并承担法律责任	海关审单批注及放行日期（签单）	
			审单	审价
报关员 单位地址		申报单位（签章）	征税	统计
			查验	放行
邮编 电话		填制日期		

9. 出口收汇核销单

未经核销此联不得撕开

出口收汇核销单

存根

（浙）编号：

（出口单位盖章）

出口单位：

单位编码：

出口币种总价：

收汇方式：

预计收款日期：

报关日期：

备注：

此单报关有效期截止到

出口收汇核销单

（浙）编号：

（出口单位盖章）

出口单位：

单位编码：

签注栏	类别	币种金额	日期	盖章

海关签注栏：

外汇局签注栏

年　　月　　日（盖章）

出口收汇核销单
出口退税专用

（浙）编号：

（出口单位盖章）

出口单位：

单位编码：

货物名称	数量	币种总价

报关单编号：

外汇局签注栏

年　　月　　日（盖章）

实训四 信用证方式 CFR 下出口单据缮制

实训目标

能够根据相关资料缮制信用证方式 CFR 下的出口单据。

实训任务

一、训练资料

(一)销售合同

SHANGHAI GARDEN PRODUCTS IMP. AND EXP. CO., LTD.

27 ZHONGSHAN DONGYI ROAD, SHANGHAI, CHINA

SALES CONTRACT

TO: LAIKI PERAGORA ORPHANIDES LTD.,   NO. E03FD121.
    020 STRATIGOU TIMAGIA AVE.,   DATE: JAN. 01, 2010
    6046, LARNAKA, CYPRUS

Dear Sirs,

    We hereby confirm having sold to you the following goods on terms and conditions as specified bellow:

Shipping mark	Descriptions of goods	quantity	Unit price	Amount
L. P. O. L. DC NO. 186/06/10014 MADE IN CHINA NO. 1-325	WOODEN FLOWER STANDS WOODEN FLOWER POTS	350 PCS 600PCS	CFR LIMASSOL PORT USD8. 90/PC USD5. 00/PC	USD3115. 00 USD3000. 00
TOTAL:		950PCS		USD6115. 00

1. Terms of Payment: L/C AT SIGHT BY NEGOTIATION WITH ANY BANK.

2. Port of Loading: SHANGHAI, CHINA

3. Port of Destination: LIMASSOL PORT

4. Latest Date of Shipment: FEB. 14, 2010

5. Partial Shipment and Transshipment: ALLOWED

6. Insurance: TO BE COVERED BY THE BUYERS

THE BUYER: THE SELLER:
LAIKI PERAGORA ORPHANIDES LTD.   SHANGHAI GARDEN PRODUCTS IMP. AND EXP. CO., LTD.
JOHNSON   王燕

（二）信用证

```
ISSUING BANK：CYPRUS POPULAR BANK LTD, LARNAKA
ADVISING BANK：BANK OF CHINA, SHANGHAI BRANCH.
SEQUENCE OF TOTAL      *27：1/1
FORM OF DOC. CREDIT    *40A：IRREVOCABLE
DOC. CREDIT NUMBER     *20：186/06/10014
DATE OF ISSUE          31C：100105
EXPIRY                 *31D：DATE100228 PLACE CHINA
APPLICANT              *50：LAIKI PERAGORA ORPHANIDES LTD.，
                           020 STRATIGOU TIMAGIA AVE.，
                           6046，LARNAKA，CYPRUS
BENEFICIARY    *59：SHANGHAI GARDEN PRODUCTS IMP. AND EXP.
               CO.，LTD.
               27 ZHONGSHAN DONGYI ROAD, SHANGHAI, CHINA
AMOUNT                 *32B：CURRENCY USD AMOUNT 6115.00
POS. / NEG. TOL.（％）   39A：05/05
AVAILABLE WITH/BY      *41D：ANY BANK BY NEGOTIATION
DRAFT AT...            42C：AT SIGHT
DRAWEE                 *42D：LIKICY2NXXX
                           CYPRUS POPULAR BANK LTD
                           LARNAKA
PARTIAL SHIPMENTS      43P：ALLOWED
TRANSSHIPMENT          43T：ALLOWED
LOADING IN CHARGE      44A：SHANGHAI PORT
FOR TRANSPORT TO....   44B：LIMASSOL PORT
LATEST DATE OF SHIP.   44C：100214
DESCRIPT. OF GOODS     45A：
    WOODEN FLOWER STANDS AND WOODEN FLOWER POTS
    AS PER S/C NO. E03FD121.
    CFR LIMASSOL PORT，INCOTERMS 2000
DOCUMENTS REQUIRED   46A：
    +COMMERCIAL INVOICE IN QUADRUPLICATE ALL STAMPED AND
    SIGNED BY BENEFICIARY CERTIFYING THAT THE GOODS ARE OF
    CHINESE ORIGIN AND THAT THE CONTENT IS TRUE AND CORRECT.
    +FULL SET OF CLEAN ON BOARD BILL OF LADING MADE OUT TO
    ORDER OF SHIPPER AND BLANK ENDORSED，MARKED FREIGHT PRE-
    PAID AND NOTIFY APPLICANT，INDICATING L/C NO.
    +PACKING LIST IN TRIPLICATE SHOWING PACKING DETAILS SUCH
```

AS CARTON NO. AND CONTENTS OF EACH CARTON.

+ CERTIFICATE STAMPED AND SIGNED BY BENEFICIARY STATING THAT THE ORIGIAL INVOICE AND PACKING LIST HAVE BEEN DISPATCHED TO THE APPLICANT BY COURIER SERVICE 2 DAYS BEFORE SHIPMENT.

ADDITIONAL COND.   47A：

+ EACH PACKING UNIT BEARS AN INDELIBLE MARK INDICATING THE COUNTRY OF ORIGIN OF THE GOODS. PACKING LIST TO CERTIFY THIS.

+INSURANCE IS BEING ARRANGED BY THE BUYER.

+ A USD50.00 DISCREPANCY FEE, FOR BENEFICIARY'S ACCOUNT, WILL BE DEDUCTED FROM THE REIMBURSEMENT CLAIM FOR EACH PRESENTATION OF DISCREPANT DOCUMENTS UNDER THIS CREDIT.

+ THIS CREDIT IS SUBJECT TO THE U. C. P. FOR DOCUMENTARY CREDITS (2007 REVISION) I. C. C., PUBLICATION NO. 600.

DETAILS OF CHARGES   71B：ALL BANK CHARGES OUTSIDE CYPRUS ARE FOR THE ACCOUNT OF THE BENEFICIARY.

PRESENTATION PERIOD   48：WITHIN 15 DAYS AFTER THE DATE OF SHIPMENT BUT WITHIN THE VALIDITY OF THE CREDIT.

CONFIRMATION   ＊49：WITHOUT

INSTRUCTION   78：ON RECEIPT OF DOCUMENTS CONFIRMING TO THE TERMS OF THIS DOCUMENTARY CREDIT, WE UNDERTAKE TO REIMBURSE YOU IN THE CURRENCY OF THE CREDIT IN ACCORDANCE WITH YOUR INSTRUCTIONS, WHICH SHOULD INCLUDE YOUR UID NUMBER AND THE ABA CODE OF THE RECEIVING BANK.

(三)相关资料

1. 发票号码:06SHGD3029   发票日期:2010 年 2 月 9 日
2. 提单号码:SHYZ042234   提单日期:2010 年 2 月 12 日
3. 船名:LT USODIMARE   航次:V. 021W
4. 集装箱号码: FSCU3214999   集装箱封号: 1295312
   1×20'FCL，CY/CY

5. 商品：

木花架，WOODEN FLOWER STANDS，H. S. CODE：44219090，中国制造

QUANTITY：350PCS，USD8.90/PC，2pcs/箱，共175箱。纸箱尺码:66×22×48cms。

毛重:11KGS/箱，净重:9KGS/箱。

木花桶，WOODEN FLOWER POTS，H. S. CODE：44219090，中国制造

QUANTITY：600PCS，USD5.00/PC，4pcs/箱，共150箱。纸箱尺码:42×42×45cms。

毛重:15KGS/箱，净重:13KGS/箱。

6. 受益人证明签发日期:2010年2月10日

7. 报检单位联系电话:88776655

8. 报检单位登记号:775566

9. 报检单编号:7856

10. 生产单位注册号:1234545671

11. 申请单位注册号:LL781120

12. 国际运费:900美元

13. 海关编号:55566

14. 境内货源地:上海

15. 生产厂家:上海园林用品进出口有限公司(7712312342)

16. 报关员:陈列　　　电话:87865544

17. 随附单据:出口货物通关单(5711888844)

二、训练要求

请以"单证员"身份,根据销售合同和补充资料缮制下列单据。

1. 商业发票

Issuer：(1)	上海园林用品进出口有限公司 SHANGHAI GARDEN PRODUCTS IMP. AND EXP. CO., LTD. 27 Zhongshan Dongyi Road，Shanghai，China

COMMERCIAL INVOICE

To：(2)		
	NO. (4)	Date (5)
Transport details：(3) From　　　　To Partial Shipments： Transshipment： By	Terms of Payment (6)	L/C No. (7)
	Country of Origin (8)	

Marks & Nos	Description of Goods	Quantity	Unit Price	Amount
(9)	(10)	(11)	(12)	(13)

TOTAL：(14)

(15)

(16) Signature

2.装箱单

Issuer：	上海园林用品进出口有限公司
	SHANGHAI GARDEN PRODUCTS
	IMP. AND EXP. CO. , LTD.
	27 Zhongshan Dongyi Road，Shanghai，China
To：	**PACKING LIST**

Invoice No.	Date

Marks & Nos.	Description of goods； kind and number of package	Gross Weight	Net Weight	Measurement

3.海运货物委托书和海运提单

(1)海运货物委托书

海运出口托运单

托运人 Shipper					
编号 No.			船名 S/S		
目的港 For					
唛头 Marks & Nos.	件数 Quantity	货名 Description of Goods	重量(千克)Weight(kilos)		
			净 Net	毛 Gross	
共计件数(大写) Total Number of Packages in Writing			运费付款方式 Mode of Freight Payment		
运费计算 Freight Charges			尺码 Measurement		
备注 Remarks					
抬头 Order of		可否转船 Transshipment		可否分批 Partial Shipment	
通知 Notify		装运期 Time of Shipment	有效期 Expiry Date	提单张数 Copies of B/L	
		金额 Amount			
收货人 Consignee		银行编号 Bank No.		信用证号 L/C No.	

制单　　　　月　　　　日

(2)海运提单

Shipper	SINOTRANS	B/L No.

中国对外贸易运输总公司
CHINA NATIONAL FOREIGN TRADE TRANSPORTATION CORP.
直运或转船提单
BILL OF LADING
DIRECT OR WITH TRANSSHIPMENT

Consignee or order	

SHIPPED on board in apparent good order and condition（unless otherwise indicated）the goods or packages specified herein and to be discharged at the mentioned port of discharge or as near thereto as the vessel may safely get and be always afloat.

Notify address	

The weight，measure，marks and numbers，quality，contents and value，being particulars furnished by the Shipper，are not checked by the carrier on loading.

Pre-carriage by	Place of loading

The Shipper, Consignee and the Holder of this Bill of Lading hereby expressly accept and agree to all printed，written or stamped provisions，exceptions and conditions of this Bill of Lading including those on the back hereof.

Vessel	Port of transshipment

IN WITNESS Where of the number of original Bills of Lading stated below have been signed，one of which being accomplished, the other(s) to be void.

Port of discharge	Final destination

Container, seal No. or marks & Nos.	Number & kind of packages	Description of goods	Gross weight (kgs)	Measurement (m³)

ABOVE PARTICULARS FURNISHED BY SHIPPER

Freight & charges	Regarding transshipment information please contact

Ex. rate	Prepaid at	Freight payable at	Place and date of issue
	Total Prepaid	Number of original B(s)/L	Signed for or on behalf of the master as Agents

4. 汇票

凭
Drawn under ....

信用证
L/C No. ....

日期　　　年　　月　　日
Dated ....

按　　　息　　付　　款
Payable with interest@ _____ % per annum

号码　　　汇票金额　　　　　　　中国上海　　　　　年　月　　日
No. .... Exchange for ▨▨▨▨ Shanghai, China 2010

见票　　　　　　　日　后　　　（本　汇　票　之　副　本　未　付）　付
At .... sight of this FIRST of Exchange (Second of exchange being unpaid)

Pay to the order of ....

金额
The sum of ▨▨▨▨▨▨▨▨▨▨▨▨▨▨▨▨▨▨▨▨▨▨▨▨▨▨▨

此致
To ....

....

....

5. 受益人证明

SHANGHAI GARDEN PRODUCTS IMP. AND EXP. CO. ,LTD.
27 Zhongshan Dongyi Road，Shanghai，China

BENEFICIARY'S STATEMENT

TO：

DATE：

RE：L/C NO.

INVOICE NO.

WE HEREBY CERTIFY THAT...

6.出境货物报检单

中华人民共和国出入境检验检疫

出境货物报检单

报检单位(加盖公章):		* 编号:_____			
报检单位登记号:	联系人:	电话:	报检日期: 年 月 日		

发货人	(中文)				
	(外文)				
收货人	(中文)				
	(外文)				

货物名称(中/外文)	H.S. 编码	产地	数/重量	货物总值	包装种类及数量

运输工具名称号码		贸易方式		货物存放地点	
合同号		信用证号		用途	
发货日期		输往国家(地区)		许可证/审批证	
起运地		到达口岸		生产单位注册号	
集装箱规格、数量及号码					

合同、信用证订立的检验检疫条款或特殊要求	标记及号码	随附单据(画"√"或补填)	
		□合同	□包装性能结果单
		□信用证	□许可/审批文件
		□发票	□
		□换证凭单	□
		□装箱单	□
		□厂检单	

需要证单名称(画"√"或补填)		* 检验检疫费	
□品质证书 ____正____副	□植物检疫证书 ____正____副	总金额	
□重量证书 ____正____副	□熏蒸/消毒证书 ____正____副	(元人民币)	
□数量证书 ____正____副	□出境货物换证凭单		
□兽医卫生证书 ____正____副	□	计费人	
□健康证书 ____正____副	□		
□卫生证书 ____正____副	□		
□动物卫生证书 ____正____副	□	收费人	

报检人郑重声明:	领取证单	
1.本人被授权报检。		
2.上列填写内容正确属实,货物无伪造或冒用他人的厂名、标志、认证标志,并承担货物质量责任。	日期	
签名:_____	签名	

注:有"＊"号栏由出入境检验检疫机关填写 ◆国家出入境检验检疫局制

7. 出口货物报关单

中华人民共和国海关出口货物报关单

预录入编号：　　　　　　　　　　　　　　　　　海关编号：

出口口岸	备案号		出口日期	申报日期
经营单位	运输方式		运输工具名称	提/运单号
发货单位	贸易方式		征免性质	结汇方式
许可证号	运抵国（地区）		指运港	境内货源地
批准文号	成交方式	运费	保费	杂费
合同协议号	件数	包装种类	毛重（千克）	净重（千克）
集装箱号	随附单据		生产厂家	
标记唛码及备注				

项号	商品编号	商品名称、规格型号	数量及单位	最终目的地国（地区）	单价	总价	币制	征免

税费征收情况				
录入员	录入单位	兹声明以上申报无讹并承担法律责任	海关审单批注及放行日期（签单）	
			审单	审价
报关员 单位地址　　　　　申报单位（签章）			征税	统计
			查验	放行
邮编　　　电话　　　填制日期				

未经核销此联不得撕开

出口收汇核销单
出口退税专用

（浙）编号：

出口单位：

单位编码：

货物名称	数量	币种总价

报关单号：

外汇局签注栏

年　月　日（盖章）

（出口单位盖章）

出口收汇核销单

（浙）编号：

出口单位：

单位编码：

类别	币种金额	日期	盖章

签注栏

海关签注栏

外汇局签注栏

年　月　日（盖章）

（出口单位盖章）

---

8. 出口收汇核销单

出口收汇核销单
存根

（浙）编号：

出口单位：

单位编码：

出口币种总价：

收汇方式：

预计收款日期：

报关日期：

备注：

此单报关有效期截止到

实训五　信用证方式 CIF 下出口单据缮制

实训目标

能够根据相关资料缮制信用证方式 CIF 下的出口单据。

实训任务

一、训练资料

（一）销售合同

CHINA SHENZHEN SEZ FOREIGN TRADE (GROUP) CORP.

2 ZHONG XING RD. ,SHENZHEN CHINA.

SALES CONTRACT

TO：KINGROCK DEVELOPMENT LIMITED　　　　NO. (00)A01-E246

RM. 1203 12/F CAPTITOL CENTER，　　　　　DATE：APRIL 24,2009

NO. 5-19 JARDINE'S BAZAAR　　　　　　　Tel. 77886655

CAUSEWAY BAY，HONG KONG.

Dear Sirs,

　　We hereby confirm having sold to you the following goods on terms and conditions as specified bellow：

Shipping mark	Descriptions of goods	quantity	Unit price	Amount
T. C. SINGAPORE NO. 1-6000	SODIUM SULPHATE ANHYDROUS	300M/T	CIF USD91. 00/MT	SINGAPORE USD27300. 00
TOTAL：		300M/T		USD27300. 00

1. Terms of Payment：BY L/C Against Beneficiary's Draft(s) at 30 Days Drawn on the Issuing Bank

2. Port of Loading：ZHANJIANG,CHINA

3. Port of Destination：SINGAPORE

4. Latest Date of Shipment：NOV. 10,2009

5. Partial Shipment：NOT ALLOWED　　　Transshipment：NOT ALLOWED

6. Insurance：to be Covered by the Sellers for 110% of CIF Value, Covering WAR RISK AND ALL RISKS

7. 3PCT More or Less in Quantity and Amount is Allowed.

THE BUYER：　　　　　　　　　　　　　　　　　　THE SELLER：

KINGROCK DEVELOPMENT LIMITED　　　CHINA SHENZHEN SEZ FOREIGN TRADE (GROUP) CORP.

JINKONG　　　　　　　　　　　　　　　　　　　　　　陈成

（二）信用证

—DATE：OCT. 18，2009

—TO：BANK OF CHINA SHENZHEN BRANCH，

SHENZHEN, GUANGDONG，CHINA.

—FROM：ABN HONG KONG/MAIN BRANCH/IB DC DEPT. Algemene Bank Nederland N. V. Hongkong

—OUR IRREVOCABLE DOCUMENTARY CREDIT NO. : CW02705

—EXPIRY DATE：NOV. 20，2009

PLACE：IN CHINA.

—APPLICANT：

KINGROCK DEVELOPMENT LIMITED

RM. 1203 12/F CAPTITOL CENTER，

NO. 5-19 JARDINE'S BAZAAR

CAUSEWAY BAY，HONG KONG.

—BENEFICIARY：

CHINA SHENZHEN SEZ FOREIGN TRADE（GROUP）CORP.

2 ZHONG XING RD. ,SHENZHEN CHINA.

—AMOUNT：USD 27,300.00

（SAY U. S. D TWENTY SEVEN THOUSAND THREE HUNDRED AND 00/ 100 ONLY. ）

—CREDIT AVAILABLE WITH ANY BANK，BY NEGOTIATION，

AGAINST PRESENTATION OF BENEFICIARY'S DRAFT(S) AT 30 DAYS, DRAWN ON US IN DUPLICATE FOR 100 PERCENT OF THE NET INVOICE VALUE, SHOWING NUMBER AND DATE OF CREDIT, ACCOMPANIED BY THE DOCUMENTS DETAILED BELOW：

—COMMERCIAL INVOICE IN TRIPLICATE IN ENGLISH INDICATING THE CREDIT NUMBER,DULY SIGNED BY BENEFICIARIES ON CIF BASIS.

—FULL SET OF MARINE BILLS OF LADING IN TRIPLICATE TO ORDER MARKED FREIGHT PREPAID ENDORSED IN BLANK，NOTIFY：STARRY INTERTRADE（FAR EAST）PTE LTD.

—INSURANCE POLICY /CERTIFICATE ENDORSED IN BLANK FOR 110％ CIF VALUE,COVERING：WAR RISK AND ALL RISKS.

—SIGNED PACKING LIST IN TRIPLICATE.

—COPY BRIEF TELEX SENT TO APPLICANT ADVISING SHIPMENT DETAILS WITHIN 3 DAYS AFTER SHIPMENT EFFECTED.

—BENEF'S CERT. CERTIFYING THAT ONE FULL SET OF NON-NEGOTIABLE SHIPPING DOCUMENTS HAS BEEN SENT TO APPLICANT BY COURIER SERVICE WITHIN 7 DAYS AFTER SHIPMENT EFFECTED.

—AMOUNT AND QUANTITY 3PCT MORE OR LESS ALLOWABLE.

—PACKING IN PLASTIC LINED PLASTIC WOVEN BAGS OF 50KGS NET EACH. PACKING LIST TO EVIDENCE SAME REQUIRED.

—DOCUMENTS IN COMBINED FORM ARE NOT ALLOWED.

—COVERING SHIPMENT OF：

300M/T OF SODIUM SULPHATE ANHYDROUS AT USD91.00/MT CIF SINGAPORE

—SHIPMENT /DESPATCH/TAKING IN CHARGE FROM/AT ZHANJIANG，CHINA TO SINGAPORE.

—LATEST SHIPMENT/DELIVERY DATE：NOV.10，2009

—PARTIAL SHIPMENTS NOT ALLOWED.

—TRANSHIPMENT NOT ALLOWED.

—DOCUMENTS TO BE PRESENTED WITHIN 20 DAYS AFTER THE DATE OF ISSUANCE OF THE SHIPPING DOCUMENT(S) BUT WITHIN THE VALIDITY OF THE CREDIT.

—ALL BANK CHARGES OUTSIDE HONG KONG ARE FOR THE ACCOUNT OF BENEFICIARY.

—ALL DOCUMENTS TO BE FORWARDED BY THE NEGOTIATING BANK IN ONE COVER BY REGISTERED AIRMAIL TO US AT 14TH FLOOR，UNITED CENTRE，95 QUEENSWAY，CENTRAL，HONG KONG. ATTENTION I/B DEPT. UNLESS OTHERWISE STATED.

—FOR THE ADVISING BANK：WITHOUT ADDING YOUR CONFIRMATION. PLEASE ACKNOWLEDGE RECEIPT.

—REIMSURSEMENT UPON RECEIPT OF YOUR DOCUMENTS IN CONFORMITY WITH THE CREDIT TERMS，WE SHALL REIMBURSE YOU AS INSTRUCTED.

—THIS CABLE IS THE OPERATIVE CREDIT INSTRUMENT AND IS ISSUED SUBJECT TO UNIFORM CUSTOMS AND PRACTICE FOR DOCUMENTARY CREDIT，2007 REVISION，ICC PUBLICATION NO.600 NO MAIL CONFIRMATION IS TO FOLLOW.

（三）补充资料

1. 发票号码.：KG1213　　　发票日期：2009 年 10 月 25 日　　签发人：陈成

2. 装箱单签发日期：2009 年 10 月 25 日　　签发人：陈成

3. 总净重：300,000 KGS

　　总毛重：301,200 KGS

　　总包装数：6,000 BAGS

　　总体积：278M³

4. 提单号码：SP-004　　提单签发日：NOV.5,2009　　提单签发地点：ZHANJIANG

5. 船名：HUANG LONG V.11

6. H. S. 编码:2833.1100

7. 报检单位联系电话:65774433

8. 报检单位登记号:1243567

9. 报检单编号:678

10. 生产单位注册号:4532156789

11. 申请单位注册号:654JJ89

12. 国际运费:1000 美元,保险费 560 美元

13. 海关编号:7685

14. 境内货源地:深圳

15. 生产厂家:深圳化工厂

16. 报关员:温理   电话:67854983

17. 随附单据:出口货物通关单(7650864675)

二、训练要求

请以"单证员"身份,根据销售合同和补充资料缮制下列单据。

1. 商业发票

Issuer:			中国深圳特区外贸集团公司 CHINA SHENZHEN SEZ FOREIGN TRADE (GROUP) CORP. 2 ZHONG XING RD. ,SHENZHEN CHINA.	
			COMMERCIAL INVOICE	
To：			No.	Date
			S/C No.	L/C No.
Transport details Partial Shipments： Transshipment： From To By			Terms of payment	
Marks & Nos.	Description of goods； kind and number of package	Quantity Unit Price Amount		

2. 装箱单

中国深圳特区外贸集团公司
CHINA SHENZHEN SEZ FOREIGN TRADE (GROUP) CORP.
2 ZHONG XING RD. ,SHENZHEN CHINA.

PACKING LIST

1) SELLER：	3) INVOICE NO. ：	4) INVOICE DATE：
	5) FROM：	6) TO：
	7) TOTAL PACKAGES (IN WORDS)	
2) BUYER：	8) MARKS & NOS.	

9)C/NOS.	10) NOS. & KINDS OF PKGS.	11) ITEM	12) QTY.	13) G.W.	14) N.W.	15) MEAS (M³)

16)

17) ISSUED BY：

18) SIGNATURE：

3. 出境货物报检单

中华人民共和国出入境检验检疫
出境货物报检单

报检单位(加盖公章)：　　　　　　　　　　　　　　　　　 ＊编号：_____

报检单位登记号：　　　联系人：　　　电话：　　　报检日期：　　年　月　日

发货人	(中文)	
	(外文)	
收货人	(中文)	
	(外文)	

货物名称(中/外文)	H.S. 编码	产地	数/重量	货物总值	包装种类及数量

运输工具名称号码		贸易方式		货物存放地点	
合同号		信用证号		用途	
发货日期		输往国家(地区)		许可证/审批证	
起运地		到达口岸		生产单位注册号	

集装箱规格、数量及号码

合同、信用证订立的检验检疫条款或特殊要求	标记及号码	随附单据(画"√"或补填)	
		□合同	□包装性能结果单
		□信用证	□许可/审批文件
		□发票	□
		□换证凭单	□
		□装箱单	□
		□厂检单	

需要证单名称(画"√"或补填)		＊检验检疫费	
□品质证书　____正____副	□植物检疫证书　____正____副	总金额	
□重量证书　____正____副	□熏蒸/消毒证书　____正____副	(元人民币)	
□数量证书　____正____副	□出境货物换证凭单		
□兽医卫生证书　____正____副	□	计费人	
□健康证书　____正____副	□		
□卫生证书　____正____副	□	收费人	
□动物卫生证书　____正____副	□		

报检人郑重声明： 1.本人被授权报检。 2.上列填写内容正确属实,货物无伪造或冒用他人的厂名、标志、认证标志,并承担货物质量责任。 　　　　　　　　　　　签名：_____	领取证单	
	日期	
	签名	

注：有"＊"号栏由出入境检验检疫机关填写　　　　　　　◆国家出入境检验检疫局制

4.海运货物订舱委托书和海运提单

(1)海运货物订舱委托书

出 口 货 物 订 舱 委 托 书				日期		月		日
1)发货人		4)信用证号码						
		5)开证银行						
		6)合同号码		7)成交金额				
		8)装运口岸		9)目的港				
2)收货人		10)转船运输		11)分批装运				
		12)信用证有效期		13)装船期限				
		14)运费		15)成交条件				
		16)公司联系人		17)电话/传真				
3)通知人		18)公司开户行		19)银行账号				
		20)特别要求						

21)标记唛码	22)货号规格	23)包装件数	24)毛重	25)净重	26)数量	27)单价	28)总价
	29)总件数	30)总毛重	31)总净重	32)总尺码	33)总金额		

34)备注

（2）海运提单

Shipper	SINOTRANS	B/L No.
Consignee or order	中国对外贸易运输总公司 CHINA NATIONAL FOREIGN TRADE TRANSPORTATION CORP. 直运或转船提单 **BILL OF LADING** **DIRECT OR WITH TRANSSHIPMENT**	

SHIPPED on board in apparent good order and condition（unless otherwise indicated）the goods or packages specified herein and to be discharged at the mentioned port of discharge or as near thereto as the vessel may safely get and be always afloat.

The weight, measure, marks and numbers, quality, contents and value, being particulars furnished by the Shipper, are not checked by the carrier on loading.

The Shipper, Consignee and the Holder of this Bill of Lading hereby expressly accept and agree to all printed, written or stamped provisions, exceptions and conditions of this Bill of Lading including those on the back hereof.

IN WITNESS Where of the number of original Bills of Lading stated below have been signed, one of which being accomplished, the other(s) to be void.

Notify address		
Pre-carriage by	Place of loading	
Vessel	Port of transshipment	
Port of discharge	Final destination	

Container, seal No. or marks & Nos.	Number & kind of packages	Description of goods	Gross weight (kgs)	Measurement (m³)

ABOVE PARTICULARS FURNISHED BY SHIPPER

Freight & charges	Regarding transshipment information please contact

Ex. rate	Prepaid at	Freight payable at	Place and date of issue
	Total Prepaid	Number of original B(s)/L	Signed for or on behalf of the master as Agents

5.投保单和保险单

(1)投保单

中保财产保险有限公司浙江分公司

THE PEOPLE'S INSURANCE (PROPERTY) COMPANY OF CHINA, LTD. ZHEJIANG BRANCH

进出口货物运输保险投保单

APPLICATION FORM FOR I/E MARINE CARGO INSURANCE

被保险人 ASSURED'S NAME			
发票号码(出口用)或合同号码(进口用) INVOICE NO. OR CONTRACT NO.	包装数量 QUANTITY	保险货物项目 DESCRIPTION OF GOODS	保险金额 AMOUNT INSURED

装载运输工具　　　　　　　航次、航班或车号　　　　　开航日期
PER CONVEYANCE _____ VOY. NO. _____ SLG. DATE _____

自　　　　　至　　　　　转运地　　　　赔款地
FROM _____ TO _____ VIA _____ CLAIM PAYABLE AT _____

承保险别：
CONDITIONS &/OR
SPECIAL COVERAGE

投保人签章及公司名称、电话、地址
APPLICANT'S SIGNATURE AND CO. 'S NAME, ADD. AND TEL. NO

备注：　　　　　　　　投保日期
　　　　　　　　　　　DATE

保险公司填写　　　报单号：　　　费率：　　　核保人：

（2）保险单

海洋货物运输保险单

发票号次	第一正本	保险单号次
INVOICE NO.	THE FIRST ORIGINAL	POLICY NO.

中 国 人 民 保 险 公 司 （ 以 下 简 称 本 公 司 ）
This Policy of Insurance witnesses that People's Insurance Company of China（hereinafter called "the company"）根据
At the request of _____
（ 以 下 简 称 被 保 险 人 ） 的 要 求 ， 由 被 保 险 人 向 本 公 司 缴 付 约 定
（hereinafter called the "Insured"）and in consideration of the agreed premium being paid to the Company by
的 保 险 费 ， 按 照 本 保 险 单 承 保 险 别 和 背 面 所 载 条 款 与 下 列
the Insured，undertakes to insure the undermentioned goods in transportation subject to the conditions of this
特 殊 条 款 承 保 下 述 货 物 运 输 保 险 ， 特 立 本 保 险 单 。
Policy as per the Clauses printed overleaf and other special clauses attached hereon.

标　记 MARKS. & NOS.	包装及数量 QUANTITY	保险货物项目 DESCRIPTION OF GOODS	保险金额 AMOUNT INSURED

总　保　险　金　额：
Total　Amount　Insured _____

保费 _____ 费率 _____ 装载运输工具
Premium _____ Rate _____ Per Conveyance S. S. _____

开航日期 自 至
Slg on or abt. _____ From _____ To _____

承保险别：
Conditions

所 保 货 物 ， 如 遇 出 险 ， 本 公 司 凭 第 一 正 本 保 险 单 及 其 有 关 证 件 给
Claims，if any，payable on surrender of the first original of the Policy together with other relevant
付 赔 款 。 所 保 货 物 ， 如 发 生 本 保 险 单 项 下 负 责 赔 偿 的 损 失 或 事
Documents. In the event of accident whereby loss or damage may result in a claim under this Policy
故 ， 应 立 即 通 知 本 公 司 下 述 代 理 人 查 勘 。
Immediate notice applying for survey must be given to the Company's Agent as mentioned hereunder:

中国人民保险公司××分公司
THE PEOPLE'S INSURANCE CO. OF CHINA
×× BRANCH

赔款偿付地点
CLAIM PAYABLE AT _____
日期
DATE _____ _____

6. 装船通知

CHINA SHENZHEN SEZ FOREIGN TRADE (GROUP) CORP.
2 ZHONG XING RD. ,SHENZHEN CHINA.

SHIPPING ADVICE

TO：

DATE：

RE：L/C NO.

INVOICE NO.

WE HEREBY INFORMED YOU THAT THE GOODS UNDER THE ABOVE MENTIONED CREDIT HAVE BEEN SHIPPED. THE DETAILS OF SHIPMENT ARE STATED BELOW.

COMMODITY：

QUANTITY：

INVOICE VALUE：

OCEAN VESSEL/ SHIPPED PER S. S. :

DATE OF SHIPMENT：

PORT OF LOADING：

PORT OF DESTINATION：

MARKS：

Signature

7.受益人证明

CHINA SHENZHEN SEZ FOREIGN TRADE (GROUP) CORP.

2 ZHONG XING RD. ,SHENZHEN CHINA.

BENEFICIARY'S STATEMENT

TO：

                              DATE：

RE：L/C NO.   INVOICE NO.

WE HEREBY CERTIFY THAT...

8. 出口货物报关单

中华人民共和国海关出口货物报关单

预录入编号：　　　　　　　　　　　　　　　　海关编号：

出口口岸	备案号		出口日期	申报日期
经营单位	运输方式		运输工具名称	提/运单号
发货单位	贸易方式		征免性质	结汇方式
许可证号	运抵国（地区）		指运港	境内货源地
批准文号	成交方式	运费	保费	杂费
合同协议号	件数	包装种类	毛重（千克）	净重（千克）
集装箱号		随附单据	生产厂家	

标记唛码及备注

项号	商品编号	商品名称、规格型号	数量及单位	最终目的地国（地区）	单价	总价	币制	征免

税费征收情况

录入员	录入单位	兹声明以上申报无讹并承担法律责任	海关审单批注及放行日期（签单）	
			审单	审价
报关员 单位地址		申报单位（签章）	征税	统计
			查验	放行
邮编　　　电话		填制日期		

未经核销此联不得撕开

9. 出口收汇核销单

出口收汇核销单
存根

（浙）编号：

出口单位：

单位编码：

出口币种总价：

收汇方式：

预计收款日期：

报关日期：

备注：

此单报关有效期截止到

出口收汇核销单

（浙）编号：

（出口单位盖章）

出口单位：

单位编码：

类别	币种金额	日期	盖章
签注栏			

海关签注栏：

外汇局签注栏

　　　　年　　月　　日（盖章）

出口收汇核销单
出口退税专用

（浙）编号：

（出口单位盖章）

出口单位：

单位编码：

货物名称	数量	币种总价

报关单编号：

外汇局签注栏

　　　　年　　月　　日（盖章）

✳ **实训指导**

一、订舱委托书缮制说明

订舱委托书各栏目的内容缮制如下。

1. 发货人（托运人）

填写出口公司（信用证受益人）。

2. 收货人

填写信用证规定的提单收货人。

3. 通知人

填写信用证规定的提单通知人。

一般在订舱委托书上会注明托运人、收货人、通知人，这三栏为提单 B/L 的项目要求。意即，将来船公司签发的提单上的相应栏目也会参照订舱委托书的写法。因此，这三栏的填写应该按照信用证提单条款的相应规定填写（具体可以参见提单条款的填制方法）。

4. 信用证号码

填写相关交易的信用证号码。

5. 开证银行

填写相关交易的信用证开证银行的名称。

6. 合同号码

填写相关交易的合同号码。

7. 成交金额

填写相关交易的合同总金额。

8. 装运口岸

填写信用证规定的起运地。如信用证未规定具体的起运港口，则填写实际装港名称。

9. 目的港

填写信用证规定的目的地。如信用证未规定具体的目的港口，则填写实际卸货港名称。

10. 转船运输

根据信用证条款，如允许分批，则填"YES"，反之，则填"NO"。

11. 分批装运

根据信用证条款，如允许分批，则填"YES"，反之，则填"NO"。如信用证未对转船和分批作具体的规定，则应该按照合同的有关规定填写。

12. 信用证有效期

填写信用证的有效期。

13. 装运期限

填写信用证规定的装运期限。

14. 运费

根据信用证提单条款的规定填写"FREIGHT PREPAID"（运费预付）或"FREIGHT TO COLLECT"（运费到付）。

15. 成交条件

填写成交的贸易术语,如:"FOB"、"CIF"、"CFR"等。

16、17、18、19 公司联系人、电话/传真、公司开户行、银行账号

按公司实际情况填写。

20. 特别要求

如托运人对所订舱有特殊要求,可以填在这一栏中。常见的特殊要求有:①对运输单据内容要求,如 B/L 须显示信用证号码;②对承运人运输要求,如货物须在香港中转;③要求外运机构提供其他议付单据,如要求出具船龄证明等;④配船指示等。

21. 标记唛码

填写货物的装运标志,即通常所说的"唛头"。

22. 货号规格

填写货物描述,一般只写统称,规格、品号、尺码无须具体列出。但同时出口两笔不同性质的货物名称,则应分别填写,而不允许仅填写其中一类的商品。

23、24、25、26、27、28 包装件数、毛重、净重、数量、单价、总价

按货物的实际情况填制。包装件数按货物的实际最大包装的件数填制,如出口货物的包装材料不同或同一批出运的货物有若干种,每种包装方式和材料不同,应先填写每种货物最大包装件数,然后统计总件数。例如,100 纸箱,50 麻袋,总计 150 件(packages)。

29、30、31、32、33 总件数、总毛重、总净重、总尺码、总金额

按货物的实际情况填写。

34. 备注

如有其他事项可填入"备注"栏中。

实训六 信用证方式下进口单据缮制

实训目标

能够根据相关资料缮制信用证方式下的有关进口单据。

实训任务

一、训练资料

（一）销售合同

SALES CONTRACT			
SELLER： LPG INTERNATION CORPORATION 333 BARRON BLVD. , OTTAWA, CANADA	**NO. ：** CONTRACT01		
	DATE： 2009-08-19		
BUYER： EAST AGENT COMPANY ROOM 2401，WORDTRADE MANSTION，JINGZHOU ROAD 47＃，HANGZHOU, P. R. CHINA	**SIGNED IN：** OTTAWA		
This contract is made by and agreed between the BUYER and SELLER，in accordance with the terms and conditions stipulated below.			
1. Commodity & Specification	**2. Quantity**	**3. Unit Price**	**4. Amount**
			CIF SHANGHAI
CANNED SWEET CORN ARTICLE NO. 01005 3060GX6TINS/CTN	800 CARTONS	USD 14. 00/CARTON	USD11200. 00
Total：	**800 CARTONS**		**USD11200. 00**
With 5％ More or less of shipment allowed at the sellers' option			
5. Total Value	SAY U. S. DOLLARS ELEVEN THOUSAND TWO HUNDRED ONLY		
6. Packing	3060G X 6 TINS/CTN EACH OF THE CARTON SHOULD BE INDICATED WITH ITEM NO. , NAME OF THE TABLE, G. W. AND C/NO.		
7. Shipping Marks	E. A. C. SHANGHAI C/NO. 1-800		
8. Time of Shipment & Means of Transportation	ALL OF THE GOODS WILL BE SHIPPED ON OR BEFORE SEP. 20，2009，SUBJECT TO L/C REACHING THE SELLER BY THE END OF AUGUST，2009. PARTIAL SHIPMENTS AND TRANSHIMENT ARE NOT ALLOWED		

9. Port of Loading & Destination	FROM TORONTO TO SHANGHAI
10.　Insurance	THE SELLER SHALL ARRANGE MARINE INSURANCE COVERING ICC(A) PLUS INSTITUTE WAR RISKS FOR 110% OF CIF VALUE AND PROVIDE OF CLAIM, IF ANY, PAYABLE IN CHINA, WITH U. S. CURRENCY.
11. Terms of Payment	BY 100% IRREVOCABLE SIGHT LETTER OF CREDIT IN OUR FAVOR
12. Remarks	

The Buyer	The Seller
	LPG INTERNATION CORPORATION
（signature）	（signature）

（二）补充资料

吴淞海关进口

买方：LPG INTERNATION CORPORATION

　　　LPG 国际公司（代码 3122240320）

船名及航次：ZAANDAM　V.203

B/L DATE：SEP. 2,2009

B/L NO.：STBLN000001

集装箱号码：TBXU3605231　规格 20 英尺　自重 1760 公斤

商品编号：20058000

船舶进口申报日：2009-09-20

进口货物申报日：2009-09-23

委托报关单位：浙江外贸报关有限公司

报关员：张三 31222800060014

二、训练要求

请根据有关资料缮制开证申请书、入境货物报检单、进口货物报关单、进口付汇核销单。

1. 开证申请书

IRREVOCABLE DOCUMENTATRY CREDIT APPLICATION

TO：   **DATE：**

Beneficiary (full name and address)	Applicant (full name and address)

Partial shipments ☐not allowed ☐allowed	Transshipment ☐not allowed ☐allowed	Issued by ☐airmail ☐brief advice by teletransmission ☐express delivery ☐teletransmission(operative)

Loading on board/dispatch/taking in charge at / from for transportation to not later than	Amount

Date and place of expiry	Credit available with ☐by sight payment ☐by deferred payment ☐by acceptance ☐by negotiation against the documents detailed herein ☐and beneficiary's draft for % of invoice value at on
☐FOB ☐CFR ☐CIF ☐or other terms	

Documents required (marked with ×)：
1. ( ) Signed commercial invoice in ____ copies indicating L/C NO. and contract NO.
2. ( ) Full set of clean on board ocean bills of lading made out to order and blank endorsed, marked "freight to [ ]collect/[ ]prepaid [ ]showing freight amount" notifying[ ]the applicant/[ ]_____.
3. ( ) Air waybills /cargo receipt/copy of railway bills issued by _____ showing "freight [ ] to collect / [ ]prepaid [ ]indicating freight amount" and consigned to _____.
4. ( ) Insurance policy/certificate in ____ copies for ____% of the invoice value showing claims payable in _____ in currency of the draft, blank endorsed, covering [ ]ocean marine transportation/ [ ]air transportation/ [ ]overland transportation All Risks/[ ]war risks/[ ] _____.
5. ( ) Packing list /weight memo in ____ copies indicating quantity, gross and net weight of each package and packing conditions.
6. ( ) Certificate of quantity/ weight in ____ copies issued by _____
7. ( ) Certificate of quality in ____ copies issued by [ ]manufacture/ [ ]public recognized surveyor/ [ ] _____.
8. ( ) Beneficiary's certified copy of fax/ telex dispatched to applicant within ____ hours after shipment advising [ ]name of vessel/ [ ]flight NO. / [ ]wagon NO. , date, quantity, weight and value of shipment.
9. ( ) Certificate of origin in ____ copies issued by _____.
10. ( ) Other documents if any：

Description of goods：

Additional instructions：
1. ( ) All banking charges outside the opening bank are for beneficiary's account.
2. ( ) Documents must be presented withindays after the date of shipment but within the validity of this credit.
3. ( ) Third party as shipper is not acceptable. Short form B/L is not acceptable.
4. ( ) Both quantity and amount % more or less are allowed.
5. ( ) Prepaid freight drawn in excess of L/C amount is acceptable against presentation of original charges voucher issued by Shipping Co. Air Line/or its agent.
6. ( ) All documents to be forwarded in one cover unless otherwise stated above.
7. ( ) Other terms, if any：

2.入境货物报检单

中华人民共和国出入境检验检疫

入境货物报检单

报检单位(加盖公章):						*编　号	
报检单位登记号:		联系人:		电话:		报检日期	
收货人	(中文)				企业性质(画"√")		□合资□合作□外资
	(外文)						
发货人	(中文)						
	(外文)						

货物名称(中/外文)	H.S.编码	原产国(地区)	数/重量	货物总值	包装种类及数量

运输工具名称号码			合同号	
贸易方式		贸易国别(地区)	提单/运单号	
到货日期		启运国家(地区)	许可证/审批号	
卸毕日期		启运口岸	入境口岸	
索赔有效期至		经停口岸	目的地	
集装箱规格、数量及号码				
合同、信用证订立的特殊条款以及其他要求			货物存放地点	
			用　途	

随附单据(画"√"或补填)		标记及号码	*外商投资财产(画"√")	□是□否
□合同	□到货通知			
□发票	□装箱单		*检验检疫费	
□提/运单	□质保书		总金额(元人民币)	
□兽医卫生证书	□理货清单			
□植物检疫证书	□磅码单		计费人	
□动物检疫证书	□验收报告			
□卫生证书	□			
□原产地证	□		收费人	
□许可/审批文件	□			

报检人郑重声明: 1.本人被授权报检。 2.上列填写内容正确属实。	领取证单	
	日期	
签名:	签名	

注:有"＊"号栏由出入境检验检疫机关填写　　◆国家出入境检验检疫局制

3.进口货物报关单

中华人民共和国海关进口货物报关单

预录入编号：　　　　　　　　　　　　　海关编号：

进口口岸	备案号	进口日期	申报日期
经营单位	运输方式	运输工具名称	提/运单号
收货单位	贸易方式	征免性质	征税比例
许可证号	起运国（地区）	装货港	境内目的地
批准文号	成交方式	运费	保费	杂费
合同协议号	件数	包装种类	毛重（千克）	净重（千克）

集装箱号	随附单据	用途

标记唛码及备注

项号	商品编号	商品名称、规格型号	数量及单位	最终目的地国（地区）	单价	总价	币制	征免

税费征收情况

录入员	录入单位	兹声明以上申报无讹并承担法律责任	海关审单批注及放行日期（签单）	
			审单	审价
报关员			征税	统计
			查验	放行
单位地址 邮编　　　电话		申报单位（签章） 填制日期		

4.进口付汇核销单

贸易进口付汇核销单（代申报单）

印单局代码：　　　　　　　　　　　　　　　　　　　　核销单编号：

单位代码	单位名称	所在地外汇局名称
付汇银行名称	收汇人国别（地区）	交易编码
收款人是否在保税区：是□　否□	交易附言	
对外付汇币种　　　　　　对外付汇总额 其中：购汇金额　　　　　现汇金额　　　　　　其他方式金额 　　　人民币账号　　　　外汇账号		

付汇性质

□正常付汇

□不在名录　　　　□90天以上信用证　　　　□90天以上托收　　　　□异地付汇

□90天以上到货　　□转口贸易

备案表编号

预计到货日期	进口批件号	合同/发票号

　　　　　/　　/　　　　　　　　　结算方式

信用证　90天以内□　　90天以上□	承兑日期　/　/	付汇日期　/　/	期限　天
托收　　90天以内□　　90天以上□	承兑日期　/　/	付汇日期　/　/	期限　天

	预付货款□	货到付汇（凭报关单付汇）□　　付汇日期　/　/		
汇 款	报关单号	报关日期　/　/	报关单币种	金额
	报关单号	报关日期　/　/	报关单币种	金额
	报关单号	报关日期　/　/	报关单币种	金额
	报关单号	报关日期　/　/	报关单币种	金额
	报关单号	报关日期　/　/	报关单币种	金额
	（若报关单填写不完,可另附纸。）			

其他□	付汇日期　/　/

以下由付汇银行填写

申报号码：　□□□□□□□　□□□□□　□□□□□□□□□　□□□□

业务编号：　　　　　　审核日期：　/　/　　　　（付汇银行签章）

进口单位签章

🌿 **实训指导**

一、开证申请书缮制说明

开证申请书通常为一式两联,申请人除填写正面内容外,还须签具背面的"开证申请人承诺书"。开证申请书其正面各栏目的内容缮制如下。

1. TO

致_____行。填写开证行名称。

2. Date

申请开证日期。

3. Issued by

①Airmail,以信开的形式开立信用证。选择此种方式,开证行以航邮将信用证寄给通知行。

②Brief advice by teletransmission,以简电开的形式开立信用证。选择此种方式,开证行将信用证主要内容发电预先通知受益人,银行承担必须使其生效的责任,但简电本身并非信用证的有效文本,不能凭以议付或付款,银行随后寄出的"证实书"才是正式的信用证。

③Express delivery,以信开的形式开立信用证。选择此种方式,开证行以快递(如:DHL)将信用证寄给通知行。

④Teletransmission (which shall be the operative instrument),以全电开的形式开立信用证。选择此种方式,开证行将信用证的全部内容加注密押后发出,该电讯文本为有效的信用证正本。如今大多用"全电开证"的方式开立信用证。

4. Credit No.

信用证号码,由银行填写。

5. Date and place of expiry

信用证有效期及地点,地点填受益人所在国家。

6. Applicant

填写开证申请人名称及地址。

7. Beneficiary

填写受益人全称和详细地址。

8. Advising Bank

填写通知行名址。

9. Amount

填写信用证金额,分别用数字小写和文字大写。以小写输入时须包括币种与金额。

10. Parital shipments

分批装运条款。填写跟单信用证项下是否允许分批装运。

11. Transhipment

转运条款。填写跟单信用证项下是否允许货物转运。

12. Loading on board/dispatch/taking in charge at/from

填写装运港。

13. Not later than

填写最后装运期。

14. For transportation to

填写目的港。

15. 价格条款

根据合同内容选择或填写价格条款。

16. Credit available with

填写此信用证可由_____银行即期付款、承兑、议付、延期付款,即押汇银行(出口地银行)名称。

如果信用证为自由议付信用证,银行可用"ANY BANK IN…(地名/国名)"表示。

如果该信用证为自由议付信用证,而且对议付地点也无限制时,可用"ANY BANK"表示。

①Sight payment

勾选此项,表示开具即期付款信用证。

②Acceptance

勾选此项,表示开具承兑信用证。

③Negotiation

勾选此项,表示开具议付信用证。

④Deferred payment at

勾选此项,表示开具延期付款信用证。

如果开具这类信用证,需要写明延期多少天付款,例如"at 60 days from payment confirmation"(60 天承兑付款)、"at 60 days from B/L date"(提单日期后 60 天付款)等等。

17. against the documents detailed herein and beneficiary's draft(s) for _____% of invoice value at _____ sight drawn on _____。

连同下列单据:

受益人按发票金额____%,作成期限为____天,付款人为_____的汇票。注意延期付款信用证不需要选择连同此单据。

"at ____ sight"为付款期限。如果是即期,需要在"at ____ sight"之间填"＊＊＊"或"____",不能留空。"drawn on"为指定付款人。注意汇票的付款人应为开证行或指定的付款行。

18. Documents required (marked with ×):

信用证需要提交的单据(用"×"标明)。

①经签字的商业发票一式____份,标明信用证号_____和合同号_____。

②全套清洁已装船海运提单,作成空白抬头、空白背书,注明"运费[ ]待付/[ ]已付,[ ]标明运费金额",并通知_____。

③空运提单收货人为_____,由签发的航空运单/承运货物收据/铁路运单注明"运费[ ]待付/[ ]已付/[ ]标明运费金额"作成_____抬头。

④保险单/保险凭证一式____份,按发票金额的____%投保,注明赔付地在_____,以汇票同种货币支付,空白背书,投保_____。

⑤装箱单/重量证明一式＿＿份,注明每一包装的数量、毛重和净重。

⑥数量/重量证一式＿＿份,由＿＿＿＿＿＿出具。

⑦品质证一式＿＿份,由[　]制造商/[　]公众认可的检验机构/[　]＿＿＿＿＿出具。

⑧产地证一式＿＿份,由＿＿＿＿＿＿＿＿出具。

⑨受益人以传真/电传方式通知申请人装船证明副本,该证明须在装船后＿＿＿日内发出,并通知该信用证号、船名、装运日以及货物的名称、数量、重量和金额。

⑩Other documents, if any

其他单据。

19. Description of goods

货物描述。

20. Additional instructions

附加条款,是对以上各条款未述之情况的补充和说明,且包括对银行的要求等。

①开证行以外的所有银行费用由受益人担保。

②所需单据须在运输单据出具日后＿＿＿天内提交,但不得超过信用证有效期。

③第三方为托运人不可接受,简式/背面空白提单不可接受。

④数量及信用证金额允许有＿＿％的增减。

⑤预付运费可凭船公司/航空公司/或其代理出具的运费收据原件,在本信用证金额外支付。

⑥除非有其他说明,所有单据应一次提交。

⑦Other terms, if any,其他条款。

二、入境货物报检单缮制说明

入境货物报检单所在列各栏必须填写完整、准确、清晰,没有内容填写栏目以"＊＊＊"表示,不得留空。入境货物报检单各栏目的内容缮制如下。

1. 报检单位、登记号、联系人、电话

填写报检单位全称并加盖公章或报验专用章,并准确填写本单位报检登记代码、联系人及电话;代理报检的应加盖代理报检机构在检验检疫机构备案的印章。

2. 编号

本栏目由出入境检验检疫机构填写。

3. 报检日期

应在检验检疫机构受理报检日现场由报检人填写。

4. 收货人

填写合同上的买方或信用证的开证人,填写中英文,中英文意思要一致。

5. 企业性质

根据收货人的性质勾选。

6. 发货人

填写合同上的卖方或信用证上的受益人,仅填写英文。

7. 货物名称（中／外文）

按贸易合同或发票所列货物名称所对应国家检验检疫机构制定公布的《检验检疫商品目录》所列的货物名称填写。

8. H. S. 编码

指货物对应的海关商品代码，填写 8 位数。

9. 原产国（地区）

指货物原始的生产／加工的国家或地区的名称。

10. 数／重量

填写报检货物的数／重量，并注明计量单位，如：×××PC。注意，该数量和计量单位既要与实际装运货物情况一致，又要与信用证要求一致。

11. 货物总值

按本批货物合同或报关单上所列的总值填写（以美元计），如同一报检单报检多批货物，需列明每批货物的总值。（注：如申报货物总值与国内国际市场价格有较大差异，检验检疫机构保留核价权利。）

12. 包装种类及数量

指本批货物运输包装的种类及件数。

13. 运输工具名称号码

填写货物实际装载的运输工具类别名称（如船、飞机、货柜车、火车等）及运输工具编号（船名、飞机航班号、车牌号码、火车车次）。

14. 合同号

指贸易双方就本批货物而签订的书面贸易合同编号。

15. 贸易方式

成交的方式，如：1 一般贸易、2 三来一补、3 边境贸易、4 进料加工、5 其他贸易，通常都为一般贸易。

16. 贸易国别（地区）

指本批货物贸易的国家或地区，即进口国。

17. 提单／运单号

指本批货物对应的提单／运单的编号。

18. 到货日期

按货物到货通知单所列的日期填写。

19. 启运国家（地区）

指装运本批货物进境的交通工具的启运国家（地区），即出口国（地区）。

20. 许可证／审批号

对国家出入境检验检疫局已实施《进口商品质量许可证制度目录》下的货物和卫生注册、检疫、环保许可制度管理的货物，报检时填写安全质量许可编号或审批单编号，一般商品可空白。

21. 卸毕日期

按货物实际卸毕的日期填写。在货物还未卸毕前报检的，可暂不填写，待卸毕后再填写。

22.启运口岸

指本批货物进境的交通工具的启运口岸名称。

23.入境口岸

指装运本批货物的交通工具进境时首次停靠的口岸名称。

24.索赔有效期至

按合同规定的日期填写,特别要注明截止日期。

25.经停口岸

指本批货物在启运后,到达目的地前中途停靠的口岸名称。

26.目的地

指本批货物预定最后抵达的交货港(地)。

27.集装箱规格、数量及号码

填写装载本批货物的集装箱规格(如 20 英尺、40 英尺等)以及分别对应的数量和集装箱号码全称。若集装箱太多,可用附单形式填报。

28.合同订立的特殊条款以及其他要求

指贸易合同中双方对本批货物特别约定而订立的质量、卫生等条款和报检单位对本批货物的检验检疫有其他特别的要求。

29.货物存放地点

指本批货物卸货时存放的仓储位置。

30.用途

指本批货物的用途,如食用、观赏或演艺、实验、药用、饲用、加工等,一般用途明确的商品也可不填。

31.随附单据

按实际向检验检疫机构提供的单据,在对应的"□"打"√",通常合同、发票、提/运单、装箱单等单据是必须提交的。

32.标记及号码

按货物实际运输包标记填写,如没有标记,填写"N/M",标记填写不下时可用附页填写。

33.检验检疫费

此栏由出入境检验检疫机构填写。

34.报检人郑重声明

必须有报检人的亲笔签名。

35.领取证单

应在检验检疫机构受理报验日现场由报验人填写。

三、进口付汇核销单缮制说明

进口付汇核销单各栏目的内容缮制如下。

1.印单局代码

为印制本核销单的六位外汇局代码。

2.核销单编号

由各印制本核销单的外汇局自行编制。

3.单位代码

应根据国家技术监督局颁发的组织机构代码填写。

4.所在地外汇局名称。

系指付汇单位所在地外汇局名称

5.付汇银行名称

通常为进口地银行。

6.收汇人国别

系指该笔对外付款的实际收款人常驻国家(地区),即出口国家(地区)。

7.交易编码

应根据本笔对外付汇交易的性质对应国家外汇管理局国际收支交易编码表填写。

0101　一般贸易

0102　国家间、国际组织无偿援助和赠送的物资

0103　华侨、港澳台同胞、外籍华人捐赠物资

0104　补偿贸易

0105　来料加工装配贸易

0106　进料加工装配贸易

0107　寄售代销贸易

0108　边境小额贸易

0109　来料加工装配进口的设备

0111　租赁贸易

0112　免税外汇商品

0113　出料加工贸易

0114　易货贸易

0115　外商投资企业进口供加工内销的料、件

0116　其他

0201　预付货款

8.交易附言

是付款人对该笔对外付款用途的描述,可不填。

9.对外付汇币种、报关单币种

应按币种的英文缩写填写。

10.对外付汇总额、购汇金额、现汇金额、其他方式金额、汇款中报关单金额

应用阿拉伯数字填写。

11.人民币账号、外汇账号

应根据如下规定填报:如所付款项系从现汇账户中支出,则在"外汇账号"栏填写该现汇账户的账号;如所付款项系从银行购得的外汇,则在"人民币账号"栏填写其用于购汇的人民币账户的账号。

12. 付汇性质

应选择适当的付汇性质打√。其中,"正常付汇"系指除不在名录、90 天以上信用证、90 天以上托收、异地付汇、90 天以上到货、转口贸易、境外工程使用物资、真实性审查以外无须办理进口付汇备案业务的付款业务;"90 天以上信用证"及"90 天以上托收"均系指付汇日期距承兑日期在 90 天以上的对外付汇业务;除"正常付汇"之外的各付汇性质在标注"√"时,均须对应填写备案表编号。

13. 结算方式

应选择适当的结算方式打"√"。其中:90 天以内信用证、90 天以内托收的付汇日期距该笔付汇的承兑日期均小于 90 天且含 90 天;90 天以上信用证、90 天以上托收的付汇日期距该笔付汇的承兑日期均大于 90 天;结算方式为"货到付汇"时,应同时填写对应"报关单号"、"报关日期"、"报关单币种"、"金额"。

14. 申报号码

申报号码由付汇银行填写,共 22 位。第 1 至第 6 位为地区标识码、第 7 至第 10 位为银行标识码、第 11 和第 12 位为金融机构顺序号、第 13 至第 18 位为该笔贸易进口付汇的付汇日期或该笔对外付汇的申报日期,最后 4 位为银行营业部门的当日业务流水码。

15. 其他各栏

均应按栏目提示对应填写。

实训七　信用证方式下单据审核

实训目标

能够根据相关资料审核信用证方式下的出口单据。

实训任务

一、训练资料

(一)信用证

THE ROYAL BANK OF CANADA

BRITISH COLUMBIA INTERNATION CENTRE

1055 WEST GEORGIA STREET, VANCOUVER, B.C. V6E 3P3 CANADA

☐CONFIRMATION OF TELEX/CABLE PER-ADVISED　　　　DATE: APR 8, 2009

TELEX NO. 4720688 CA　　　　　　　　　　　　　　PLACE: VANCOUVER

IRREVOCABLE DOCUMENTARY CREDIT	CREDIT NUMBER: 01/0501-FCT	ADVISING BANK'S REF. NO.
ADVISING BANK: NANJING FINANCE CORPORATION 59 HONGKONG ROAD NANJING 210002, CHINA	APPLICANT: NEO GENERAL TRADING CO. ♯362 JALAN STREET, VANCOUVER, CANADA	
BENEFICIARY: DESUN TRADING CO., LTD. ROOM 2501, JIAFA MANSTION, BEIJING WEST ROAD, NANJING 210005, P.R. CHINA	AMOUNT: USD35,229.00 (US DOLLARS THIRTY FIVE THOUSAND TWO HUNDRED AND TWENTY NINE ONLY)	
EXPIRY DATE: MAY 15, 2009	FOR NEGOTIATION IN BENEFICIARY 'S COUNTRY	

GENTLEMEN:

WE HEREBY OPEN OUR IRREVOCABLE LETTER OF CREDIT IN YOUR FAVOR WHICH IS A-VAILABLE BY YOUR DRAFTS AT SIGHT FOR FULL INVOICE VALUE ON US ACCOMPANIED BY THE FOLLOWING DOCUMENTS:

+ SIGNED COMMERCIAL INVOICE AND 3 COPIES.

+ PACKING LIST AND 3 COPIES, SHOWING THE INDIVIDUAL WEIGHT AND MEASURE-MENT OF EACH ITEM.

+ ORIGINAL CERTIFICATE OF ORIGIN AND 3 COPIES ISSUED BY THE CHAMBER OF COMMERCE.

+ FULL SET CLEAN ON BOARD OCEAN BILLS OF LADING SHOWING FREIGHT PREPAID CONSIGNED TO ORDER OF THE ROYAL BANK OF CANADA INDICATING THE ACTUAL DATE OF THE GOODS ON BOARD AND NOTIFY THE APPLICANT WITH FULL ADDRESS AND PHONE NO. 77009910.

+ INSURANCE POLICY OR CERTIFICATE FOR 110 PERCENT OF INVOICE VALUE COVER-ING: INSURANCE CARGO CLAUSES (A) AS PER I. C. C. DATED 1/1/1982.

COVERING SHIPMENT OF:

4 ITEMS OF CHINESE CERAMIC DINNERWARE INCLUDING:

30-PIECE DINNERWARE AND TEA SET, 544SETS, USD17.50/SET, 1260KGS (G. W.), 1010KGS(N. W.), 19M^3

20-PIECE DINNERWARE SET, 800SETS, USD15.00/SET, 1590KGS (G. W.), 1320KGS (N. W.), 27.8M^3

45-PIECE DINNERWARE SET, 443SETS, USD19.00/SET, 950KGS (G. W.), 780KGS (N. W.), 17.8M^3

95-PIECE DINNERWARE SET, 245SETS, USD21.60/SET, 920KGS (G. W.), 790KGS (N. W.), 17.3M^3

N/M, PACKAGE: ONE SET PER CARTON

DETAILS IN ACCORDANCE WITH SALES CONTRACT NO. HSDS03027 DATED APR. 3, 2009.

[ ] FOB / [ ]CFR / [X] CIF/ [ ]FAX VANCOUVER CANADA.

SHIPMENT FROM NANJING	TO VANCOUVER	LATEST APRIL 30, 2009	PARTIAL SHIP-MENTS PROHIBITED	TRANSSHIPMENT PROHIBITED

DRAFT AT SIGHT TO BE PRESENTED FOR NEGOTIATION WITHIN 15 DAYS AFTER SHIP-MENT, BUT WITHIN THE VALIDITY OF CREDIT. ALL DOCUMENTS TO BE FORWARDED IN ONE COVER, BY AIRMAIL, UNLESS OTHERWISE STATED UNDER SPECIAL INSTRUCTION.

SPECIAL INSTRUCTION:

+ALL BANKING CHARGES OUTSIDE CANADA ARE FOR ACCOUNT OF BENEFICIARY.

+ ALL GOODS MUST BE SHIPPED IN ONE 20'CY TO CY CONTAINER AND B/L SHOWING THE SAME.

+ THE VALUE OF FREIGHT PREPAID HAS TO BE SHOWN ON BILLS OF LADING.

+ DOCUMENTS WHICH FAIL TO COMPLY WITH THE TERMS AND CONDITIONS IN THE LETTER OF CREDIT SUBJECT TO A SPECIAL DISCREPANCY HANDLING FEE OF US $35.00 TO BE DEDUCTED FROM ANY PROCEEDS.

DRAFT MUST BE MARKED AS BEING DRAWN UNDER THIS CREDIT AND BEAR ITS NUM-BER; THE AMOUNTS ARE TO BE ENDORSED ON THE REVERSE HEREOF BY NEG. BANK. WE HEREBY AGREE WITH THE DRAWERS, ENDORSERS AND BONA FIDE HOLDER THAT ALL DRAFTS DRAWN UNDER AND IN COMPLIANCE WITH THE TERMS OF THIS CREDIT SHALL BE DULY HONORED UPON PRESENTATION.

THIS CREDIT IS SUBJECT TO THE UNIFORM CUSTOMS AND PRACTICE FOR DOCUMENTA-RY CREDITS (2007 REVISION) BY THE INTERNATIONAL CHAMBER OF COMMERCE PUBLI-CATION NO. 600.

Yours Very Truly,

Joanne Hsan

David Jone

AUTHORIZED SIGNATURE

AUTHORIZED SIGNATURE

（二）汇票

BILL OF EXCHANGE

No. 　52589D41

For 　USD35229.00 　　　　　　　　　　　2009-05-05，NANJING，CHINA

　　　(amount in figure) 　　　　　　　　　　(place and date of issue)

At 　************************* 　sight of this FIRST Bill of exchange (SECOND being unpaid)

pay

to 　　NANJING FINANCE CORPORATION 　　　　　　 or order the sum of

U.S. DOLLARS THIRTY FIVE THOUSAND TWO HUNDRED AND TWENTY ONLY

　　　　　　　　　　　(amount in words)

Drawn under 　　　　　THE ROYAL BANK OF CANADA

L/C No. 　　　01/0501-FTC 　　　dated 　　APR 8，2009

To：THE ROYAL BANK OF CANADA

BRITISH COLUMBIA INTERNATION CENTRE

1055 WEST GEORGIA STREET，VANCOUVER，

B.C. V6E 3P3

CANADA

For and on behalf of

DESUN TRADING CO.，LTD.

　　　　　　　　　　　(Signature)

（三）商业发票

DESUN TRADING CO. , LTD.

ROOM 2501，JIAFA MANSTION，BEIJING WEST ROAD，

NANJING 210005，P. R. CHINA

TEL：025－77009910 025－77008820 FAX：025－77009930

COMMERCIAL INVOICE

To：NEO GENERAL TRADING CO.

♯362 JALAN STREET，VANCOUVER, CANADA

From：NANJING

Letter of Credit No. :01/0501-FCT

Invoice No. :2003SDT007

Invoice Date：2009-04-20

S/C No. :HSDS02703

S/C Date：2009-04-03

To：VANCOUVER

Date：2009-04-08

Marks and Numbers	Number and kind of package Description of goods	Quantity	Unit Price	Amount
				CFR VANCOUVER CANADA
N/M	ABOUT 544 CARTONS OF 30-PIECE DINNERWARE AND TEA SET	544SETS	USD17. 50	USD9520. 00
	ABOUT 800 CARTONS OF 20-PIECE DINNERWARE SET	800SETS	USD15. 00	USD12000. 00
	ABOUT 443 CARTONS OF 45-PIECE DINNERWARE SET	443SETS	USD19. 00	USD8417. 00
	ABOUT 245 CARTONS OF 95-PIECE DINNERWARE SET	245SETS	USD21. 60	USD5292. 00
	TotaL：	2032SETS		USD35229. 00

Say Total：U. S. DOLLARS THIRTY FIVE THOUSAND TWO HUNDRED AND TWENTY NINE ONLY

（四）装箱单

DESUN TRADING CO. , LTD.

ROOM 2501，JIAFA MANSTION，BEIJING WEST ROAD，

NANJING 210005，P. R. CHINA

TEL：025－77009910 025－77008820 FAX：025－77009930

PACKING LIST

To：NEO GENERAL TRADING CO.

＃362 JALAN STREET，VANCOUVER，CANADA

From：NANJING

Letter of Credit No. :01/0501-FCT

Invoice No. :2003SDT009

Invoice Date：2009-04-20

S/C No. : HSDS03027

S/C Date：2009-04-03

To：VANCOUVER

Date：2009-04-26

Marks and Numbers	Number and kind of package Description of goods	Quantity	Package	G. W	N. W	Meas.
N/M	ABOUT 544 CARTONS OF 30-PIECE DINNERWARE AND TEA SET	544SETS	544 CARTONS	1260KGS	1010KGS	19M³
	ABOUT 800 CARTONS OF 20-PIECE DINNERWARE SET	800SETS	800 CARTONS	1590KGS	1320KGS	27.8M³
	ABOUT 443 CARTONS OF 45-PIECE DINNERWARE SET	443SETS	443 CARTONS	950KGS	780KGS	17.8M³
	ABOUT 245 CARTONS OF 95-PIECE DINNERWARE SET	245SETS	245 CARTONS	920KGS	790KGS	17.3M³
	TOTAL：2032SETS		2032 CARTONS	4740KGS	3900KGS	81.3 M³

SAY TOTAL：TWO THOUSAND AND THIRTY TWO CARTONS ONLY

（五）保险单

中国人民保险公司南京市分公司
The People's Insurance Company of China Nanjing Branch

总公司设于北京　　　一九四九年创立
Head Office Beijing　　Established in 1949

货物运输保险单
CARGO TRA NSPORTATION INSURANCE POLICY

发票号（INVOICE NO.）	2003SDT007	保单号次 POLICY NO.	PICCSH034582
合同号（CONTRACT NO.）	HSDS03027		
信用证号（L/C NO.）	01/0501-FCT		
被保险人： Insured：	DESUN TRADING CO.，LTD.		

中国人民保险公司（以下简称本公司）根据被保险人的要求，由被保险人向本公司缴付约定的保险费，按照本保险单承保险别和背面所载条款与下列特款承保下述货物运输保险，特立本保险单。

THIS POLICY OF INSURANCE WITNESSES THAT THE PEOPLE'S INSURANCE COMPANY OF CHINA（HEREINAFTER CALLED "THE COMPANY"）AT THE REQUEST OF THE INSURED AND IN CONSIDERATION OF THE AGREED PREMIUM PAID TO THE COMPANY BY THE INSURED, UNDERTAKES TO INSURE THE UNDERMENTIONED GOODS IN TRANSPORTATION SUBJECT TO THE CONDITIONS OF THIS POLICY AS PER THE CLAUSES PRINTED OVERLEAF AND OTHER SPECIL CLAUSES ATTACHED HEREON.

标记 MARKS&NOS	包装及数量 QUANTITY	保险货物项目 DESCRIPTION OF GOODS	保险金额 AMOUNT INSURED
N/M	2032 CARTONS	4 ITEMS OF CHINESE CERAMIC DINNERWARE	US$ 35229.00

总保险金额 TOTAL AMOUNT INSURED：	SAY U. S. DOLLARS THIRTY EIGHT THOUSAND SEVEN HUNDRED AND FIFTY ONE POINT NINE.				
保费： PERMIUM：	AS ARRANGED	启运日期 DATEOF COMMENCEMENT：	AS PER B/L	装载运输工具： PER CONVEYANCE：	JIN YOU
自 FROM：	NANJING	经 VIA		至 TO	VANCOU-VER
承保险别： CONDITIONS：					

INSURANCE CARGO CLAUSES (A) AS PER I. C. C. DATED 1/1/1982
WAR RISKS

所保货物，如发生保险单项下可能引起索赔的损失或损坏，应立即通知本公司下述代理人查勘。如有索赔，应向本公司提交保单正本（本保险单共有＿＿份正本）及有关文件。如一份正本已用于索赔，其余正本自动失效。

IN THE EVENT OF LOSS OR DAMAGE WHICH MAY RESULT IN A CLAIM UNDER THIS POLICY, IMMEDIATE NOTICE MUST BE GIVEN TO THE COMPANY'S AGENT AS MENTIONED HEREUNDER. CLAIMS, IF ANY, ONE OF THE ORIGINAL POLICY WHICH HAS BEEN ISSUED IN ORIGINAL(S) TOGETHER WITH THE RELEVANT DOCUMENTS SHALL BE SURRENDERED TO THE COMPANY. IF ONE OF THE ORIGINAL POLICY HAS BEEN ACCOMPLISHED. THE OTHERS TO BE VOID.

中国人民保险公司南京市分公司
The People's Insurance Company of ChinaNanjing Branch

赔款偿付地点 CLAIM PAYABLE AT　　VANCOUVER
出单日期 ISSUING DATE　　2009-04-25　　Authorized Signature

地址（ADD）：中国南京石鼓路 225 号　　　　　　　　　电话（TEL）：(025)6521049
邮编（POST CODE）：210029　　　　　　　　　　　　　传真（FAX）：(025)4404593

（六）海运提单

Shipper		B/L No.

DESUN TRADING CO., LTD.
ROOM 2501, JIAFA MANSTION, BEIJING WEST
ROAD, NANJING 210005, P. R. CHINA

中国外运江苏公司

SINOTRANS JIANGSU CO.

OCEAN BILL OF LADING

Consignee or order

TO ORDER OF THE ROYAL BANK OF CANADA

SHIPPED on board in apparent good order and condition (unless otherwise indicated) the goods or packages specified herein and to be discharged at the mentioned port of discharge or as near thereto as the vessel may safely get and be always afloat.

Notify address

NEO GENERAL TRADING CO.
#362 JALAN STREET, VANCOUVER, CANADA

The weight, measure, marks and numbers, quality, contents and value, being particulars furnished by the Shipper, are not checked by the Carrier on loading.

The Shipper, Consignee and the Holder of this Bill of Lading hereby expressly accept and agree to all printed, written or stamped provisions, exceptions and conditions of this Bill of Lading, including those on the back hereof.

IN WITNESS whereof the number of original Bills of Lading stated below have been signed, one of which being accomplished the other(s) to be void.

Pre-carriage by	Port of loading
	NANJING

Vessel	Port of transshipment
JIN YOU	HONGKONG

Port of discharge	Final destination
VANCOUVER	

Container. seal No. or marks and Nos.	Number and kind of package	Description of goods	Gross weight (kgs.)	Measurement (m³)
N/M	544 CARTONS	30-PIECE DINNERWARE AND TEA SET	1260KGS	19M³
	800 CARTONS	20-PIECE DINNERWARE SET	1590KGS	27.8M³
	443 CARTONS	45-PIECE DINNERWARE SET	950KGS	17.8M³
	245 CARTONS	95-PIECE DINNERWARE SET	920KGS	17.3M³

WE HEREBY SHOWING THAT ALL THE GOODS HAVE BEEN SHIPPED IN ONE 20' CY TO CY CONTAINER

Freight and charges	FREIGHT PREPAID
REGARDING TRANSHIPMENT INFORMATION PLEASE CONTACT	SHIPPED ON BOARD

Ex. rate	Prepaid at	Freight payable at	Place and date of issue
			2009-04-28
	Total prepaid	Number of original Bs/L	Signed for or on behalf of the Master
		THREE	
			As Agent

实训指导

一、单据审核注意事项

1. 纵向审核法

指以信用证或合同（在非信用证付款条件下）为基础对规定的各项单据进行——审核，要求有关单据的内容严格符合信用证的规定，做到"单证一致"。着重审核：

(1)检查规定的单证是否齐全，包括所需单证的份数；

(2)检查所提供的文件名称和类型是否符合要求；

(3)有些单证是否按规定进行了认证；

(4)单证之间的货物描述、数量、金额、重量、体积、运输标志等是否一致；

(5)单证出具或提交的日期是否符合要求。

2. 横向审核法

在纵向审核的基础上，以商业发票为中心审核其他规定的单据，使有关的内容相互一致，做到"单单一致"。

参考文献

1. 朱春兰,俞岑. 外贸单证(第二版). 杭州:浙江大学出版社,2008.

2. 陈伟芝,潘旭强. 国际商务单证. 广州:暨南大学出版社,2009.

3. 国际商会中国国家委员会. ICC 跟单信用证统一惯例(UCP600). 北京:中国民主法制出版社,2006.

4. 全国国际商务单证培训认证考试办公室. 国际商务单证理论与实务. 北京:中国商务出版社,2009.

5. 海关总署报关员资格考试教材编写委员会. 报关员资格考试统一教材. 北京:中国海关出版社,2009.

6. 国家质检总局报检员资格考试委员会. 报检员资格全国统一考试教材. 北京:中国标准出版社,2009.

7. 中国国际货运代理协会. 国际货运代理理论与实务. 北京:中国商务出版社,2009.

8. http://www.bjciq.gov.cn/Contents/Channel_782/2010/0601/22005/content_22005.html,北京出入境检验检疫局网

9. http://www.safe.gov.cn/model_safe/index.html,国家外汇管理局

10. http://www.licence.org.cn,中华人民共和国商务部许可证事务局

图书在版编目（CIP）数据

外贸单证实训 / 朱春兰主编. —杭州：浙江大学
出版社，2010.11（2020.1 重印）
ISBN 978-7-308-08084-2

Ⅰ.外… Ⅱ.①朱… Ⅲ.①进出口贸易－原始凭证
Ⅳ.①F740.44

中国版本图书馆 CIP 数据核字（2010）第 213108 号

外贸单证实训

朱春兰　主编

责任编辑	周卫群	
封面设计	卢　涛	
出版发行	浙江大学出版社	
	（杭州天目山路 148 号　邮政编码 310007）	
	（网址：http://www.zjupress.com）	
排　　版	杭州中大图文设计有限公司	
印　　刷	临安市曙光印务有限公司	
开　　本	787mm×1092mm　1/16	
印　　张	14.75	
字　　数	360 千	
版印次	2010 年 11 月第 1 版　2020 年 1 月第 5 次印刷	
书　　号	ISBN 978-7-308-08084-2	
定　　价	27.00 元	